MODERN BONDS

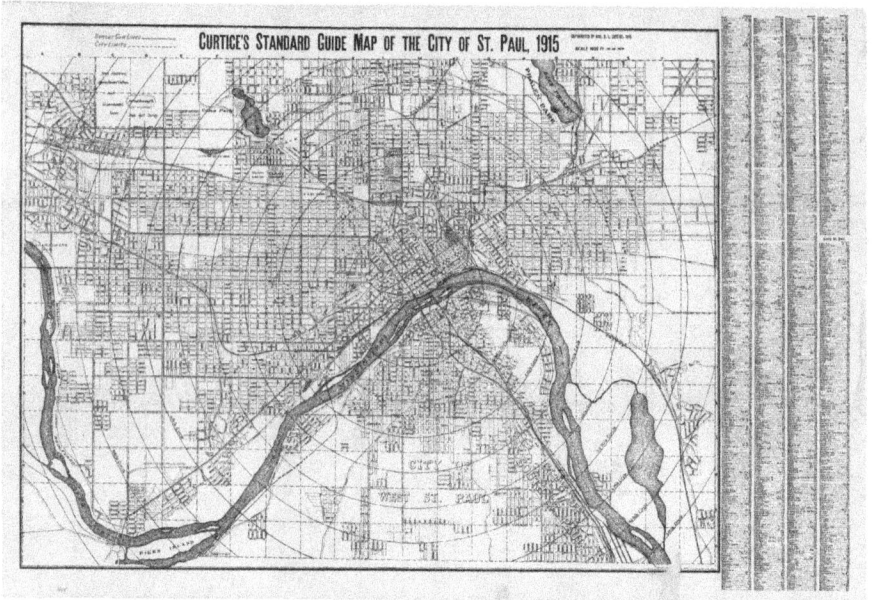

Map of St. Paul in 1915. The bold lines mark streetcar routes. D. L. Curtice, *Curtice's Standard Guide Map of The City of St. Paul, 1915.* Courtesy of the Minnesota Historical Society Map Collection.

MODERN BONDS

Redefining Community in Early
Twentieth-Century St. Paul

ELIZABETH ANN
DUCLOS-ORSELLO

University of Massachusetts Press
Amherst and Boston

Copyright © 2018 by University of Massachusetts Press
All rights reserved
Printed in the United States of America

ISBN 978-1-62534-335-2 (paper); 334-5 (hardcover)

Designed by Sally Nichols
Set in Monotype Dante and Josefin Sans
Printed and bound by Maple Press, Inc.

Cover design by Milenda Nan Ok Lee
Cover art: (Foreground) Colorized photograph of *Wahasha [i.e. Wabasha] Street,
St. Paul, Minn.*, c. 1908, published by Detroit Publishing Company.
Courtesy of Library of Congress.
(Background) Detail from 1915 map of St. Paul by D. L. Curtice,
Curtice's Standard Guide Map of The City of St. Paul, 1915.
Courtesy of the Minnesota Historical Society Map Collection.

Library of Congress Cataloging-in-Publication Data
Names: Duclos-Orsello, Elizabeth Ann, author.
Title: Modern Bonds : Redefining Community in Early Twentieth-Century St.
Paul / Elizabeth Ann Duclos-Orsello.
Description: Amherst : University of Massachusetts Press, [2018] | Includes
bibliographical references and index. |
Identifiers: LCCN 2017050247 (print) | LCCN 2018017766 (ebook) | ISBN
9781613765722 (e-book) | ISBN 9781613765739 (e-book) | ISBN 9781625343345
(hardcover) | ISBN 9781625343352 (pbk.)
Subjects: LCSH: Community life—Minnesota—Saint Paul—History—20th century.
| Saint Paul (Minn.)—Social life and customs—20th century.
Classification: LCC F614.S4 (ebook) | LCC F614.S4 D83 2018 (print) | DDC
977.6/581—dc23
LC record available at https://lccn.loc.gov/2017050247

British Library Cataloguing-in-Publication Data
A catalog record for this book is available from the
British Library.

For my son, Luca.
Thank you for allowing me to
see the world anew.

CONTENTS

Photo gallery follows page 138.

vii

PREFACE

When I headed to Kansas City, Missouri, in August 1995 to join the Jesuit Volunteer Corps (JVC), I never imagined that my year of service would spawn a book nearly a quarter century later. It did. The challenge to maintain connections with communities in my former life and to live in community with my housemates, in community with the women I served at a nonprofit agency, in community with members of my own and other faith traditions, and in community with residents of my neighborhood became one of the transformative experiences of my life. I grappled with what community meant, how I fit into these various communities, and what my responsibilities were to each. I asked whether community and individuality (both American traditions) were compatible. I wondered how the United States could call itself a community even as poverty continued to ravish lives and racial, ethnic, economic, and gender-based injustices persisted. I questioned the ways in which clothing, houses, music, and the paths of city bus lines defined or reinforced communal identities or borders. I realized I had few answers. At times the barriers of community seemed fluid; at other times they were rigid. On some days I could articulate who and what constituted parts of my community (singular), and on others I was overwhelmed by and surprised at the intersecting and even concentric communities (plural) to which I could or did claim some attachment.

This was supposed to be the easy part, I remember thinking. I was a member of a large family, and I'd spent my life engaged in social justice and community service. I'd always had a passion for being part of efforts and entities bigger than myself. Why couldn't I shake the questions about this aspect of my year? Why wasn't I able to easily identify the requirements for members of an American community? Why did I keep stumbling over the awkward compatibility between the rhetoric of community and the realities of the structural inequalities I saw around me? After my year with JVC ended, I left Kansas City and embarked on the next phase of my life's journey, where I continued finding ways to bridge doing and theorizing. Yet the questions from that year stayed with me and multiplied, and for some twenty years they have shaped nearly all of the civic engagement, teaching, research, and co-created public-facing work I have done in the many places I have called home across the United States and around the world.

In the years since my experiences in Kansas City, I have become increasingly attuned to the fact that the word *community* is omnipresent in the global, transnational, diverse United States of the twenty-first century. Social media posts, corporate mailings, newspaper headlines, coffee-shop boards, church bulletins . . . the list is endless. Yet ask a hundred people to define *community,* and you will get a hundred different answers. Challenge your friends or neighbors or relatives to identify which individuals or places make up their community, and the conversation will quickly gain complexity far beyond their initial responses, revealing that the term is flexible, fluid, changeable, hard to nail down. It is suitable to both a knitting group and a gathering of activists; it has been appropriated by sports fans and block-party organizers, by nations, faith traditions, elementary schools, and groups based on nearly every imaginable combination of demographic characteristics and interests and geographic boundaries. The term does not discriminate, even if the groups using it might. The one common denominator? *Community* always has a positive connotation. And as I have read and thought and talked with others about all of this, I have tried to better understand not only how we have come to talk about community in these multifaceted ways but also why, and through what mechanisms, its expansiveness has been maintained and at what opportunity or cost.

These nagging questions motivate *Modern Bonds.* My search for answers led me to a previous moment of great change and into the daily lives of residents in the nation's booming cities. In this book, I demonstrate how and why people in one diverse U.S. city in the opening decades of the twentieth century reoriented Americans' understanding of what community would be and how it would be understood and enacted in the

modern and postmodern eras. Their concerns and reactions to changing demographic and economic conditions—at times deliberate, at times
accidental—profoundly shaped ideas about and practices of community
in ways that have direct implications for our daily life today. In St. Paul,
as in many other American cities between 1900 and 1920, groups and individuals were struggling to make sense of life in a modernizing nation.
In the process, they redefined and complicated the concept of community through a range of actions and cultural productions in private and
public spaces. These were mostly unremarkable activities and commonplace events and products, part and parcel of how cities and city life functioned at the time. The reproduction of photographs, decisions about park
design, choices about housing styles, the planning of public festivals—
each remade the way in which the term *community* was used and how the
concept was experienced. Such activities changed where and with whom
individuals felt they belonged (or were allowed to feel they belonged),
and they reflected and reinforced ideas about how race, class, gender, ethnicity, and a person's position vis-à-vis the centers of power factored into
those possibilities. Today, Americans live with the legacy of both the *what*
and the *how* of this remaking. The bonds these midwesterners forged a
century ago still empower and constrain us.

ACKNOWLEDGMENTS

Far from being a solitary venture, researching and writing are inherently communal projects, and this book exists because of the numerous communities that have sustained both it and me through its progression from idea to artifact. Years ago, as a young thinker, activist, and emerging scholar, I found intellectual homes in intensive, dynamic, flexible, and interdisciplinary programs at Connecticut College and Boston University, where scholar-mentors such as Cathy Stock, Kim Sichel, Anita Patterson, Richard Fox, Marilyn Halter, and the faculty in the Focus Program nurtured my unorthodox questions and pathways and allowed me to draw new lines between academic disciplines and approaches even as I fought to bridge academic and real-world work. This book benefited from that base as well as from the multidisciplinary group of friends and colleagues at Salem State University and elsewhere. All helped me refine my questions and my writing in important and timely ways, offering feedback and giving me the confidence to do what I thought I could not do when the project became larger than I had imagined. Trying out ideas at conferences in places near and far has allowed me to think about community on a global scale, and in recent years I've been fortunate to develop and teach courses at several institutions about the theory and cultural construction of community while also engaging in community-based teaching and learning. I am grateful to the hundreds of students and off-campus co-creators who have helped me test and refine much that appears in this book. My deepest professional thanks is reserved for Bruce Schulman, whose scholarly acumen and editorial prowess have made this a much better book and whose unwavering confidence in the project gave me the courage to see it through. I am honored to call him a friend.

Trying to write about a specific place with texture and depth requires access to archives—lots of them—and I have been blessed with many wonderful resources. First and foremost, I owe a debt of gratitude to the team of reference librarians at the Minnesota Historical Society, who cheerfully responded to thousands of obscure queries and helped me track down materials that at times no one knew existed. Elsewhere in St. Paul, the staff of the State Historic Preservation Office, Steve Granger at the Archdiocesan Archives, Ruth Schumi and Patrice Bass at the St. Paul Parks and Recreation Department, and the staffs of both St. Peter Claver Church and the Ramsey County Historical Society facilitated my access to their important archival collections. In Sauk Center, the guides at the Sinclair Lewis home helped me see and feel the complexities that shaped his novel *Main Street*. Finally, I thank Evelyn Hill and Rosella Limon for allowing me to analyze and reproduce items from their family photo albums. Without their generosity, I would never have been able to write chapter 2, and I will be forever grateful to them and their extended family.

My research and writing has been supported by funding from the Minnesota Historical Society, Boston University, and Salem State University as well as by an Argyll Rice Phi Beta Kappa Delta of Connecticut fellowship. In addition, I was privileged to live, teach, and consider community in a global context thanks to two Fulbright fellowships and a Whiting fellowship. While on a Fulbright in Thessaloniki, Greece, in 2016, I was able to carve out precious time around my teaching to draft the manuscript that has become this book. I wish to thank the amazing staff at the University of Massachusetts Press for shepherding the book at every stage—in particular, my editor, Matt Becker, who championed the project from day one and offered sage advice at several junctures. Thanks also to the anonymous reviewers who read the manuscript and offered insightful suggestions for strengthening it.

Final thanks are reserved for my family and friends. I send a heart full of gratitude to my fearless women friends, including my HERS sisters, my JVC housemates, my fellow American Studies Association women leaders, members of my former women's spirituality group, and the group of Ph.D. mother-scholar-educators with whom I shared a basement office some years back. Collectively you have shown me that anything is possible if we support one another. Because I've been writing about St. Paul without living there, I've regularly descended on extended family and friends, and this has been one of the delights of the process. Bruce and Linda Orsello, the Olson and Ochocki families, and Bill Dinon have all repeatedly fed and housed me, providing sounding boards, moral support, running partners, and camaraderie over hot and cold beverages at all hours. At critical times they have helped ground me in a place that is truly my second home.

For my family of origin, I am thankful. They were my first team, my first group, my first community. My mother, Elaine, has not only has provided cozy fires and much coffee for last-minute writing visits but tremendous inspiration. She is an example of perseverance par excellence. So was my late grandmother, Alice Lacasse Olivier, who shared with me stories about her life and her parents—immigrants who were sacrificed to the logic of early twentieth-century industrial capitalism—and in this way shaped my earliest interest in the issues and era of this book. My siblings, Rebecca, Jeremy, Nathan, Joshua, and Benjamin, have each in their own way made this book possible. Along with my mother they have provided childcare, moral support, long talks, and a healthy dose of reality as my work progressed.

To my husband, Chase, who knows more than he ever wanted to know about community and who has lived this book as much as I have for far longer than he ever imagined, thank you for recognizing that my academic trajectory will never be linear and that I wish to lead ten different lives at once. Thank you for letting me use weekends and vacations to get this book done, for living amid the piles of papers, and for believing in me always. And finally, to my son, Luca, my heart and my soul: I began thinking about this book before you were part of my life, so it has been with me as long as you have. You have brought joy to challenging days. You have taught me what it is to love unconditionally and how to live in the moment despite looming deadlines. Your ability to navigate cultures and peoples and places and ideas and build communities as we've upended and trekked you across the globe has inspired me. I marvel at the amazing young man you have become. While I am proud of launching this book into the world, I am even prouder of you. I hope to make you proud too.

MODERN BONDS

INTRODUCTION

From January 27 to February 3, 1917, the city of St. Paul, Minnesota, buzzed with activity. Business and political leaders were enjoying the success of their annual winter carnival, the second they had staged after reinvigorating a tradition begun in the 1880s. Children and adults raced down large toboggan slides set up around the city; costumed members of social clubs and employees from the city's largest businesses marched in formation through the streets; the parks filled with revelers; parties, balls, and pageants entertained locals, regional boosters, commercial counterparts, and curious outsiders alike who flocked to the capital city from across the nation. The festivities included the crowning of a Queen of the Snows, a sled-dog race, and even a mythical battle over the weather between King Boreas and his archenemy, the Fire King. Intended to shore up communal bonds among residents and to build, represent, and reaffirm connections among economic and political leaders across municipal and state lines, the carnival of 1917, like the one the year before, captured the city's—and the nation's—imagination. Photographers, moviemakers, and journalists documented the festivities, depicting the frivolity sweeping across the city and underscoring the organizers' production of a St. Paul that was both unified and nationally (even globally) significant.

Parades were central elements of this midwinter celebration of St. Paul's climate, industry, and people, and perhaps none of the 1917 parades was grander than the one staged on the carnival's last full day, when nearly a thousand cars snaked through the city's business district despite below-freezing temperatures. The tremendous scale of the event owed much to the hundreds of cars driven by Minneapolis-based auto dealers, who had crossed the Mississippi to join the parade as a declaration of support and as a gambit to boost attendance at their upcoming auto show. Both the St.

Paul-based carnival organizers and the Minneapolis businessmen deemed this greatest of all auto parades an unqualified success.

What stands out about this parade of cars is that the Minneapolis men who rode in them and mingled with revelers throughout the afternoon came dressed in what the leading St. Paul daily called "white-hooded robes such as were worn by the Ku Klux Klan." This description had first appeared two weeks earlier in a newspaper article accompanying a photograph of three men (apparently soon-to-be parade members). The celebratory headline above the image read proudly, "Minneapolis Ku Klux Clansmen Coming in Force."[1] The hooded assembly dramatically highlighted the apparent embrace of nonresident economic partners in the city's festival and suggested the exclusion of the city's African American population. Yet St. Paul's African Americans were not to be deterred; instead, they embraced the opportunity to celebrate another version of vibrant community. Immediately after the 1917 carnival ended, the black population staged its own multi-day festival in which organizers replicated some of the events of the citywide carnival, offered additional unique experiences for their revelers, and provided a time and place for black residents and nonresidents to share in and reinforce their own understanding of community as tied to geographic proximity and racial identity. Thus, in dramatic fashion, the winter carnival of 1917, the blending of economic, political, and social agendas, the unsettling parade featuring night rider costumes, and the African American response formed and reflected threads of a larger story as residents of St. Paul—and Americans everywhere—struggled to make sense of life in a modernizing, urbanizing, industrialized nation. Communal bonds and identities were being renegotiated in and through everyday practices, and place of residence was becoming only one among many competing factors in the definition and experience of community.

Reflecting fairly common practices in cities across the United States, the winter carnival of 1917 also demonstrated that, in the first two decades of the twentieth century, as modernizing Americans worked in new ways to define, identify, and nurture communal relationships in an increasingly mobile and complex society, activities in the cultural sphere were critical components of their efforts to renegotiate and redefine bonds of fellowship. After all, while the 1917 carnival events were dramatic, they were more postscript than prelude. As this book will lay out, the general contours of the winter carnival story had been present in practices surrounding the production and circulation of personal and public photographs; the city's changing residential, ecclesiastical, and civic architecture; and the design of and access to open space. Activities and decisions in these areas reflected residents' attempts to articulate their ideas about the nature of community and where or with whom they found it, a struggle that simultaneously played out in everyday decisions and actions, in intellectual circles, and even in popular fiction of the era. In some cases, residents of St. Paul and other American cities imagined community in terms of the entire city; in others, they envisioned it as something much narrower or broader. In some cases, community required emotional intimacy and reciprocity; in others, it was comfortably imagined and universal in scope. Contradictions abounded, yet somehow rival understandings of community coexisted. Again and again, efforts at uniting all of St. Paul's residents proved to be a challenge, but efforts persisted for a generation. Far from obscuring a hidden message, these contradictions and complications, embedded and reflected in the everydayness of life in modernizing America, embodied a clear message: the concept of community itself was in flux in the opening years of the twentieth century, and it was being renegotiated to serve the needs and reflect the realities of a new era.

The complex interplay between ideas and experience, conceptions of place and understandings of affinity, lies at the heart of this book. Although some version of these tensions had existed in previous generations, their contours and intensity in the early twentieth century were unprecedented, and their impact was profound. For urban Americans in the 1900s and 1910s, the locality-based community of nineteenth-century humanism had become as much imagined as real. Americans increasingly separated communal relationships from a requirement of shared residency, even though many also longed for a communal experience that remained tied to their place of residence. Locality did not become completely irrelevant, but city limits related only partially to experiences of community. During the first decades of the twentieth century, the notion of shared identities or experiences linked to demographic variables and one's relationship with capitalism and commerce competed with geography as the central marker of community. On the rise were ideas of affinity that operated both in smaller geographic areas within the city and across much wider ones. Imagination and experience overlapped most often in city neighborhoods in which informal ties survived. Even in these instances, however, structural forces often reinforced limited, affinity-based experiences of community such as those marked by shared class or by ethnic or racial identities. The well-documented rise of race-based residential segregation in St. Paul and other northern cities in the early twentieth century is one such example. Others include zoning laws that regulated size, type, and use of structures and the proliferation of urban parishes (Catholic and otherwise) that served specific linguistic, immigrant, or racial groups.

This book advances a new interpretation of the opening years of the twentieth century by exploring the myriad ways in which the residents of St. Paul created, experienced, and navigated an emerging, multifaceted conception of community and how the cultural products they produced and consumed reflected and shaped that conception. A number of central questions drive this investigation. How did Americans imagine community in an era of great transition? What role did cultural production play in shaping or representing these shifts? What impact did the era's anxiety about and renegotiation of community have on subsequent American ideas and experiences? For early twentieth-century Americans, community had become an increasingly ambiguous concept—imaginatively connected to place of residence for some but increasingly experientially linked to affinity groups of one sort or another. Attending to the ways in which the concept of community was renegotiated and made manifest, this book works to weave together the era's seemingly diverse political, social, cultural and economic changes, many of them linked to efforts to transform urban places and improve the lives of their residents. This analysis also strive to shed new light on the conflicts and coalitions that defined the Progressive Era by explaining how the discourse of community motivated and delimited the public efforts of women, African Americans, immigrants, laborers, and the urban industrial elite while also emerging as a crucial component of the apparatus that shored up the logic and structures of industrial capitalism and nation building that defined the modern United States.

Furthermore, this book engages two important areas of scholarship: the historical investigation of community as a concept and the search for unifying threads that link the wide range of activities that marked urban life in the early twentieth-century United States. Not since Thomas Bender's 1978 *Community and Social Change in America* has there been a sustained historical exploration of community, and his account ends in 1900.[2] Historians, social scientists, and humanities scholars regularly write about community, but most assume a definition of the term and then read the evidence through that lens. Historians largely use the word as a synonym for town, neighborhood, or city or as a notion through which to explore the lives of a group sharing a racial, gender, linguistic, ethnic, or religious identity. While neither approach is inherently problematic, the former has helped to sustain a persistent declension narrative about community in America while the latter has downplayed the power of place and made intersectional analysis challenging. Both have led to a hollowed-out concept of community as an analytical tool available to scholars. In this book, the very definition and use of the term is assumed to be fluid.

The declension narrative owes a great deal to recent scholarly trends as well as to those of the early twentieth century. Beginning in the 1980s, popular books such as Robert Putman's *Bowling Alone* and Robert Bellah and colleagues' *Habits of the Heart,* along with a proliferation of writing from the communitarian camp, helped place the term *community* at the center of American popular and scholarly discourse. These works consistently emphasized the loss of a kinder, gentler, more communal America.[3] By comparing the present to some imagined past, they shored up a belief that contemporary Americans lack community and that community itself is the product of an earlier, simpler, better time—one often contrasted with "modern" or "society." Scholars, politicians, and activists interested in contemporary social change often wax poetic about the virtues of community, even as they deliver its eulogy.

To change this pattern requires investigating the ideal of community itself. Yet unlike other major historical concepts such as nation, whiteness, and identity, community has received little critical examination.[4] In the early years of the twentieth century, when increasing urbanism intersected the rise of professional sociology, many social scientists and policymakers began to equate communal relationships (defined as those based on mutuality and reciprocity) with premodern lifestyles and their demise in present-day America.[5] As one of the era's most respected sociologists argued, "powerful forces are more and more transforming community into society, that is, replacing living tissue with structures held together by rivets and screws."[6] Many social scientists and policymakers embraced this idea, even though other, more nuanced views of communal relationships in urban America were emerging around them.[7] By the late 1930s, the notion that urban life was antithetical to communal relationships had become intellectual orthodoxy. In his canonical 1938 essay, "Urbanism as a Way of Life," Louis Wirth asserted that urban life consisted "of the substitution of secondary for primary contacts, the weakening of bonds of kinship, the declining social significance of the family, the disappearance of the neighborhood, and the undermining of the traditional basis of social solidarity."[8]

Born in a particular time and linked to specific social and cultural changes, this declension theory has nonetheless persisted in academic circles and continues to shape historians' approach to the subject of community in the United States. The result is a body of historical writing that has overwhelmingly embraced a continuous decline, one that began as soon as European colonists set foot on the North American continent.[9] Not until the late 1970s did scholars explicitly question the validity of this narrative. In what seemed to be a challenge to the prevailing approach, Bender pointed out that preindustrial small towns did not always or even usually comport with idealized sites of community and that modernization did not necessarily kill community.[10] Pushing that notion further, Craig Calhoun argued that formal groups could, and perhaps did, have significance in people's lives that would warrant viewing them as sources and places of communal relationships. He instructed scholars of community to refrain from pairing irrationality or subjectivity with *communal* and rationality or instrumentality with *noncommunal*.[11]

The rise of social history in the 1970s expanded some of the scholarly discourse about community, bringing with it a proliferation of studies about various groups of individuals linked by similarities in their demographic profiles and daily lives. This new approach highlighted the need to look beyond locality (especially in the industrial and modern eras) to recognize the various ways in which Americans have identified with one another in the past. Following classic works such as Carroll Smith-Rosenberg's "The Female World of Love and Ritual" and Herbert Gutman's *Work, Culture and Society in Industrializing America,* many scholars embraced this important conceptual shift, taking up the study of immigrant and religious groups

and examining the collective histories of people linked by race, class, ethnicity, gender, sexual orientation, and many other identities.[12] Such works
emphasize the unique bonds that exist among members of a specific demographic group, whether or not they share a residence in a specific location,
and often imply that all individuals with the chosen characteristic form part
of a community. Yet however valuable these works may be, they cannot tell
the whole story of community in America any more than locality-based
studies can. In recent years, feminist and poststructuralist scholars have
challenged this trend, recognizing that identity-based community rhetoric
can erase difference and exclude some actors or subjects while claiming
to integrate and, in this way, reinscribe privilege.[13] Postcolonial scholarship has also done much to encourage a rethinking of the use of the term
community. Benedict Anderson, whose articulation of the "imagined community" as a way to understand national sentiment shaped a generation of
scholars, has helped unhinge the notion from either a specific geographic
referent or an identity narrowly defined and connect it to more ephemeral
connections that inspire and support concrete loyalties and actions through
mechanisms that include activities in the cultural sphere.[14]

Rather than assume that any one form of community or site of communal bonds contains the sum total of communal options, I aim here to
"recognize community as a social process predicated on relationships and
therefore susceptible to change over time." This approach aligns with the
tradition of the nineteenth-century humanists who wrote about community as well as the goals and methods of network theorists, whose strategy,
many have argued, is indispensable to historians of community.[15] Only by
thinking about community as a set of relationships can we "break free of
the value laden assumptions of the 'community saved' and 'community
lost' paradigms" in which "the historical process becomes teleological."[16]

Thinking about community as an experience or process allows twenty-
first-century scholars to attend to the ways in which a wide range of historical actors have constructed, reorganized, reimagined, and negotiated
it. This approach allows us to perceive a nuanced history of community
in America that challenges the ubiquitous declension narrative, breaks
up the so-called "commonsense" pairing of location and community, and
undermines the tendency to see modernity and community as incompat-
ible.[17] For as this book will show, in the spaces of American cities, at a time

of transition, in and through a range of cultural products, there emerged a complex, multifaceted practice and understanding of community that could support and balance the wider range of meanings and messages that today's use of the word implies. The early years of the twentieth century marked a period of widespread intellectual and political concern with the idea and experience of community. The era influenced how many contemporary Americans continue to think about community and its decline. But it was also a time when a new understanding of community emerged in the urban struggles and transformations that made and remade everyday life.

Certainly there was no lack of writing about community in those years. In fact, it was a hallmark of works by the era's leading philosophers, sociologists, and educators, who believed that the pace and scope of changes in the lives of most Americans—especially in cities—required attention, documentation, and response. The settlement house movement, the labor movement, the rise of urban and city planning, and transformations in public education each reflected anxiety about community lost, sought, or renegotiated. Yet for most city residents, daily life was lived rather than studied, and it required interactions with others. Their choices, innovations, and reactions to change also sustained, reimagined, and renegotiated community.

Middle-class anxiety about modernizing America fueled the rush to put pen to paper and develop actionable responses to change. In retrospect, that reaction seems almost frantic, but it reflected the mood and tenor of the age. Trains crisscrossed the nation. In massive factories, machinery hummed and clanked and pumped and wove and stitched and smelted; on massive farms, reapers and combines carved the landscape. Migrants from around the world arrived at Ellis and Angel islands or crossed and re-crossed northern and southern borders. Sharecropping families left their tenancies and headed north toward cities at the other end of railroad lines. The new motion pictures drew crowds to theaters, and even the art of the era moved. The influence of impressionist training on Robert Henri and other Ashcan School painters is omnipresent in their American cityscapes. Thanks to short brushstrokes, color and light flickered, figures pulsed, and flags and laundry flapped in almost-palpable breezes.

The movements of people, the rise of cities, the ascendancy of industrial wage labor, the rush of immigration, the growth of mass culture and leisure culture, and the emergence of national and international markets on a larger scale than ever before caused anxiety and concern for native-born Americans and academics as well as for religious, business, municipal, and national leaders. All of this movement meant change and raised questions about the nature of the good life in this new order and what it meant to be American in this new century.

Because cities underwent these transformations more dramatically than other places did, responses to them there were swift, expansive, and palpable. Perceived overcrowding led to slum clearances and the creation of green spaces. The arrival of significant numbers of non-English speakers, new immigrants, and African Americans from the South bolstered Americanization efforts and the development of social services aimed at education and integration. An emergent middle class spurred the growth of suburbs as well as social and political clubs. A desire to be competitive in a globalizing economy encouraged business leaders to look across the nation and the world for networks and opportunities. For those outside the traditionally sanctioned white, Anglophone, male, middle-class power structures—in particular, African Americans, immigrants, and the poor—the movements and changes of this era presented possibilities for renewal even as nativism and racism offered daily reminders of what had not changed. Navigating life in the cities of modernizing America was new for everyone, and there were few guidelines. Regardless of your position or your past, to make a life in an American city between 1900 and 1920 was to cut a path. This could be liberating for some, but it also created anxiety among the largely middle-class, white, native-born Americans who felt that their nation was shifting underneath them.

These shifting landscapes and rapid changes were especially notable in the cities of the Middle West, which in the opening years of the twentieth century ascended from regional to national prominence: Chicago, Milwaukee, Cleveland, Indianapolis, Omaha, Detroit, Des Moines, Kansas City, and the Twin Cities of Minnesota, Minneapolis and St. Paul. The influx of immigrants from southern and eastern Europe and Scandinavia as well as the northern migration of southern blacks was transforming much of the Midwest but was most noticeable in its cities, increasing not only the number of non-English speakers but also the non-white, non-Protestant populations. In all of these urban centers, ethnic and racial enclaves emerged, places where poverty intersected with nativist tendencies and life was challenging even as opportunities grew for low-wage, low-skilled work.

These changes forced a reassessment of what community could mean in an urbanizing, modernizing United States, and many of the era's leading intellectuals, located in the Midwest, focused on discussing, theorizing, and trying to create, re-create, or shore up the concept. An overriding concern was that community was disappearing (or could not be properly fostered) in American cities. Some thought it might be possible to create new forms of relationships unhampered by geographic referent or ones that were much narrower than a city as a whole, but not all of them saw *city* and *community* as synonyms. Instead, many continued to revere a nineteenth-century humanistic notion of community as tied to intimacy and reciprocity, as a relationship that most often required face-to-face interactions. At the same time, they believed that something lesser—preference or affinity—bound together people in cities. Most had been raised in small towns in homogeneous settings, so they were struggling to make sense of life in what they saw as an increasingly heterogeneous, chaotic society, one in which their intimate communities and their public or instrumental communities seemed to be comprised of separate people gathered in separate spaces that required different skills to negotiate. Anxiety about this bifurcation stimulated much of the period's writing about the loss of community.

In 1901 the sociologist Edward Ross wrote what amounted to a eulogy for community. In his seminal work, *Social Control,* he proclaimed that cities would never become communities in the sense that small towns had been and that emotionally driven communal relationships could not naturally develop among urbanites who formed only instrumental relationships.[18] The import of this work for early twentieth-century policymakers, scholars, and civic leaders cannot be overstated. Powerful national figures such as Theodore Roosevelt and Oliver Wendell Holmes, Jr., praised the book, and many readers embraced Ross's notion of community decline and saw his work as a blueprint for urban social reform.[19]

Yet at the same time other people were hopeful about the possibility of retaining or creating intimate connections in cities and thereby fostering broader civic unity and identity. These communitarians included activists, philosophers, and reformers such as Jane Addams, Mary Parker Follett, and Josiah Royce, whose early experiences in small towns had led them as adults to, in the words of the historian Jean Quandt, "search for new and wider forms of community."[20] As they strove to nurture relationships among smaller, narrower groups of city dwellers (such as residents of specific neighborhoods) through community centers and settlement houses, Addams and Follett worked in the belief that broader unity would develop in due time. They viewed the two types of interactions as mutually reinforcing. In fact, Addams was convinced that the unity that she saw developing among diverse ethnic groups in impoverished city neighborhoods could and should provide a model for an international community, and Follett argued persuasively that intimate, personal experiences of human connection were not restricted to those within a person's "nearest group" because "community [was] a process." Uniting with the "nearest group" would lead to "an urge to embrace more and more," and thus community could be understood as one among many possible "modes of associations."[21]

Progressive Era philosophers, social scientists, and reformers grappled with the meaning of community in a fast-changing nation in which neither face-to-face interaction nor place of residence seemed to define the sum total of Americans' meaningful social experiences. Still, they neither abandoned the term nor removed from its definition a sense of placedness. Rather, they increasingly invoked *community* to describe the broad, free connections, based on shared aspects of life (that is, culture), among members of a society that stretched ever outward from the location of daily living (neighborhoods and cities) to the whole world. In these new incarnations of community, place of residence remained important, but individuals increasingly belonged to and embraced more than one community simultaneously. In an important way these new understandings were an attempt to integrate what we now call the local and the global.

While focused broadly on unpacking the historical understanding, production and experience of community in the early twentieth-century United States, this study is grounded in a particular place—St. Paul, Minnesota—and is intended to contribute to the growing interest in and attention paid to the Middle West by scholars of many disciplines. St. Paul's scale and size, too, figures prominently in this study of the early twentieth-century United States. Many discussions of urban America in the modernizing period have focused on prominent cities such as Chicago. Yet St. Paul, a second-tier city in the Midwest, allows us investigate the complexity of modernizing America on a more manageable scale in a region that was emerging as particularly American in the national consciousness. By the turn of the twentieth century, Americans no longer regarded the East Coast as representative of the nation at large. Instead, they increasingly looked west—not to the Far West but to the Middle West—for images and ideas about the nation; and between 1900 and 1920, the region had ascended to a position of grandeur and prominence in the national imagination. A 1908 *Scribner's* article proclaimed that the Middle West had "more pride of individual opinion and less reliance on tradition and corporate habits" than the East, so "the East is more fairly judged by the West than the West is by the East. . . . [Consequently] . . . the national spirit is more strongly developed in the West than in any other part of the country."[22]

On the intellectual front, the Midwest also asserted its importance. Its large universities were home to some of the most renowned scholars and thinkers the United States has ever produced, with scholars at Michigan, Minnesota, Wisconsin, and the University of Chicago taking the lead in theory and activism. But whether championing the Middle West as "a kingdom of plenty . . . in the sturdy, healthy, full-blooded heyday of its strength," or celebrating its academic prominence, many saw the region as the most American part of America, as emblematic of the nation as a whole.[23] As James Shortridge asserts, "Americans [in the 1910s] placed a high value on the pastoral traits of morality, independence and egalitarianism, and they saw the Mid West as a symbol for these ideals."[24] In fact, in a speech in St. Paul in 1918, the famous historian Frederick Jackson Turner praised the prairie historians for their studies of the establishment of democracy in the Middle West. This work and this place, he proclaimed, "'tied together' the 'past and the future' of the American republic."[25]

Jon Lauck's strident 2013 celebration of this revival, *The Lost Region: Toward a Revival of Midwestern History*, is a welcome reminder of the ways in which the region and its people, places, and institutions have "mattered to the course of historical events" and "can help us see the totality of our national past."[26] *Modern Bonds* situates itself among an impressive number of recent monographs and articles that engage the region in new ways and through such lenses as labor, gender, race, immigration, ethnicity, working-class culture, consumerism, art and literature to expand our understanding of the origins and trajectories of the United States as a whole.[27]

In the nineteenth century, the Middle West was largely comprised of small towns; but by the turn of the twentieth century, the region's residents, like all Americans, were moving in increasing numbers to nearby urban areas, a phenomenon captured in period fiction such as Stephen Crane's *Maggie* and Theodore Dreiser's *Sister Carrie.* In midwestern cities, diverse groups of people—black, white, immigrant, native-born, Jew, Protestant, Catholic, wealthy, working class, desperately poor—came into contact with one another, and negotiations over belonging and exclusion were played out in dramatic fashion.

And so it was in St. Paul. The city never became a metropolis like Chicago, nor did it match the cultural prominence or commercial-industrial potential of its twin city, Minneapolis. Yet its ordinariness is precisely what makes it so rewarding to investigate. By scaling back on the size of the city examined it becomes possible to investigate the experiences of the majority of Americans without losing the nuance and detail of a case study.

By 1900, St. Paul was home to about 160,000 people. Having quadrupled its population during the previous twenty years, it was a city on the make, one that had emerged from its origins as a trading post on the Mississippi River into the capital of Minnesota. Its economy featured a mixture of finance-, industry-, and trade-related commerce that was supported by the railroad and the city's fortuitous location. Businesspeople made money in enterprises linked to cities and industry from Chicago to the Pacific Coast; furs, transportation, lumber, banking, real estate, breweries, and dry goods were critical.[28] The inhabitants included second- and third-generation St. Paulites, often of German ancestry; a large and growing Irish and Irish-American population with political, ecclesiastical, and religious clout; newly arrived migrants from the South; immigrants from Scandinavia, Canada, Eastern Europe, and Southern Europe; an emerging middle class of young professionals; a small but significant black middle class; a large wage-labor pool of black and ethnic white residents; and one of the leading industrialists of the era, James J. Hill, the owner of the Great Northern Railroad, who lived in a grand mansion at the top of Summit Avenue, the toniest address in town.[29]

Ethnic enclaves were scattered on the edges of St. Paul, and a working-class culture had taken shape. Churches of many denominations dotted the city. The stockyards, Hamm's brewery, and the railroad culture (with its ancillary commercial and financial industries) ensured a need for laborers, though city did not ultimately emerge as an industrial powerhouse in the way that Minneapolis did. Cultural institutions—libraries, concert halls, and universities—as well as private social clubs had claimed space in the downtown and on the emerging margins, adding a decidedly middle-class air to what had been an outpost of white settlement only fifty years earlier. In 1920, the city reached an apex of sorts: with the addition of another 70,000 residents, it had now established itself as a solidly democratic town with all the ethnic and racial diversity that was common in midwestern cities but with fewer explicit class- or race-based tensions. Mansions lined all of Summit Avenue, parks dotted the landscape, civic organizations were working to record and address perceived social ills, and new businesses (among them 3M) had relocated to the city. The reemergence of the winter carnivals in 1916 and 1917 reflected leaders' vision of the city as a prosperous and healthful place to live, visit, conduct business, and celebrate.

The numerically small size of St. Paul's African American population belied the richness of its cultural, intellectual, and economic role, not only in this city but in the nation as a whole. Outside of the South and the largest northern metropolitan areas, the percentage of blacks in St. Paul (1 to 1.5 percent of the population between 1900 and 1920) differed little from the percentage in the non-South as a whole. Even when compared with a large city like Chicago, the difference was far from dramatic.[30] But St. Paul had long been home to a substantial, stable middle-class black population that included national figures such as John Q. Adams, the editor of the *Appeal,* an influential black newspaper, and Frederick McGhee, the first black attorney west of the Mississippi and a key figure in the creation of the NAACP. In this era, Minnesota twice strengthened its civil rights legislation. In the same period, William (Billy) Williams, a black St. Paul resident and a former baseball star, was hired to serve as an assistant to the white governor, a post he held for half a century. Clarence (Cap) Wigington began his thirty-year tenure as the nation's first African

American municipal architect. In 1902, the city hosted a meeting of the National Afro-American Council, attended by Ida B. Wells, Booker T. Washington, William Munroe Trotter, W. E. B. Du Bois, and many others.

Culturally and politically, the black population of St. Paul seemed to have advantages unavailable to other African Americans in the urban North and therefore might have appeared to be in a position to be accepted into the imagined community of St. Paul. Yet race-based discrimination was real and present. Despite the early adoption of civil rights laws and a perception of cooperation between white leaders and black residents, St. Paul's white population had a history of discrimination and intimidation that persisted into the twentieth century. Furthermore, the black elite's desire to retain some level of favor with white residents sometimes meant that they distanced themselves from the less prominent black majority.[31] Despite the façade of a "colorless" St. Paul, African American residents and their cultural productions powerfully shaped the renegotiation of community in urban America.

This book offers an intensive look at the transformation of community as both a concept and an organizing principle for daily life, political and social activism, urban planning, and economic boosterism and, in doing so, engages with a renewed scholarly interest in the history of the United States at the turn of the twentieth century that seeks to integrate the political, social, cultural, economic, and intellectual history of the era.[32] At the same time, this book build on important work about the power of place and civic identity in St. Paul.[33] My particular focus is on the analysis of activities and products that occupied a broadly inclusive cultural sphere. It was in and through cultural production and consumption (culture with a small *c*) of many types that the renegotiation of community occurred and was made manifest. Moving beyond (although not ignoring) traditional historical sources such as census records, diaries, and newspapers, this study combines social history methods with the techniques and sources of cultural historians, literary critics, and art historians. My interdisciplinary approach is intentional, conceived as an attempt to get at the experiences and ideas of community that shaped the lives of elite and nonelite St. Paulites. In other words, this book engages in a "reading of community that incorporates all signs that convey meanings . . . including non-linguistic signs."[34] By placing literature, photographs, homes, city buildings, parks, and public festivals at the center of my inquiry (and letting written records illuminate them rather than the other way around), I have tried to understand the experiences and voices of a vast array of St. Paulites who created or felt the impact of those cultural products.[35] By way of an interdisciplinary lens *Modern Bonds* uses and integrates diverse ways of seeing in order to expose and bring to bear new perspectives on a well studied era, seemingly familiar cultural products, and existing debates. Its purposeful engagement across disciplinary boundaries and multiple humanistic and social scientific methodologies reveals new sight lines onto the past.[36] Yet it also sheds historical light on the current anxiety and debates about community, political and ideological division, identity politics, and distress over the state of social capital in contemporary America. It demonstrates that fears about the decline of civic life long predated contemporary concerns about bowling alone or the impact of social media, technology, globalization, and transnationalism on communal bonds.

In 2018, *community* can mean nearly anything. My recent Google search for the term resulted in nearly 4 billion hits—from neighborhood gatherings to transnational networks, from people living in diaspora to the tweets of those who follow a particular Netflix show. The concept is at once meaningless and deeply meaningful. It is endowed with positivity, though it possesses no clear boundaries and can be used to affirm nearly any group or relationship. Its expansiveness sometimes becomes a benign platitude compatible with boundary making.[37] It means many things to many people, but most of them deeply desire it.

By focusing attention on the way a renegotiation of community was carried out and made manifest in an earlier era of economic, political, racial, ethnic, and social fragmentation and transformation, it becomes clear that our current, expansive use of the term *community* owes much to that moment's attempts to integrate ideas of the past with realities of the present and future. By 1920, what was in many ways a new understanding of the concept (as both broader and narrower than city limits, as both intimate and imagined, as both solid and fragile) itself harkened to an earlier time. Yet it was also fully compatible with industrial capitalism and its attendant political, social, and economic ethos, and it continues to shape the discourse about and experience of community in the United States today.

Nonetheless, our current climate of deep divisiveness and bitter antagonisms is regularly attributed to loss of community. For instance, Marc Dunkelman's 2014 *The Vanishing Neighbor: The Transformation of American Communities* argues that massive changes in the second half of the twentieth century have hollowed out the presence of "middle ring" relationships in the places where Americans live and work, hollowing out "communities" in favor of close sets of intimates and far-flung networks linked by social media and the like. This process, he asserts, has had devastating consequences for civic life as a whole.[38] But Dunkelman's argument ignores both contemporary and historical fact. He does not engage the economic, ideological, and work realities of contemporary American life in which global forces are at play, borders are questioned, jobs are scarce, the economy is unstable, and models of residential living that rest on home ownership, fixedness of place over the long term, and excess human capital to engage in civil society remains inaccessible to those outside of the professional classes. He also ignores the ways in which connections to place *do* matter to many Americans, even if not in the ways that marked the lives of their parents or grandparents. J. D. Vance's 2016 *Hillbilly Elegy* has exposed a wide readership to the deep class divisions in the United States and to the complicated and painful attempts of poor rural whites to integrate identities tied to place (of birth, of family origin, of familiarity) and to groups of people, ideas, belief systems, and generationally embedded practices that, deeper than place, are not easily dislodged no matter how far one travels from the locations that formed and shaped them. Similarly, in her 2016 *Strangers in Their Own Land*, Arlie Russell Hochschild reveals divisions in the electorate and a lack of national identification among some on the right, even as these same people celebrate a strong regional identity and a connection—thanks to the cultural product that is cable news—to those who share their political and religious beliefs, no matter how far removed geographically.[39]

Divisions and tensions between here and there, us and them, local and global are everywhere in such accounts of contemporary America. Yet in their deep acts of listening and in their elegiac tone, the authors construct a rallying cry for a richer, more subtle, more generous conversation about who belongs in or to which communities in the United States and how daily actions (or inactions) along with policies shape the answers. As Elena Pulcini has recently pointed out, "the rise of community should not be considered as an archaic and pre-modern residue running counter to the development of a global society but as a *new* product of globalization. Accordingly, community, and the 'local' must be reconsidered from a fresh perspective, not as *resisting* residues but as *co-existing* with the global dimension creating a complex and multifaceted setting."[40]

This book suggests an alternative organizing principle for the opening years of the twentieth century when technological change, immigration, population shifts, ethnic and racial strife, class conflict, and urban growth shaped life in the United States. But in so doing, I also hope to offer a new lens onto our own era of change, conflict, divisiveness, and uncertainty. In the conclusion to *A Fierce Discontent,* Michael McGerr's important book on Progressive Era reform efforts, the author recounts the ways in which progressive reform efforts began to wane after World War I and how, by the 1920s, a focus on individualism had overcome progressive ideas.[41] I reject such a sharp line, such a marked shift. By focusing on the renegotiation of community as a concept and an experience, this book challenges common assumptions about a dramatic postwar break during which the nation eschewed community and unity in favor of an alternative that stood in opposition to it.

And so, in urban America in the opening decades of the twentieth century, we find the anxieties, actors, and activities (among the everydayness of life in urban places) that gave birth to an understanding of community that holds to the present day: one that is both incredibly expansive and malleable and one that has great power to unite as well as divide. The types of activities that were omnipresent a century ago in cities—urban planning, circulation of photographs, public festivals, social reform, residential growth along ethnic, racial, and class lines—can be understood as the renegotiation of an existing understanding of community and the concurrent development of one that could coexist with life lived in urban locales structured by the political, cultural, economic, and ideological logic of industrial capitalism and nation-building while still offering up the hope, desire, place, and experience of close, shared bonds of fellowship.

Chapter 1 of the book focuses on Sinclair Lewis's best-selling novel *Main Street* (1920), whose publication at the tail end of the era made manifest the new and complex understanding of community that had arisen in urban, modernizing America during the previous two decades. Attending to Lewis's symbolic juxtaposition of a fictional small town with his portrayal of communal life in St. Paul—where the novel begins—this chapter highlights the shape of the protagonist's communal relationships in Minnesota's capital city, the more limited experiences she has in the novel's well-known small-town setting, and the way in which Lewis's work intersects with and responds to writings of contemporary social scientists and critics. By proposing that cities were the site of the most desirable experiences of community in the modernizing United States, the novel challenged any simple declension narrative and made a case for the value of new, complex, and multifaceted understandings and forms of communal experience.

At two key points in *Main Street*, photographs appear to influence the protagonist's ideas about where and with whom she might find joy and meaning in life.[42] Far from being a mere literary trope, these scenes suggest the increasing currency of photographic evidence in debates over community in the opening years of the twentieth century, a relationship that is the subject of chapter 2. Examining three types of photographs—family photography, social reform photography, and newspaper photography—I outline a series of ways in which the photographic record speaks about and participates in community and community making in a modernizing American city. Of particular interest are the community-building and community-limiting possibilities of framing, capturing, and circulating representations of St. Paul's people, places, and events.

To the extent that photographs of the built environment were part of the act of constructing communities, so, too, was the built environment itself. Chapter 3 revisits the relationships among race, class, neighborhood, and community through the lens of ecclesiastical, residential, and municipal buildings. In addition, through a close examination of the city's architecture, this study bring ethnicity and religion into focus as important aspects of communal experience.

Chapter 4 investigates efforts to create a grand plan for city parks focusing on the shift from an early emphasis on building large municipal parks with diverse recreational facilities to a campaign to also create small neighborhood-based playgrounds and green spaces. At a time when city managers, mayors, and business interests across the nation were embracing urban parks and green spaces as a solution to any number of urban challenges, the politics of park design in St. Paul illuminated deep-seated questions about how residents of the city should or could or wished to be brought together or kept apart in their private lives.

Chapter 5 returns to the winter carnivals of 1916 and 1917 to illustrate the process of renegotiating community in modernizing America. It also considers the emergence, on the eve of the U.S. entry into World War I, of a more complex understanding of community as created by and reflected in cultural activities such as public festivals and the public responses to them. In particular, the carnivals refute the prevailing idea that instrumental and communal relationships, collective and individual gain were isolated in modernizing America. Inherent in this finding is the place of the market and commerce in shaping both the experience and the definition of community in modernizing America.

As my book demonstrates, a malleable understanding of community, brought about by and made manifest in a range of activities and cultural productions (some of the very things that other scholars see as hallmarks of the era), nourished a modern celebration of community that did not require limiting or downplaying individual gain, goals, or identities. Yet it was painfully compatible with racism, class divisions, and the logic of industrial capitalism, even as it allowed for the development of deep and broad bonds among narrow groups within locales and across great distances. We are living this legacy still.[43]

CHAPTER 1

"GENEROUS INDIFFERENCE"

Realism, Sociology, and the Experience of Urban Community in Sinclair Lewis's *Main Street*

Early in Sinclair Lewis's blockbuster novel *Main Street* (1920), the protagonist, Carol Kennicott, has become the object of the insipid but silent scorn of the Gopher Prairie inhabitants she hoped to reform. She realizes that her life in the small northern Minnesota town of Gopher Prairie is being shaped by what she calls the "hidden derision" of its citizens. Her ideals have been dashed, her character has been attacked, and, after a humiliating walk through the center of town, she compares her experience of community life to "being dragged naked down Main Street."[1] The image aptly embodies the banal parochialism and lethal prejudice of Carol's adopted town. Her every move, like those of the other townsfolk, is fodder for gossip. She cannot be an individual, for the other inhabitants of Gopher Prairie understand her only through the ways in which she does or does not fit their expectations and conform to the established social order. Small-town life offers her none of the protection or security its promoters proclaim. Rather, its hypervigilance and strict conformity leave her isolated and scorned when she dares to challenge tradition. She longs for life in another place, one where she feels she belongs.

Scholars have long focused on Lewis's indictment of small-town Middle America, yet Carol is not a character with vague dreams of an imaginary better place, nor did the author entirely denigrate the town. Rather than simply longing to escape *from* Gopher Prairie, Carol wants to go *to* a specific place, and she makes her wish clear to the readers shortly after her humiliating walk down Gopher Prairie's central thoroughfare. Carol has a particular destination in mind as she surveys her situation. She seeks not a smaller town nor an unknown East Coast city (although she does this later) but St. Paul, Minnesota's state capital, where she lived before marrying Gopher Prairie's doctor, Will Kennicott. In St. Paul, she will be able to hide in the "generous indifference" that marks city life and, in so doing, feel as if she belongs.[2]

By situating St. Paul and Gopher Prairie in symbolic opposition—two poles representing the opposite extremes of Carol's experience as she searches for community in Middle America—Lewis signaled that his novel is not solely concerned with the general ills of small-town life, a topic that many American authors had already taken up.[3] Rather, *Main Street* is specifically about the relationship among place, affinity, demographics, and community in American life in the early twentieth century. It is less significant that the novel rejects Gopher Prairie than that it celebrates St. Paul. For by celebrating St. Paul, Lewis articulated the value and desirability of a vision of community that he saw in the nation's burgeoning urban areas. As the novel vividly illustrates, the city's "generous indifference" creates an atmosphere in which fulfilling relationships and desirable experiences of community can flourish alongside a feeling of place-based solidarity, especially for those closest to the era's centers of power. In other words, Lewis's portrayal of community life in St. Paul positioned the novel within wider sociological and popular debates about and renegotiations of community in modernizing America.

Main Street burst onto the scene just as social scientists, scholars, and social reformers were debating the viability of community in the nation's growing metropolitan centers—the very places that, in the novel, offer a desirable alternative to the problems of relationships and conformity in the small town of Gopher Prairie. At the center of these debates was a concern about whether cities could provide place-based experiences of community and even if such a thing was desirable. Unfortunately, however, Lewis scholars have largely ignored *Main Street*'s emphasis on urban community and thus have failed to recognize its significance within the era's national reassessment of attitudes toward community in early twentieth-century America. *Main Street* not only offered Americans an accessible entrée into the scholarly discourse of their age but also a fictional representation of some of their own reality in a rapidly transforming world.

By the time Lewis took up these issues in *Main Street*, concerns about the relative value of town versus city life had been a staple of American social thought for more than a century. Ever since industrial modes of production had begun to replace older systems, Americans had been trying to make sense of and adjust to the rapidly industrializing world that was fast overtaking small towns.[4] Worries about the social impact of this transition came to the fore in the early twentieth century. By this point Americans had begun to internalize a decades-long celebration of the small town as the site of all that was good and right about the nation—a celebration that the works of many American novelists encouraged.[5] As cities began to dominate the political and cultural landscapes, this mythic idealizing of the American small town reached its zenith.[6] Lewis was well aware of these general attitudes when, in 1905, he began to chafe at what he later called the "village virus." Some thirty years later, in the preface of a special 1937 edition of *Main Street,* he wrote:

> Back in 1905, in America, it was almost universally known that cities were evil and though even in the farmland there were occasional men of wrath, our villages were approximately paradise. They were always made up of small white houses under large green trees; there was no poverty and no toil worth mentioning; every Sunday sweet-tempered, silvery pastors poured forth comfort and learning; and while the banker might be a pretty doubtful dealer, he was inevitably worsted in the end by the honest yeomanry. But it was Neighborliness that was the glory of the small town. In the cities, nobody knew or cared; but back home the Neighbors were one great big jolly family.[7]

In the opening decades of the century, numerous paeans to the small town verified Lewis's assessment of the conventional wisdom. Among the most influential was Meredith Nicholson's 1918 *The Valley of Democracy,* a collection of magazine articles celebrating everything that an idealized small-town Midwest could offer. Even its flaws were not problematic. "The people of the Valley of Democracy," Nicholson explained, ". . . do a great deal of thinking and talking; they brood over the world's affairs with a peculiar intensity and beyond question they exchange opinions with a greater freedom than their fellow citizens in other parts of America. . . . In the smaller Western towns . . . lines of social demarcation are usually obscure to the vanishing point."[8] For him and like-minded authors, the small town was a site of democratic camaraderie and healthy introspection.

Even a cursory reading shows that Lewis's novel debunks the views put forth by Nicholson and like-minded enthusiasts. More subtly, however, it challenges the apocalyptic myth about the devastation of communal values and bonds in large U.S. cities, another piece of conventional wisdom that was widely circulating at the time. In the late 1890s, leaders in American sociology and social reform began expressing concern about the status of community in the large industrial centers of the growing nation. In their view, personal connections and relationships in cities were discussed and categorized in opposition to those present in small-town or rural America. Small-town relationships were understood to have been built on a reciprocity with roots as deep and broad as the boundaries of the locality. In cities, by contrast, relationships were increasingly seen as limited and often merely associational, an assumption that created great concern among many Progressive Era scholars, activists, and leaders, who interpreted this shift as the end of an age of community in America. Cities were seen as sites of communal discord where no natural forces bound people to deal kindly with others and where a sense of responsibility to and for others was limited at best.[9]

In 1901, the sociologist Edward Ross published *Social Control,* a work that he labeled *social psychology.* His ostensible goal was to offer suggestions for ordering life in cities that he perceived as largely chaotic. In the book, he contrasted *community* with *society,* using the former term to refer to experiences in the past, the latter to refer to the experience of relationships in urban America. Attributing a decline in community to the rise of cities, Ross emphasized the degree to which both cities and their organizational life were devoid of organic communal links. He mourned the loss of an idealized communal past and argued that the resulting forms of society were inherently less desirable than the experience of community found in small towns. He announced that, in a general sense, "powerful forces are more and more transforming community into society, that is, replacing living tissue with structures held together by rivets and screws."[10]

At the core of Ross's argument was a claim regarding the shift he observed in the types of bonds that drew people into association with one another in cities. "Local solidarity," he wrote, "perishes because bonds of fellowship are woven which unite a man to distant co-religionists, or fellow-partisans, or fellow-craftsmen, or members of the same social class."[11] Although he conceded that "in this way fresh social tissue forms and replaces, perhaps, the tissue that dies," he warned that "these communions do not fit people to deal kindly and honestly by one another because, instead of resting on neighborhood or economic intimacy, they rest on preference. Like friendship they are founded on affinity and selective choice."[12] For Ross, "fresh social tissue" was not communal tissue; anything less than a locality-based sense of obligation did not add up to an understanding of what constituted natural order or community. Thus, the types of relationships that tended to form in cities—those based on shared interests, affinity, or professional ties—made up something less than true community.

Although this general theme persisted in one form or another throughout the Progressive Era, some important intellectuals challenged its pessimistic conclusion. Members of this group, later known as *communitarians,* reformulated the experience of community for city dwellers. They argued that, although true community would continue to be found in intimate, face-to-face interactions, cities did not preclude such interactions. They were usually willing to concede the difficulty of extending this intimacy to an entire city or region and instead focused on nurturing the smaller communities that did sustain intimate urban relationships. Yet they believed in the potential of these small communities, developed from shared experiences, demographics, and affinity, to strengthen and sustain wider forms of community in an increasingly mobile, global, industrial age. At Chicago's Hull House, for example, Jane Addams sought to strengthen American democracy by nurturing relationships in one particular area of the city. Similarly, in Boston, Mary Parker Follett theorized that neighborhood revitalization was essential for the smooth functioning of the larger urban society. The sociologist Robert Park found in 1915 that "positive law" was shaping many urban interactions but that a wonderful variety of vital intimate groups continued to flourish.[13] These thinkers and activists believed that such small, intimate, limited communities might ultimately save urban America and would offer models for building community in the future.[14]

Thus, by the late 1910s, the academic world had begun to move away from an all-out assault on relationships in cities. Intellectuals were accepting that, while community might never again look the same as it had in nineteenth-century small towns (if that version of community had ever even existed), communal relationships would persist. For instance, in *Community: A Sociological Study* (1917), the sociologist Robert MacIver refused to engage in the same old debate.[15] Instead, he altered his terminology to fit the reality. He made it clear that modernizing, urban American society was made up of small reciprocal groups that he called "associations." In his view, far from being a threat to civil society, these narrow connections were the most important elements of it.[16] That is, these limited groups of intimates made the experiences of much larger, unified, place-based community possible.[17] In MacIver's formulation, a person did not have to choose between intimate reciprocity and a sense of place-based community: the two were symbiotic and dialectically related. In this way he was in line with the thinking of people such as Addams and Follett, whose writings between 1900 and 1920 had proposed that community was a continuum in which connecting with those nearest to you would encourage the desire to, in Follett's words, "embrace more and more."[18]

The debate over associational and place-based community highlights a critical point regarding Lewis's *Main Street*—namely, that he had produced a novel that reflected the way in which Americans had come to both think about and experience community by 1920. The novel's central symbolic opposition, between Gopher Prairie and St. Paul, repudiates the notion of community declension that shaped Ross's views while holding up a mirror to the newer notions of community that were shaping American civil society and that MacIver's book and the ideas of the communitarians suggested. In his portrayal of community in St. Paul, Lewis's novel seems to have been informed by some of the major concerns of the era's key thinkers and reformers. Whether these public figures ultimately believed that some form of intimate community could be created in cities or not, their analysis and activities derived from acknowledging that cities posed particular problems for those interested in pursuing communal relationships based on residence in a shared locality. Locales were becoming less relevant in modern relationships, but the desire for place-based unity had not disappeared. As a result, the solution to this quandary lay in MacIver's formulation. By celebrating the reality of affinity-based relationships and offering a way for people to link themselves imaginatively to others with whom they shared some space or locality, place-based community could be preserved (if only in the imagination) amid a reality that allowed for more than one understanding of community and increasingly made affinity central for all experiential forms of community, whether they were broader or narrower than a city's borders. The story of Carol Kennicott exemplified the new possibilities for and understandings of communal experience in America's cities.

In *Main Street,* Lewis constructed an urban environment in which communities exist and thrive. Yes, they are both limited and overly expansive or abstract, but the novel holds these multiple, contradictory understandings in balance and portrays them positively. It confirms the fact that intimate reciprocal relationships need no longer be tied exclusively to place, even as places can still be imagined as communities. When Lewis created Carol and began exploring the reasons behind her longing for St. Paul, he knowingly or not relied on and re-created the multifaceted notion of community that MacIver had illuminated only a few years earlier. Carol desires the freedom to associate with people who share her worldview but also longs for and imagines an older notion of place-based unity. She, like other Americans, discovers this in one of America's growing urban centers.

At the end of *Main Street,* Carol finds neither acceptance nor tolerance in Gopher Prairie, merely a sense of resignation to her fate for as long as she lives there. On the last page of the novel, as she and Will turn in for the night, she bravely states (with a tone of consigned acceptance), "I'll go on, always. And I am happy. But this [latest event in town] makes me see how thoroughly I'm beaten."[19] In certain respects, her quest and failure resemble Lewis's own search for community. Scholars have spoken of the many ways in which his writings reflect the general cultural values of the time in which he lived. He gave voice to the experiences of the men and women who had come of age in the first decades of the twentieth century and were trying to make sense of the changes around them as the nation transformed from a rural to an urban environment.[20] But *Main Street,* perhaps more than his other novels, mirrors his own personal trials, which dated from his childhood.[21] Lewis spent much of his life searching for a positive experience of community, a failed quest that found its nearest fulfillment in cities such as St. Paul. In the words of his wife, Grace, who traveled the globe with him, "he wanted fame and he wanted Love and he had both but he found they were not enough. . . . He continued to seek love as a fulfillment to a scientific experiment, to hurl himself from city to city, never pausing long enough to taste their true flavor, acquiring hardly more than a train-window observation, and from no one and nowhere ever came peace."[22]

Lewis was searching for people who would accept him and take him into their community, yet he was skeptical about claims that a given place could or would be the community he wanted. While his nomadic lifestyle suggests that he had at least partly dismissed any notion of place-based community, his constant searching shows that he still believed that such an experience might be possible. These ideas fueled the central theme in *Main Street,* and the novel's success proved that Lewis's life was perhaps not significantly different from the lives of millions of other Americans.

Thanks to the work of generations of scholars, Lewis's life has been well documented.[23] The best of these draw on Lewis's own writings and diaries as well as those of his wife, and all reveal a persistent sense of alienation and loneliness. He was born Harry Sinclair Lewis in February 1885, the son of a physician and his wife, who lived in the small Minnesota town of Sauk Centre. From his youngest years, he was a child outside the mainstream. As Mark Schorer writings in the opening of his massive biography, "he was a queer boy, always an outsider, lonely . . . with only one real friend in a town full of boys, laughed at by girls." The biography's second paragraph concludes with the terse statement: "He was lonely. He became Sinclair Lewis."[24]

In the 1860s and 1870s, small towns such as Sauk Centre were sprouting in the Minnesota countryside like so many newly planted trees. As the railroad crept northward, connecting these outposts to the Twin Cities and the world beyond, an increasing number of Americans began to call the Minnesota prairie home. Yet by 1885, Sauk Centre was still a small, raw city of 2,807 residents, with one school, a railroad station, a library, a hotel, an opera house, and a newspaper. In short, it had all the amenities that represented small-town America. What it didn't offer Harry Lewis was a sense of comfortable belonging. He was not completely ostracized; but as his diaries and his wife's recollections attest, he never felt as if he were at the center of the town's life. Even years later, on a return trip with his new wife, she recognized that "he was nervous . . . [because he felt] he would be as much of a stranger as I was."[25] Although he did not wholeheartedly dismiss or hate Sauk Centre, the small-town solidarity that social scientists such as Ross held so dear was far from a reality for him. In the late 1930s, an interviewer came away from a conversation with Lewis with the image of "a shy, sensitive, solitary, . . . homely, gawkey [sic] boy, who was keenly aware of the social shortcomings he fancied afflicted him."[26]

After matriculating at Yale in 1903, Lewis spent two years trying to find an outlet for what had become his driving interest—writing—but the school's literary editors repeatedly rejected his submissions. Despite the presence of a few close friends, he became increasingly resigned to solitude and began turning to alcohol for comfort. Determined to avoid spending another summer in Sauk Centre with the carriers of the "village virus," he signed on for his second tour with a cattle boat and took the chance that "the fallacy of elsewhere" would prove more hospitable.[27]

After returning to New Haven at the end of July, Lewis took up his studies, but by October he was ready to strike out once more for some place, some experience, that would make him feel connected to others. This time he had a short stint as a janitor at Helcion Hall, Upton Sinclair's utopian community in Englewood, New Jersey. The idea behind the Home Colony Association (as Helcion Hall was officially incorporated) was to demolish the notion of the single-minded, self-serving family unit that marked American life. By sharing all resources and work, the residents would have to rely on a larger form of community that transcended the bounds of democratic individualism.[28] But their community was limited: the "club members," as the residents were called, were all skilled artists or intellectuals. This element was central to Sinclair's design.[29] He wanted the colony to foster a community of intimates who shared interests, affinities, and physical location. Lewis's attraction to Helcion Hall seems to have been linked in part to this combination. According to Schorer, he "met in intimacy and equality so many thoroughly worthwhile people" during his short stay, and their likeness to himself helped make the experience positive.[30] He had found a geographic location where he could feel connected, and he could imagine himself as part of the community because he could see daily what he had in common with the other residents.

Although Lewis enjoyed his time at Helcion Hall, he continued his pattern of frequent moves and seeming indecision: he stayed there for only a month before moving on to New York, and he did not return to Yale until December 1907. After graduating, he held various jobs as a freelance writer, got married, and wrote and published five novels: *Hike and the Aeroplane* (1912), *Our Mr. Wrenn* (1914), *The Trail of The Hawk* (1915), *The Job* (1917), and *The Innocents* (1917). In the meantime, he moved from Washington, D.C., to New York, to California, to Washington State, to Iowa. He even returned to Sauk Centre for a summer stay in 1916, a decision that suggests he might have thought, even in passing, about the possibility of finding a sense of belonging in his own hometown. In a letter he wrote for the local *Sauk Centre Herald* during this brief visit, he proclaimed:

> But I wish to recommend the prescription to Drs. Wallace and Huba who say "Take one homecoming week to restore your faith in Mankind," for a reason which should peculiarly appeal to all who have gone from Sauk Centre to some large city—It will give you friends again! The urbanites who used to live in Sauk Centre will understand what I mean when I say that out of the hundreds or thousands or millions of people in their city, they can have but few friends. The distances, the nervous tension, forbid. When I returned to Sauk Centre the other day after eight years of absence it was astonishing and delightful . . . [t]o go down the pleasant streets in the sunshine and be able to say "Hello, Fay!" "Mornin' Charley!" . . . without receiving in return the congealed state of the big city.[31]

Yet at the same time, he was taking notes for what would become *Main Street* and, as Grace would later record, was again feeling the scorn of the townsfolk as they expressed shock at his desire to take long walks for picnics and made their dullness and rigid view of propriety clear.[32]

Lewis continued to search for a location that would satisfy his need to be connected, and in the winter of 1917–18 he found himself in St. Paul with his wife and their first child. In a November 1917 letter to Upton Sinclair, he noted, "We've come out for the winter and spring . . . in this middle-western environment, watching the solid, stolid Real America in its faults and virtues, its stability and reluctance. And there is an easy friendliness about here rather pleasant."[33] The "here" that he referred to was the beautiful large home he and his wife were renting on St. Paul's prestigious Summit Avenue. His neighbors were some of the most well respected citizens in the city, and they received him with open arms.[34] While in St. Paul, Lewis completed his play *Hobohemia*, in which he elevated midwestern virtues over eastern airs, and in January he wrote a letter to his editor at Holt declaring, "We've made hundreds of good friends in St. Paul—enough parties, despite the war; skating and skiing; all feel well. . . . I'm more 'n happy in Sinpaul."[35] In St. Paul, as at Helcion Hall, his satisfaction and sense of community were related to the degree to which he was surrounded by people whose lives matched his and who actively encouraged his participation in theirs. The social life in St. Paul suited him; there was no doubt that the city's savvy elites admired his intellect.

But Lewis's satisfaction did not last long. By the end of March he had set out again, this time to New York City's Greenwich Village. (His wife and child would follow a few weeks later.)[36] There is some controversy as to whether or not he began *Main Street* in earnest during that summer of 1918, but it is certain that by the time he returned to Minnesota—this time to Minneapolis and then to Mankato—later that year, the time had come for him to crystallize his ruminations about the problems of small-town America and the loneliness that it had nurtured in him.[37]

During this prolonged stay in the Gopher State (1918–19), *Main Street* finally came to fruition. But the success of the novel did not end Lewis's restlessness. His letters to the editors at Harcourt, Brace chronicle his movements across the nation and the world, often making reference to his "boredom" and his desire for new experiences.[38] Underscoring this sentiment was a sentence he wrote in a third-person self-portrait composed in Berlin in 1927: "He detests polite dinner parties. As he listens to the amiable purring of amitrons, he is afflicted with ennui as with disease."[39] More than ten years later, a young admirer who was dining with him at a Madison, Wisconsin, party remarked, "Society had taken him up, but Lewis was never at home in society. Even the subject was distasteful to him, and he changed it before it had been exhausted. He spoke of a trip to Paris."[40]

Yet even though Lewis had left Sauk Centre, Sauk Centre would never leave him. His early years shaped his life and left him searching for an experience of community that apparently was just out of his grasp. It was not that he was avoiding connection with others; he simply did not seem capable of accepting it when it appeared. Even though he had periodic flashes of connection, as at Helcion Hall and in St. Paul, he was unable to translate them into permanent experiences. He sought community throughout his life, and in *Main Street* he worked to explore its limits, its possibilities, and its definition in the new sites of modernizing America. Nonetheless, although the novel was a popular sensation, critics and reviewers seemed to be split with regards to the validity of the story Lewis was telling about small-town America. Some scholars have since offered insight into the relationship between Lewis and his protagonist.[41] But given the centrality of community to both Lewis's life and the contours of this novel, it is striking that in the eleven decades since publication no one has specifically addressed the way in which competing ideas about community shape the work.

Lewis's awkward position in the world of realist writers is partly to blame for this lack of attention.[42] Critical responses to *Main Street* were, from the beginning, tied to the fact that he had produced a realist novel at the tail end of realism's peak, when responses to such works were shifting. By the 1920s, the Howellsian realism of the 1870s and 1880s had given way to naturalistic realism such as Dreiser's *Sister Carrie* (1900), and it was into this second category (sometimes known as *naturalism*, sometimes simply as *realism*) that *Main Street* was grouped.[43] Lewis, like Dreiser, wrote not about the "drama of a broken teacup [or] the tragedy of a walk down the block" but about "the unplumbed depths of the human heart, and the mysteries of sex, and the problems of life, and the black, unsearched penetralia of the soul of man."[44] *Main Street* challenged the complicity of middle-class American ideals and their ability to enrich the nation's moral or social fabric. And into the 1920s and 1930s, Lewis's work reaped the benefits of a still-positive critical climate for realist fiction even as the genre's heyday was drawing to a close.[45]

Even the famous critic H. L. Mencken weighed in on the newly released *Main Street*'s merits. His review in the January 1921 issue of *Smart Set* recommended that readers pay "polite attention" to the new novel: "It is, in brief, good stuff." The article included many favorable comments on Lewis's control of an American realism that "presents characters that are genuinely human [and] . . . also authentically American [and] it carries them through a series of transactions that are all interesting and plausible; it exhibits those transactions thoughtfully . . . in the light of the social and cultural forces underlying them." He noted that the novel was "well written, and full of a sharp sense of comedy, and rich in observation, and competently designed." But "the virtue of the book," he wrote, "lies in its packed and brilliant detail . . . [and its ability] to depict with great care a group of typical Americans."[46]

As Donald Pizer has noted, literary criticism during the 1920s and 1930s was far from monolithic or static and was often influenced by the shifting import of economic stressors and political leanings.[47] Thus, not every *Main Street* critic agreed with Mencken's accolades. For instance, T. K. Whipple, in his 1925 review in the *New Republic,* condemned the novel's "lumpy plot, flat characters, coarse composition, and excessive length."[48] Speaking more generally of Lewis's work, he argued that "the excellence of his rare intervals of real writing is lost in the general glare . . . [and] even *Arrowsmith,* though an artist's as well as a scientist's book, is the work of a mangled artist."[49] Yet even though Whipple claimed that Lewis's works show a "poverty of imagination" he, like most other early reviewers, praised him for offering the public a significant sociological look into an American small town. When Carl Van Doren wrote his biographical sketch of Lewis in 1933, he, too, furthered the image of Lewis as a brave crusader who was using the "vigorous hands of realism" to challenge the "pattern of thought" that had preserved the sacredness of the small town.[50]

Even this tepid form of adoration disappeared as New Criticism and Cold War–influenced scholarship came to the fore after World War II. Primarily interested in formal analysis, not social commentary, these scholars tended to shun fiction that threatened the myth of American progress and democratic superiority.[51] For the next two decades, they continued to ignore many works that could be grouped, by virtue of genre, with the corpus of left-leaning writers such as Lewis and John Dos Passos.[52] A major exception was Alfred Kazin, whose 1942 *On Native*

Grounds: An Interpretation of Modern American Prose Literature includes a chapter on Lewis.[53] Yet Kazin's voice was not loud enough to reverse the trend.[54] Not until the 1970s did scholars begin to heed his advice about the importance of these new realists. But they did, and in the past half-century there has been a general resurgence of interest in and serious criticism of realist works as scholars have begun to take notice of the enduring presence of the form in the twentieth century.[55] Nevertheless, even though scholars have since helped to bring attention back to *Main Street,* academic writing about the novel remains limited, and few have paid attention to the experiences of community that shape life in Lewis's depictions of St. Paul and Gopher Prairie.

This is surprising, for Carol's inability to adjust to the new experience of community that greets her in Gopher Prairie lies at the center of her transition and struggle. She is forced to give up her belief that place and community can be synonymous and faces instead divisiveness and divisions within town boundaries. Undergirding her tribulations is the issue of defining and negotiating the unfamiliar definition of ascribed community while longing for the experiences of a volitional one.

To understand Lewis's view of community in modernizing American, it is essential to understand why and how St. Paul (and, by extension, other American urban centers) made community possible and desirable. What created the "generous indifference" in St. Paul, and why is it absent in Gopher Prairie? Although he structured his novel as a symbolic opposition between town and city, Lewis took care not to paint Gopher Prairie as the actual antithesis of St. Paul. In fact, the novel makes it clear that, in modernizing America, even the smallest town was influenced by an urban worldview. By the late 1910s, both towns and cities across American housed a diverse citizenry and were socially stratified. In both places, residents formed intimate relationships with narrow segments of the population.

In the novel, the size of the two locales is an obvious difference, but Gopher Prairie's problem is not that it is small or provincial. The real problem lies in the impact of those factors on Carol's life—how they thwart her ability to build or experience meaningful community. The city, in contrast, offers her a freedom of association that leads to a more emotionally rewarding experience of community. Importantly, however, the scale and population density of St. Paul make it impossible for any one resident to know all the others, and Carol does not even try: "She went to dances and suppers at the houses of college acquaintances. . . . During her three years of library work several men showed diligent interest in her [but] none of them made her more than pause in thought."[56] Anonymous to most of the city, Carol is able to choose her intimate associates at will, free from the peering eyes of the entire population.

In Gopher Prairie, by contrast, the small number of inhabitants makes such freedom of association impossible and any deviation from the norm difficult. The pressures of social stratification, more than her heart, dictate the makeup of Carol's intimate relationships. Thus, she is unable to nurture the relationships that might make her life happy in Gopher Prairie. Moreover, the town's small size means that all residents have close knowledge of everyone else's private life, which forces Carol to confront the internal divisions around her. In St. Paul, Carol can imagine herself part of the city as a whole. Here, in her husband's beloved hometown, her place-based idealism is dashed, her intimates are limited by social custom, and she finds it impossible to construct desirable communities, either real or imagined.

Lewis might have chosen to construct Gopher Prairie and St. Paul as two poles in a symbolic opposition, much as Carol herself sees them. Instead, his narrator maintains a skeptical, ironic, though sympathetic distance from her viewpoint. After all, the power of the book's discussion of community arises from a careful delineation of the ways in which the two venues are both similar and divergent.[57] This becomes clear only by examining Carol's experiences in each location.

When the narrator first introduces readers to Carol's life in St. Paul, he appears to denigrate the communal life of cities. He tells us that she is alone most of the time, that "she read[s] scores of books, . . . [takes] walks, and [is] sensible about shoes and diet."[58] "It [is] a frail and blue and lonely Carol" who arrives at the dinner party where she first meets Will Kennicott.[59] She is not isolated per se, but her indifference about her job has cast a pallor over her life. She is missing something—a vocation, a purpose. Yet this solitude does not indicate a lack of community. On the contrary, the novel links Carol's apparent loneliness to a vocational quest;

not once does it imply that she lacks a sense of connection to other human beings. In fact, it presents her isolation as a virtue of the city; it is merely a side-effect of the forces that allow her to live an independent and otherwise fulfilling life in St. Paul.

In St. Paul Carol is free to move in, out of, and around a variety of groups, events, and circumstances. She goes to dances, takes long walks, dines at the homes of college acquaintances, and reads voraciously. She makes decisions and chooses acquaintances without the interference of overbearing social controls. This freedom becomes the gold ring that she grasps at from the confines of Gopher Prairie. There, she longs for the anonymity that allowed her to dream and take up new interests without feeling the weight of a hundred eyes on her every move. In St. Paul she was free to associate with whom she wished. More importantly, she was free to end relationships if they did not suit her—as she did with the men who pursued without making her "more than pause in thought."[60]

Among her St. Paul comrades Carol could count her fellow librarians, a traveling insurance company representative and his wife, and a variety of college acquaintances. Without fanfare, the novel offers an eclectic yet telling picture of the familiar crowd gathered at the Marburys' home on the night Carol meets Will. On arrival she sees her hosts, a woman who teaches gymnastics in a high school, a chief clerk from the Great Northern Railway offices, and a young lawyer. The scene depicts Carol among a group of intimates whom she considers part of her community but whom she is free to reject if they do not suit her. Through such casual, expansive, and flexible social networks and relationships, she becomes more fully herself. Her loneliness, happiness, and sense of community are within her own control.

All this changes once she takes up residence in Gopher Prairie. The town is far from being a major urban center, but it does boast a diverse citizenry. It has its own "smart set" as well as a struggling Scandinavian radical, the evangelical Mrs. Bogart, and the philosophical Eric Valbourg. The small town does not fit into any definition of a traditional or natural community—if one defines *community* as being marked by commonality more than difference.[61] Yet Carol's life becomes circumscribed. Written and unwritten rules, spoken and implied, dictate the organization of the social hierarchy and place extraordinary pressure on citizens to conform or be snubbed. The town's social circles have been long established, and Carol quickly learns that personal desire has little to do with how one chooses a group of intimates.

Even before Carol and Will marry, readers learn about these strata. As the lovers talk over their future together, Will runs down a list of the nine individuals he most wants her to meet in his beloved prairie town. The list includes not only the town's wealthiest citizen but also its well-read Latin teacher, its storeowner, its Congregationalist preacher, and its leading attorney.[62] Taken as a whole, this grouping reveals some of the characteristics that Will sees as necessary for inclusion in his intimate community. While diverse in some ways, all of his chosen few are well educated, native-born, and financially well-off. Importantly, they are also acceptable to one another. They and Will believe that their social circle constitutes the sum total of the individuals with whom Carol, as Will's wife, should form close relationships.

After marrying, the new Mrs. Kennicott is the honored guest at a party at the home of Sam Clark, who owns the town's main hardware store. The *Gopher Prairie Weekly Dauntless* describes the gathering as "one of the most charming affairs of the season [attended by] many of our most prominent citizens."[63] Lewis took pains to paint capsule portraits of the guests. In addition to some of the prominent folk on Will's list, the assembly includes Harry and Juanita Haydock, the informal leaders of the younger smart set; Ezra Stowbody, the local bank president; and Chet Dashaway, the furniture-store owner and undertaker, who, according to Will, can "talk your arm off, about religion or politics or books or anything."[64] The only attendee who is neither a wealthy businessman nor a well-educated professional (or a wife) is Nat Hicks, the town tailor. Still, Will accepts his presence; after all, they have known each other for years. Will impresses upon Carol that Nat's presence proves that the townsfolk are "democratic"; yet when pushed on the topic, he admits that he would hunt with Nat but not with his barber. He wants her to understand that "there's no use running this democracy thing into the ground."[65] The sentence is telling. For, as Carol soon discovers, those who attempt to challenge the town's power structure, belief system, or social boundaries are asking to be ostracized. After the couple leaves the party, Will chastises Carol for discussing unsavory topics with the "conservative" crowd. He claims to be pointing out this faux pas for her own good but makes it clear that she "ought to be more careful about shocking folks." His reason: "Juanita Haydock is such a damn cat [that] I wouldn't give her a chance to criticize me."[66]

Thus begins Carol's lesson in the politics of community in Gopher Prairie. There were limited groups to which any resident could belong, each with its own culture and boundary. Blurring the boundaries was unacceptable. But she has brought with her the ideas that shaped her life in St. Paul. She firmly believes that communities are, by definition, made up of people with whom one feels a sense of affinity and connection. Choosing or rejecting such social intimates had been commonplace in St. Paul, and she tries to re-create the experience in Gopher Prairie. Yet as she works to establish relationships with social outcasts—among them, Eric Valbourg, the sexually ambiguous artist and dreamer; Guy Pollock, the romantic attorney; Fern Mullins, the spinster schoolteacher—the opinions of the leading townsfolk become a serious impediment. For instance, over the course of the novel, she becomes close to her maid, Bea Sorenson, and the man who will become Bea's husband, Miles Bjornstrom, otherwise known as the Red Swede. They are relatively poor and have strong ethnic ties. Bea arrives in Gopher Prairie aboard the same train that Carol does, finds employment in the Kennicott house, and becomes a confidante and a dear friend. But the townspeople are suspicious of Carol's relationship with Bea: they see her and the town's many other poor and laboring immigrants as necessary problems, not as potential friends. In time Carol yields to this social pressure and drops Bea.

During tea at a meeting of the Jolly Seventeen, the local elite ladies' club, Carol voices her support for higher wages for the Swedish female laborers who cook, clean, and take care of the wealthy women's children. The other members respond with surprise and intense opposition. After Carol insists that honest work deserves honest pay, Mrs. Dave Dyer retorts, "Honest? Do you call it honest to hit us up for every cent they can get?" Her response underscores the sentiments she uttered moments before, when she proclaimed that the Swedes were "simply ghastly hired girls," as bad as the problematic male "Svenkas" who work in the town's planing mill.[67]

This blatant attitude underscores the fact that there are clear limits to belonging in this town, and Carol learns that anyone who protests such marginalization is doubly ostracized. The clubwomen's anger stems not

only from the hired girls' status as foreigners but also (and more importantly) from the knowledge that the girls are unwilling to passively accept
their marginalization. "I don't know what the country's coming to," fumes
Juanita Haydock, "with these Scandahoofian clodhoppers demanding
every cent you can save, and so ignorant and impertinent, and . . . demanding bath-tubs and everything—as if they weren't mighty good and lucky
at home if they got a bath in the wash-tub."[68] Juanita claims that "all that
class of people" is "ungrateful," apparently because they are not content
to receive the remains of other people's dinners or to have their social
lives dictated by their employers. The problem is that they embrace their
self-worth.

After Carol voices support for the Scandinavian laborers, she is all but
blacklisted from the inner circle of Gopher Prairie. But in fact her reaction
to the servant question is merely the final straw for members of the Jolly
Seventeen and their compatriots. From the day she arrived, her behavior, her background, even her clothes had disturbed the establishment.
She learns of her myriad flaws from a confidante, the schoolteacher, Vida
Sherwin:

> The illiterate ones resent your references to anything further away than
> Minneapolis. . . . [T]hey think you dress too well, . . . [they think] you're
> affected, . . . [t]hey think you're showing off when you say "American"
> instead of "Ammurrican" [and] they think you're too frivolous. . . . Mrs.
> Elder thought you was patronizing when you said she had a "pretty
> little car" . . . [and] every housewife in town is doubtful about your
> being so chummy with . . . Bea.[69]

It appears that all the traits that made Carol acceptable in a St. Paul
crowd are doing just the opposite in Gopher Prairie. Her wit, her sense of
fashion, and her interest in the working class all make her, in Vida's words,
"suspect." Most damning of all is her intellect. As Carol herself says much
later in the novel, "the respectability of the Gopher Prairies . . . is reinforced by vows of poverty and chastity in the matter of knowledge."[70] She
has ended up in a town where everyone watches her constantly, discusses
her goings-on in detail, and eventually retreats into interactions that are
purely utilitarian.

Whether she entered a store or swept the back porch, or stood at the bay-window in the living-room, the village peeped at her. . . . [D]aily she was thrown into panic. She saw curtains slide back into innocent smoothness, old women who had been entering their houses slipped out again to stare at her. . . . [One morning] she had the shock of shame as she entered Ludelmeyer's. The grocer, his clerk, and neurotic Mrs. Dave Dyer had been giggling about something. They halted, looked embarrassed, babbled about onions. Carol felt guilty. . . . Except Dave Dyer, Sam Clark and Raymie Witherspoon, there were no merchants of whose welcome Carol was certain. . . . [Furthermore,] [w] hen she dared to go shopping in her new checked suit with the black-embroidered sulphur collar, she had as good as invited all of Gopher Prairie . . . to investigate her.[71]

Lewis's narrator ends this recitation of Carol's struggles by affirming that she "could not endure it."[72] Freedom of thought, dress, and association was grounds for persecution. She was paralyzed by the knowledge that she was seen as a foreigner, an oddity, and a woman to be avoided. She was an outsider in the Gopher Prairie community. Escape seemed to be the only solution.

In many ways, Lewis's portrayal of Gopher Prairie supports Ross's belief that city life fundamentally changes the nature of human relationships that marked small-town life. Yes, diversity creates division as localities grow. Yes, intimate communities are more associational than natural; they do not necessarily correspond with place-based experiences or understandings of community. But, in a dramatic break from Ross, and in apparent solidarity with the newer reality of affinity-based community, *Main Street* repudiates the tendency to see these changes as problematic. Like MacIver and the communitarians of his day, the novel hints that it is possible for intimate communities to thrive in urban America.

If the possibilities for forming desirable affinity-based communities are identifiably different in St. Paul and Gopher Prairie, then the contrast between relative possibilities for forming place-based communities in each locality are even more dramatic. True, neither venue offers Carol an actual experience of place-based community (if the entirety of the municipality was the benchmark); in neither is she engaged in reciprocal relationships with every other resident of the town or city. But Carol, like most modern Americans, is not so much interested in trying to create a lived experience of geography-as-community as she is in reinforcing a notion that it is present in an abstract sense. To this end, Lewis chose to portray her as a white middle-class American who is able, despite her narrow intimate communities of daily life, to imagine herself as part of a group united by a shared place of residence and committed to its survival in modern America. In St. Paul, Carol comes close to this place-based ideal; in Gopher Prairie, she is unable even to imagine it.

In Gopher Prairie, Carol's decision to interact with other shunned towns-folk buoys and reinforces her indignation and sense of alienation. As much as she wants to blur barriers and associate freely, she has begun to internalize the pattern of isolating distinct demographic groups. In time, she herself begins to participate in, even embrace, the norms that divide the town. This is most obvious in her relationship with Bea. For months after first arriving in the Kennicott home, she is Carol's sole confidante. Carol thinks of her much as she had thought of her girlfriends in college: "As a companion [she was] altogether superior to the matrons of the Jolly Seventeen."[73] However, Carol's own prejudices against the "Lower Classes"—ingrained since childhood—soon begin to surface; and when Bea marries the town anarchist, she becomes embarrassed by the friendship with her maid. Although Carol "hate[s] herself for it," she hopes no one is watching her visit Bea and Miles's shanty.[74] Most distressing to any reader who hopes to see Carol rise above the town's stratification is the harrowing scene in which, bowing to peer pressure, she chooses not to attend Bea's funeral. Instead, she stands in her window watching from a distance as Miles marches alone behind the caskets of his wife and infant son. Carol's guilt tears at her heart, but her actions cannot be reversed. Her decision to remain home reinforces the ways in which diversity (rendered as relative distance from the centers of economic, political, and social capital) creates divisions in Gopher Prairie.

By this time the novel has made it clear that the more interest Carol takes in the town's outcasts, the more she internalizes and accepts the town's social divisions. She can still intellectualize the need for cohesion, but she finds it increasingly difficult to challenge the status quo or imagine that it can be changed. After spending so much time in the Juanita Haydock crowd, she discovers that it is impossible to transcend the social stratifications of Gopher Prairie without risking her own social status. So she embraces the Jolly Seventeen, becomes "part of the town. Its philosophy and its feuds dominat[e] her."[75] As guilty as she feels about avoiding Miles and Bea in their time of greatest need, she chooses to preserve her status and appears to give up her dream of place-based unity along with any chance at having truly fulfilling communal relationships. Miles's departure and his forced, gruff "goodbye" confirm that future.[76]

Conversely, Carol's experiences in St. Paul illustrate the degree to which such petty divisions can be reversed—at times, even avoided—in places with more dramatically diverse demographics and significantly larger populations. In Gopher Prairie class divisions are insurmountable, but Carol seems to be able to overcome them in St. Paul. Ironically, her observations of the capital city's marginalized citizens do not create a sense of division but support her belief that a community can exist based on place of residence. In Gopher Prairie, her concern for outsiders pushes her to reinforce the very class, ethnic, and ideological divisions and alienating behavior she abhors. Yet in St. Paul, she feels that she is part of a broad, diverse whole that is the city. The key: St. Paul gives her the ability to distance herself from many of the difficult moral quandaries with which she must engage directly in the small town.

In two critical passages Carol takes a visual inventory of her respective hometowns. Taken together, they establish that only in an urban setting can a geographic definition of community be imagined. The first is set on a cold February day, not long after she has arrived in Gopher Prairie. Venturing out on her own, Will Kennicott's new bride turns to view the town from a distance. It is a lonely Carol who walks into the wind that day for, even after only a few months in her new hometown, she is overwhelmed with the fear that she will "never become an authentic part of the town."[77] As the young wife of a well-respected doctor, she feels she should be accepted into the bosom of the smart set and feel at one with the business owners and town leaders who have such a comfortable rapport with her husband. Yet as each day passes, the town and its inhabitants come to feel more and more like her enemies. So, on the second day of her husband's business-related absence, she flees "from the creepy house for a walk," heading for the edge of town as though she is searching for physical distance as an antidote to the psychic distance she had begun to internalize. After stopping to catch her breath in the warmth of a barn, she "struggle[s] past the earth-banked cottages to open country, to a farm and a low hill corrugated with hard wood." The narrator tells us, "In her loose nutria coat, seal toque, virginal cheeks, unmarked by lines of village jealousies, she was as out of place on this dreary hillside as a scarlet tanager on an ice-floe." The simile is important, for it reinforces that Carol's outward appearance is a key source of village scorn.[78] Every aspect of her being, from the color of her cheeks to her choice of a coat, marks her and makes her feel like an outsider—a feeling that is reinforced when she turns her attention back to the place she has just escaped.

On this hillside, far away from other human life, Carol's sense of isolation becomes visible. When she looks down on Gopher Prairie, onto Main Street itself, she does not see anything she knows or holds dear. Instead, she sees "the snow, stretching without break from streets to devouring prairie beyond, wip[ing] out the town's pretense of being a shelter." Even the houses do not hint at life or hospitality; they are "bleak specks on a white sheet. . . . [And] her heart shiver[s] with that still loneliness as her body shiver[s] with the wind."[79] In this scene, Lewis chose to draw on images of savage wilderness and the "devouring" prairie common to earlier midwestern writers as he painted a panorama of an alienating location that carries the name *Gopher Prairie*. This empty, inhospitable spot has cast out one of its inhabitants and offers only a chilly snub as a send-off. From her perch Carol experiences not a feeling of ownership or a feeling of admiration at seeing the town to which she ostensibly belongs. She is overwhelmed instead by a renewed sense of isolation and distance between herself and all those who also call Gopher Prairie home. Lewis's compelling metaphor of a voracious beast drives the scene's finale. Left with nowhere else to go, Carol runs back into the town—into the monster that would devour her—"all the while protesting that she want[s] a city's yellow glare of shop windows and restaurants."[80] In this way, the novel reestablishes that Carol sees urban spaces as redemptive, safe, and embracing.

By this point in *Main Street,* readers are not surprised to learn that, after a survey of Gopher Prairie, Carol might wish to return to the city. For, in an earlier scene, set less than two years before, readers see her looking out over a different hometown—the city of St. Paul—and responding in a nearly opposite manner. Thus, Lewis created a memory for Carol (and the reader) against which to judge her relationship with Gopher Prairie.

Not two years before her solitary survey of Gopher Prairie, on a bright, sunny day, Carol and Will decided to go "tramping" into the hills overlooking the city, walking "from St. Paul down the river to Mendota, . . . Carol youthful in a tam-o'-shanter of mole velvet, a blue serge suit with an absurdly and agreeably broad turndown linen collar, and frivolous ankles above athletic shoes."[81] Notably, her appearance carries no negative connotations, nor does it result in the type of isolation she will experience in Gopher Prairie.

The pair crosses the St. Paul High Bridge, and from the bluffs on the opposite bank they look "back at St. Paul on its hills; an imperial sweep from the dome of the cathedral to the dome of the state capital."[82] In this line the narrator positions Carol as a grand overseer, as one who knows the city and feels that it knows her. She is at home with what she sees from her perch; she can absorb its majesty without questioning her place in the life and times of the city before her. She is part of all of it, and it is part of her.

Carol's sense of peace and security leads her not to flee from her visage and return to the town (as she would later do in the Gopher Prairie scene) but to continue her walk along the hills of Mendota all the way to the fort and house that mark the area's earliest permanent European settlements. There, in "the bold stone house which General Sibley, the king of fur-traders, built in 1835, . . . Carol and Kennicott found prints from other days which the house had seen." The place "had the air of centuries. . . . It suggested to them a common American Past."[83] The historical setting and authorial choice to link it to a description of her grand view of contemporary St. Paul serves to enhance Carol's sense of belonging, connection, and community with the people and places that had played a role in creating her city.

Whereas viewing downtown Gopher Prairie from a distance leaves Carol feeling like a social outcast, regarding St. Paul from a similar vantage point does just the opposite. It links her urban life to both the near and far past: she is part of all the places and people she can see or reach from the bluffs; and she is part of the place called St. Paul, which is also the place she calls home. In other words, this is Carol's imagined community of St. Paul. Not only can she conceive of the unity of all residents, despite her personal distance from most of them and their distance from one another, but she can picture, in Benedict Anderson's words, a "deep, horizontal comradeship" despite "the actual inequality and exploitation that may prevail."[84]

Importantly, the factors that make Carol's imagined sense of place-based community possible in St. Paul are the same that make fulfilling affinity-based community possible. In her mind, the size, heterogeneity, and anonymity of the city mute the ever-present divisions in St. Paul and allow her to imagine it as an organic whole and herself as part of it. This type of distancing is not possible in Gopher Prairie.

Another poignant scene in *Main Street* reveals the ways in which proximity and small scale limit the possibility of imagined place-based community while reinscribing affinity-based communal bonds. On that same February day that Carol first sees Gopher Prairie from a distance, she also sees the immigrant settlements along its edge. Yet rather than offer readers a sense that the two are connected, the novel clarifies that in Carol's mind they are not. By separating the descriptive passages detailing the immigrant settlement from the rest of the account of Gopher Prairie, readers understand that Carol sees the area and its inhabitants as something foreign to her and to the town. First, the novel separates Carol's narrative perception of the area (called "Swede Hollow" by the townsfolk) from her view of the town proper.[85] It does not flow directly from her discussion of the main areas of downtown but is inserted only after readers learn that his protagonist has fled back toward the town's "huddle of streets" and after she reflects on the townspeople's prejudices. By creating these topographical and narrative boundaries, the novel formally positions Swede Hollow as a separate entity and emphasizes its division from the community of Gopher Prairie. The segregation is reinforced by the passages detailing what Carol sees in Swede Hollow on that gray winter day:

> She circled the outskirts of the town and viewed the slum of "Swede Hollow." . . . In Gopher Prairie the Sam Clark's boasted, "you don't get any of this poverty that you find in cities—always plenty of work—no

need for charity—man got to be blame shiftless if he don't get ahead."
But now that the summer mask of leaves and grass was gone, Carol
discovered misery and dead hope. In a shack of thin boards covered
with tar-paper she saw the washer-woman, Mrs. Steinhof, working in
the gray steam. Outside, her six-year-old boy chopped wood. He had
a torn jacket, muffler of a blue like skimmed milk. His hands were
covered with red mittens through which protruded his chapped, raw
knuckles. He halted to blow on them, to cry disinterestedly. A family
of recently arrived Finns were camped in an abandoned stable, a man
of eighty was picking up lumps of coal along the railroad.[86]

The passage evokes desolation and isolation, not only with regard to
the subjects and to the townsfolk who see them as "shiftless" but also to
Carol, who is isolated from the people she is looking at. Even her good
intentions become reasons to leave these others alone. "She did not know
what to do about [what she saw]. She felt that these independent citizens,
who had been taught that they belonged to a democracy, would resent
her trying to play Lady Bountiful."[87] Ironically, the fact that Carol knows
some of these others personally is the very thing that enhances her sense
of division and pushes her to distance herself from them. Her guilt and
angst stem from recognition of the lines that the town has drawn.

The novel reinforces this idea in a description of an encounter between
Carol and Miles Bjornstrom on the same day. Passing a shack amid the
jumble of homes in Swede Hollow, she meets the town handyman "in a
rough brown dogskin coat . . . [and with a] square face [that was] confident."[88] After learning his name, Carol is invited into the warmth of his
home and engages in a lengthy discussion about politics and the town
personalities. Yet even as she comes to see Miles as a possible friend, her
image of him is based not on his place within the town but on the way in
which he offers her a vision of life outside of it. Her closeness with this
outsider reinforces the limits of her own position.

In contrast, Carol's first two encounters with the poor and destitute
of St. Paul show us an image of a city in which even the downtrodden
can be understood in some way as members of a larger place-based community called St. Paul. These encounters dramatize the "generous indifference" that make such understandings possible. They suggest that, in

cities, difference can be appropriated or erased to allow a vision of city-as-community to coexist alongside narrower daily experiences. In the first Carol is a senior at Blodgett College. Trailing after their handsome sociology professor, she and a class full of "giggling" co-eds trek through the prisons, charity offices, and employment agencies of the Twin Cities. As Carol follows the other students, she feels "indignant at [their] prodding curiosity . . . their manner of staring at the poor as at a Zoo. She felt herself a great liberator. She put a hand to her mouth, her forefinger and thumb quite painfully pinching her lower lip, and frowned and enjoyed being aloof."[89] Here in the city the poor and the needy are nameless, faceless objects of study; they exist in relation to her as "liberator" (a title she does not reject). While they draw out empathy, they do not engage her deep emotions. She approaches them as a scholar, an observer. Yet, paradoxically, it is precisely this indifference that allows her to imagine them as part of her community. She can envision some future moment when her life and theirs might intersect, when their presence in the city might give hers meaning or offer her some redemption. For the time being, however, there is no need to "do" anything for or with them. She can remain "aloof" and still fold them into the catalog of people and places that exist in her general landscape. In this way they are part of an abstraction called "St. Paul."[90] To be separate yet feel connected and in control: this articulates the novel's most basic point of contrast between the large city and the growing town. In the city a sense of distance is a positive force in a reimagined understanding of how community might be understood in modern America.

Conversely, Carol's familiarity with Gopher Prairie's poor residents and their critics leaves her unable to escape established social norms. Unlike in St. Paul, the fact that she sees them up close and notes their suffering only distances them further. Because she understands the delicate balance of power and lines of influence in Gopher Prairie, it is impossible for her to conflate "the poor" and "Gopher Prairie" even in her mind. She knows there is no possibility for mere cursory involvement in the life of a Swede Hollow resident. To engage in any way is to commit to upending the power structures. In St. Paul, however, the poor are so numerous and so anonymous and so separate from Carol's everyday life that she does not have to risk a challenge to her own experience of intimate community in order to accept them into her image of city-as-community. As a nameless mass, the St. Paul poor can be absorbed into the abstraction of "St. Paul" without forcing Carol to abandon either her imagined place-based idea of community or her intimate community of fellow professionals and free thinkers.

Carol's expansive and dialectical understanding of community is rendered most poignantly in the scene with Will on the Mendota bluffs, as they take in the panorama below. The novel carefully connects Carol's view (and thus her sense of identity) of a historic St. Paul to the lives of the city's residents who fit into social strata that are vastly different from hers. Here, in the authorial decision to have Carol visually embrace St. Paul's poor as part of the larger, historic, romantic scene without a sense of personal involvement or culpability, we understand best the novel's contribution to a modern notion of community in America: that is, an urban resident's ability to simultaneously hold a *belief* in locale as community alongside a lived *experience* of affinity-based community.

As she crosses the High Bridge, her eyes are drawn "far down beneath it on the St. Paul side, upon mud flats," to "a wild settlement of chicken-infested gardens and shanties patched together from discarded sign-boards, sheets of corrugated iron, and planks fished out of the river."[91] Perched above the river, "Carol leaned over the rail of the bridge to look down at this Yang-Tse village, [and] in delicious imaginary fear she shrieked that she was dizzy with the height; and it was an extremely human satisfaction to have a strong male snatch her back to safety." Here, in contrast to her Swede Hollow experience, she at once identifies the St. Paul poor as an unknown mass far removed from the ethnic makeup of "her" St. Paul, and quickly shifts her focus to other, more pressing concerns such as ensuring her safety and shoring up a romantic relationship. By highlighting the otherness of the poor, Carol is able to maintain her intellectual and physical distance from the impoverished residents of the river-edge settlements even as she demonstrates that she needs them to be there: she relies on their presence to motivate specific desires about her chosen life with Will. By translating an unknown into a playful and romantic scenario, she incorporates the poor into her imaginary world and thus into her view of St. Paul, embracing the "Yang-Tse village" as she will later embrace orientalism in dress and food.

Lewis links this scene directly to Carol's grandiose description of the "imperial sweep" of St. Paul "from the dome of the Cathedral to the dome of the state Capitol." In Carol's St. Paul, the poor—kept at a safe distance, marked as unknowable, and appearing only in the aggregate—are much easier to imagine as part of the larger entity represented by St. Paul's grandest facades than Miles Bjornstrom is to the "black specks" of downtown Gopher Prairie. In short, the extensive diversity that marks life in St. Paul is what allows Carol to identify herself as a member of a place-based community without giving up the ability to develop intimate communities of choice. The city, because of its heterogeneity and the related social distance among many of citizens, allows inhabitants to imagine the feeling of place-based unity that social scientists such as Ross believed was limited to small towns but that MacIver assured readers was possible in modern America. It allows people like Carol to reimagine and hold in balance multiple ideas and experiences of community.

In Lewis's rendering of this St. Paul setting, then, he suggests that it is only in the city of St. Paul (an urban place) that Carol can even imagine being connected to all residents of a given locale. Ironically, only in the large city, where narrow, affinity-based networks shape her intimate, reciprocal relationships, is she able to envision any sense of connection based on shared residence. Importantly, the novel suggests that the relative anonymity or "indifference" of the city combined with the freedom of knowing that she cannot know everyone there makes it possible for Carol to welcome all residents into her mind's-eye view of the place she calls home.

Through the experiences of Carol Kennicott, Lewis constructs a complex definition of community, one that was useful for understanding life in urban America by 1920. In his view, community is absent if it is defined as physical or political unity among *all* residents of a geopolitical locale; it is present if it is defined as self-selecting groups of intimates (that can extend beyond the boundaries of the locale) and/or as an imagined unity with everyone in the locale, past and present. Rather, narrow affiliations and broad imagined communities are symbiotically related and can comfortably coexist. By contrast, Lewis describes community in Gopher Prairie as limited but divisive. There, Carol tries to make links between antagonistic individuals and groups but she is unable to ever fully incorporate every one into either her experience or her vision of the town as a whole.

She knows and understands too much about the town's inner workings; the other residents know and understand too much as well. Her anxiety on that first day in Gopher Prairie had resulted from being both unable to hide from the gaze of others and unable to avert her own gaze from the otherness everywhere around her. Her experience is the experience of her fellow townsfolk. There is no "generous indifference" to be found. As a result, not only is there no *experience* of town-as-community but there is no way to *imagine* it into being. And by the end of the novel Carol has resigned herself to this fact.

Lewis scholars agree that his greatest feat was his ability to portray particular angles of the nation he readers knew so well. On the issue of community, one of the most pressing social concerns of the day, he entered boldly into the debate, challenging those such as Ross, who trumpeted the small-town ideal, and supporting those such as MacIver and the communitarians, who saw modern city life as desirable and argued that community could survive within it, albeit in new forms.

Main Street highlights the way in which middle-class, white, native-born Americans thought about, negotiated, and experienced communal life in one of the nation's growing urban centers, and Lewis's portrayal of and questions about community life in cities and small towns positioned the novel squarely within wider sociological and popular debates about the nature and future of community in modernizing America. Of course, *Main Street* cannot be read as a sociological record of life in early twentieth-century Minnesota or anywhere else, but its popularity suggests that the writer's view of community and Carol's experience of it may have been familiar to his readers. Like Carol, they were renegotiating and reimagining what community could mean in the modern age. Yet as the novel reveals, not all modernizing Americans had access to the multiple meanings that the concept was coming to include. For instance, Carol embraces the diversity of St. Paul from a distance, but that diversity is not represented in her intimate, experiential community. It is real only in her imagination. In everyday life, at her dinner parties and on her long walks, her confidants are all people who share key economic and lifestyle characteristics with her. They include no seem of the working class, no newly arrived immigrants, no one who appears to be anything other than white. They are all more or less like Carol: middle-class, well-educated, native-born, and white. They, too, are a smart set. They, too, are the Jolly Seventeen.

The point is that Carol is able to rationalize this stratification in St. Paul because *she* can *imagine* herself as part of something larger as well. She can integrate members of many other demographic groups into her mind's-eye view of the St. Paul community, even as she remains comfortably situated in her relatively homogeneous daily life. And she can do this because of her privileged position near the centers of power.

For those she embraces without knowing, what does community mean and where does one find it? We do not hear the voices of the poor, the homeless, or the immigrants in the St. Paul of *Main Street*. Their intimate communities and the ways in which they understand them do not appear in its pages. At their mealtime gatherings would they host a group that shared the demographic characteristics of the Marburys' guests? Their imagined communities and the ways in which they understood them do not appear on its pages. Crucially, if they were standing on the bluffs overlooking the city, would they feel as if they had earned a spot in its dramatic sweep?

What Lewis failed to acknowledge explicitly in *Main Street* is that in St. Paul Carol occupies a unique and privileged position. The ideal experience of community that she has—one in which imagined place-based unity and intimate, affinity-based community coexist and commingle—was not a universal experience in modernizing America, even if it was a commonly articulated definition. It may have been true for white, middle-class, native-born Americans, even women. But other groups in American cities found this hard to realize. Affinity-based communities were real for everyone—Lewis was on target here—but members of marginalized groups often found restrictions (either de jure or de facto) placed on their freedom to enter into communal relationships, not unlike what Carol saw in Gopher Prairie.

Importantly, not only were experiences of community in modernizing America circumscribed by one's position vis-à-vis the various hierarchies of urban places, but the ability to imagine oneself as a member of a place-based community was limited in the same way. What Lewis's novel suggests is that those whose affinity-based communities were similar in form and membership to the individuals and groups at the center of the political, economic, and social structures that shaped life in a place and time driven by the logic of industrial capitalism were more likely than others to imagine themselves to be part of anything resembling place-based community. Although marginalized St. Paulites may have wished for something resembling city-as-community, by the time *Main Street* was published these men and women (most noticeably the poor and/or non-white residents) had become increasingly aware that this was less and less possible for them, either experientially or in the abstract. So, different groups of St. Paulites moved through the opening years of the twentieth century searching for, negotiating, recasting, re-creating and transforming what community was to mean for them and for the nation as a whole. Cultural products and cultural production were at the center of this work.

CHAPTER 2

IMAGES AND IMAGINING

Photographing Community

Cameras pervaded early twentieth-century America, and in St. Paul photographs appeared everywhere. Standard studio portraits remained popular with many of the city's residents; but as the new century dawned, other photographic forms challenged their ubiquity. More St. Paulites were snapping their own photos of family, friends, and surroundings, thanks to the increasingly inexpensive and accessible camera technology, while serious amateurs experimented with larger-format cameras and developed their own images at the St. Paul Camera Club.[1] The city's progressive reformers used photographs to document and dramatize their accounts of the area's social problems—notably, in printed reports about the city's poverty and poor housing conditions. The leading local newspapers, too, added to the volume of circulating images. Savvy editors and publishers took advantage of improved reproduction techniques and replaced hand-drawn illustrations with photographs to accompany their news stories. On a daily basis, then, the majority of St. Paul citizens, like their counterparts elsewhere in the nation, were active participants in the creation, dissemination, and interpretation of photographic representations of themselves and their city.[2]

In 1900, photos were still somewhat of a novelty, and the camera—an instrument that could capture a moment in time and produce an object that would reflect that moment back to the viewer—still fascinated many

Americans. Much of the attraction had to do with the technology's apparent ability to capture and re-create reality in a way nothing else at the time did. Yet photographic images were far from being representations of any objective reality, for in one way or another all were intended to create and record a reality that a specific photographer alone saw through the lens. Because photographs capture only a portion of the real while purporting to show reality, they inherently embody the ideas and worldviews of their creators or disseminators. Every photograph, as John Berger has argued, "bear[s] witness to a human choice being exercised in a given situation . . . [for] photography is the process of rendering observation self-conscious." A photograph "uses the *given* to *explain* its recording."[3]

Beyond the photographer's conscious decisions, the accompanying text and arrangement of images work together to create the connoted meaning of a photograph or set of photographs. Consequently, as they are recording and disseminating particular images of their world, photographers, album organizers, editors, and publishers are also shaping that world into something they believe or hope to be true. When presenting their work to others and themselves, they offer viewers the chance to re-interpret an image in the context of their own lives so as to make sense of their own worlds.[4] In modernizing St. Paul, private citizens, organizations, and civic leaders pressed photographers and photographs into service to depict and promote specific experiences and definitions of communal life in the city. Yet in spite of some photographs' efforts to illustrate a notion of place-based community, there was a persistent message about the limits of that type of community in St. Paul.[5]

Examining three different types of photographs will bear out this argument. First, from a close examination of two family collections—one from a white, professional, middle-class family (the Dunns), one from a working-class African American family (the Gardners)—it is possible to outline some of the boundaries of intimate community in St. Paul and to flesh out how family photographs worked to reinforce them. Clearly, increasing residential and structural segregation made it possible and common for St. Paulites to pursue both class- and race-based forms of communal interaction without actively excluding other classes or races. Family photographs provided a cultural parallel for this limiting.

The second grouping, social reform photographs, offers a variation on this theme. Those under study were disseminated during a large, well-funded 1917 housing survey published by the city's leading charitable organization, a fact that suggests the centrality of photography to the goals of the reform movements that were sweeping the nation in the early twentieth century. These survey photographs managed to complicate any simple understanding of the mechanisms for establishing community boundaries in St. Paul. An investigation of the interaction between text and image and an inquiry into the purpose of the report and its findings reveal that, in contrast to the more passive imagining done in and by family photographers, some St. Paulites were actively involved in using photographs to define and reinforce the characteristics of two communities: the report's lower-class subjects versus its middle- and upper-class viewers.

The third type of photograph shows less intentionality but just as much concern about a public image of the St. Paul community. By the turn of the twentieth century, the city's newspapers had begun to take advantage of the increased ease of photography reproduction and made images a focal point of their publications. At the time St. Paul had a range of newspapers (including a labor publication and several representing immigrant and white ethnic residents). But four papers—and their many photographic images—played a crucial role in community discourse and renegotiation: the *St. Paul Pioneer Press*, the *St. Paul Dispatch*, the *Daily News*, and the *Appeal*. The first two were part of the mainstream white press: they were morning and evening papers owned by the same company and edited by the same man. The *Daily News* was their leading challenger and billed itself as focusing on local news, while the *Appeal* was the city's only African American paper and had a reach beyond St. Paul. Each publication used photographs in ways that offered readers a particular and limited view of who constituted the imagined community of St. Paul.[6]

Turn-of-the-century photographs reveal much about the structure of community in modernizing America, and both the photographs and the photographers became active participants in the renegotiation and restructuring that was taking place. Ultimately, due to such diverse issues as framing, image-text pairings, and choice of publishable images, both public and private photographic representations of St. Paul between 1900 and 1920 indicate an experience of community and produce an image of the same that was tightly—though not simply—linked to racial and class distinctions much more so than to locale.

Many St. Paul families took photographs during the first two decades of the twentieth century. While these collections belonged to families with different racial, ethnic, and class identities, the images had a great deal in common. And while the specific individuals or recorded sites differed from collection to collection, an overall survey of family albums illustrates that family communities were closed: that is, the idea of family as an entity did not extend far beyond the bonds of blood ties or the four walls of the family home.[7] St. Paul family photograph collections most often include images of immediate family members, the family home, and the family's neighborhood surroundings. These visual boundaries indicate the general limits of the most intimate communities that existed in the city, limits that appear to be consistent regardless of the family demographics.

In some ways this obvious limitation would seem to render family albums useless in an investigation of the larger issue of community formation or negotiation in a city. However, the very unreliability of personal pictures and the fact that they are always constructed within broader institutional gazes, can be invaluable aids when one is trying to reveal the most intimate ideas and experiences of a group of people and their complex relationships to other groups, structures, institutions, and social-cultural pressures and norms.[8] Family collections, then, offer particularly valuable data precisely because they are intended to be intimate, private mediations of the family community. In particular, in such collections, those photographs that depict subjects *other* than the expected closed circle are instructive.[9] That is certainly true in both of the collections discussed here.[10] Importantly, they offer clear evidence of the ways in which race and class combined with urban development in the early twentieth century to shape limited communal relationships.

In 1910, William J. Gardner, Sr., and his wife, Ida Gardner, were living with their ten children, ages one to twenty-two, in a modest Victorian-style home at 369 Jay Street (now Galtier Street) in St. Paul's Rondo neighborhood.[11] William was a custodian at a white club in St. Paul, and his two eldest daughters, Ella and Carrie, were employed as a dressmaker and a stenographer while Ida stayed home with their growing family. By 1920, William had left his custodial job for a position as a waiter in a local restaurant, Ida had given birth to one more child (a daughter named Dorothy, now age eight), and both Ella and Carrie had moved out of their parents' home.[12] The family photograph collection traces the family during this decade of change and provides a relatively rare self-constructed glimpse into the private world of an African American St. Paul family.[13]

The collection as a whole supports bell hooks's argument that, in a segregated America, "the camera was the central instrument by which blacks could disprove representations of us created by whites. . . . More than any other image-making tool, it offered African-Americans disempowered in white culture a way to empower [themselves] through representation."[14] For hooks, "the camera became in black life a political instrument, a way to resist misrepresentation as well as a means by which alternative images could be produced."[15] The alternative image of community made manifest in the Gardner collection is at once obvious and subtle. Rather than reinforcing a narrative of race-based community forced on the family by the actions and desires of whites, the collection, filled with pictures of black men, women, and children, depicts a community of African Americans whose intimacy appears to be at least partly self-created rather than completely ascribed. By choosing to include and exclude specific elements of St. Paul life, the Gardner photographs imply that the city environment provided opportunities for even marginalized citizens to include or exclude others from their idea of community. Yet this argument must not be taken to an extreme. In the end, there can be no doubt that the Gardners lived in a city in which the experience of community was tightly linked to race and class and the power to alter it was limited by structural forces.

Like many of the city's African American families, and like many African Americans across the urban North, the Gardners were members of what could be called the working middle class. By 1900, there was an increasing number of black professionals in St. Paul, but the vast majority of the city's black workers were employed in low-wage, low-skilled jobs. Most men worked for the railroads or, as William did, in the service industry.[16] The Gardners were not wealthy but they were financially stable, and the family's photographs indicate great pride in their accomplishments and in the lifestyle their efforts had made possible. This is particularly evident in one of the earliest photographs in the collection, depicting the three youngest Gardner children at Christmastime 1912 in the family home (fig. 1).[17] Unlike most of the others, this print is a full 8 by 10 inches, thus indicating its importance at least to its developer. The tightly cropped frame is filled top to bottom and corner to corner with the trappings of a middle-class Christmas celebration. At the center of the image sit Ralph, Dorothy, and William, Jr., their laps and the foreground filled with what appear to be gifts—among them, three dolls and a toy horse and wagon. Behind them is an elaborately decorated tree, its ornaments and garland highlighted against the darker expanse of the left side of the frame and blending into the elaborately patterned wallpaper and lace curtains that cover the wall and the window behind the tree. The children look calmly and directly at the camera, indicating a level of comfort both with the photographer and their surroundings. This may be Christmas, and they may be a bit unused to posing, but they are apparently familiar with the environment.

This sense of pride and relative comfort is almost universally apparent in other photographs in the collection, most of which depict two or more related subjects in and around the Gardner family home. In dozens of photos, all posed in front of their Jay Street residence, the subjects look at the camera with a sense of ownership and confidence. The house—visible at least in part in the majority of the images—is a solid structure with Victorian massing and architectural details. The subjects, young and old, own each frame and the representation of themselves that each captures. In a photo labeled "With the Youngsters," from 1912, William and Ida Gardner sit on the steps with three of their children, claiming their place in the neighborhood (fig. 2).[18] The relaxed arms thrown over a sister's shoulder in a cluster of images from 1920 project security and self-confidence, while the jaunty hats, cocked heads, broad smiles, and hands on hips in another from that year assert the sisters' delight in controlling their image (fig. 3).[19]

It is no surprise that these images reflect the family's comfort and sense of belonging in the context of kin and home. More important is discovering whether their sense of self-confidence and mode of self-presentation persisted when the subjects moved away from the security of that private and familiar environment. The collection does include a number of photographs that visually extend the geographic referent of the Gardner's community outside the walls of the family home and beyond their property to the streets nearby. In pictures such as figures 4, 5, and 6, family members pose on Rondo's streets and in the bountiful garden of their relatives who lived nearby.[20] The photographs include almost all of the children at one time or another, depicting them confidently navigating the neighborhood they called home—one that appears to be accessible and welcoming to black residents. Here, gardens are possible, freedom of movement seems protected, and extended African American families share lives, backyards, and leisure time.

But a few images place the family in more public and less familiar spaces in St. Paul, and these photos hint at the borders of the Gardners' understanding of place-based community. "While on a Family Outing at Como in 1912" shows six of the Gardner children standing in front of a flower garden at St. Paul's Como Park (fig. 7).[21] As a city park, Como had been designed and maintained for the recreational use of all St. Paul citizens, beginning in the late nineteenth century. By 1912, the park, located in the northwest section of the city, was accessible by streetcar from almost every section of St. Paul, and that was most likely how the Gardners arrived there. In this photo, the children smile at the camera, some shyly, as they stand in a line that moves from tallest to shortest, left to right. This image is one of only a handful in the collection that pose the children in such a contrived manner, yet the children appear to be as much at home in this environment as they are in the photographs taken near their home. It is likely, then, that the Gardners understood the park to be available and accessible to them as St. Paul residents, regardless of their racial identity. However, the formality of the photograph and the absence of other images from that outing (no candid shots at all) indicate that the outing might have been a rare-enough occasion in 1912 to warrant a formal image, at least in the mind of the photographer (most likely the elder William). The children may have felt comfortable in Como Park, but it may not have had the same connotation for their parents.[22]

Yet one photograph in the collection challenges any straightforward argument for interpreting this formality as evidence of a generation gap.

It is the only one that clearly situates family members in or near the commercial district of St. Paul (fig 8).[23] Dressed in what could be winter carnival costumes (although nowhere identified as such), the two youngest Gardner boys stand in front of a closed store on a street, deserted save for the streetcar behind them.[24] Their light-colored clothing blends with the snowy urban landscape, thus formally integrating them into this public commercial space. At the same time, however, the similar tonalities make the boys appear to be floating in the landscape—as if not anchored there at all. In addition, their stiff poses and unsmiling faces raise questions about their sense of connection to this location or to the event in which they appear to be participating. Unlike photos such as figure 9 and numerous other images of the brothers in winter scenes near their home, the photograph in figure 8 reveals a lack of ease in the surroundings, again raising questions about the geographic limits of community as experienced by St. Paul's African American citizens.[25] Away from the streets of Rondo, the boys appear literally and metaphorically to be standing in a landscape less hospitable than that of which their home is a part. Because so few images from this era depict the Gardners far outside the reaches of Rondo, it is hard to draw clear conclusions from the image. Yet those that do exist hint at the way in which the Gardner family photographer tried to create a record of the family's claim on a place in the broader St. Paul community. By deliberately capturing images of family members in public, not identifiably black sections of the city, the photographs make a statement about the family's sense of rightful membership in an imagined community of St. Paul as a whole.

By law, the Gardners were free to move around the public spaces of St. Paul; the photographs taken in Como Park and downtown make this clear. In fact, unlike African Americans in some other northern cities, those in Minnesota were, in theory, protected from outright discrimination by a state-level 1899 civil rights bill that prohibited discrimination based on race, color, national origin, or religion and included provisions for punishing offenders.[26] Yet the photographs in the Gardner collection seem to reflect a narrower experience of everyday community, suggesting that access to all spaces remained precarious. The family was undoubtedly aware of the many acts of discrimination that had long plagued African American residents and visitors in their city since the passage of

the first anti-discrimination law in 1885, and it is likely, too, that they recognized there was no guarantee that the 1899 amended law would resolve
the situation. Certain white residents continued to work to bar African
American visitors from public accommodations, and in 1909 some white
parents attempted to legally segregate the elementary schools. Thus, the
Rondo neighborhood was in many ways both the actual and imagined
spatial referent for the Gardners' community within the boundaries of
their hometown.[27]

If it can be said that community was linked to place for the Gardner
family, that place was much narrower than the city limits. This is not
surprising, given the increasing racial tension in the city. In the second
decade of the twentieth century, African Americans in most northern cities were becoming more and more concentrated in certain neighborhoods
as racial prejudice became more explicit and restrictive housing practices
more common.[28] One can get a sense of some of the broad contours of
these issues of race and class by noting the people who appear in the
Gardner photographs. Who besides family members was let in, and how
well did they appear to be integrated into that closed circle? The answer is
at once predictable and unexpected. Just as the Rondo district, as a place,
provided an alternative geographic definition of community, racial identity seems to have been an integral factor in determining which Rondo
residents were part of that community. Yet by looking at the non-family
members who appear in the Gardner collection, one sees that race was a
primary factor but not the only one. Fair-skinned or white St. Paulites do
appear in some of the photographs, whereas certain wealthy members
of the black community are absent. This gives us room to speculate that
that the Gardners also took class into consideration when developing or
nurturing communal relationships.

If Rondo had been a racially homogenous neighborhood, the relationship between geographic and racial solidarity might have been a given. Yet
both census data and firsthand accounts indicate that between 1900 and
1920 the neighborhood was racially diverse.[29] By 1930, more than 50 percent
of the residents were black, but the trend toward this black majority was
slow. According to the 1910 census, the majority of the Gardners' immediate neighbors were white immigrants and their first generation children
from Germany, Sweden, Austria, and Canada.[30] The Gardners' block was

not unique. As a boy in the 1900s and 1910s, Roy Wilkins, future leader of the NAACP, lived in Rondo with his aunt and uncle, not far from the Gardners. In his autobiography, *Standing Fast,* he recalls that in his particular neighborhood there were only three other black families: "The men who owned the tidy frame houses in my neighborhood were white: First and second generation Swedes and Norwegians, Poles, Germans, and Irish—first-and-second-generation immigrants." He sees in this multiracial upbringing the foundation for his life's work: "The faith I have in integration comes from the days I spent . . . chasing around the quiet tree-shaded lanes that stretched off and away from our little cottage." He mentions his mother's relationship with the Irish next-door neighbor and his own close friendship with a white boy, painting a picture of a neighborhood in which people, black and white, felt connected with and concerned about one other based on their shared status as working-class residents who were trying to support a "middle-class outlook." Gardner family descendants, too, affirm the multiethnic, multiracial realities of the neighborhood.[31]

Yet the Gardner photographs, reflecting the immediacy of the moment, present a slightly different view of Rondo and, in so doing, suggest the complexity of class status within a racially stratified society. It seems that the family photographers made deliberate decisions about whom to picture in their photographs of neighborhood life and whom to exclude. If, as the census data make clear, the majority of their immediate neighbors were not black and most of the other black subjects of their photos (including their relatives Billy Williams and his sister Ella) lived at least a short walk away, the photographs simultaneously worked to extend the family's geographic limits of community while narrowing the racial limits.[32]

Rather than offering viewers a sense that there was an actual or imagined St. Paul that was all-inclusive, the Gardners' personal photographs offer just the opposite. For this family, not even neighborhood solidarity trumped racial identity. While the Gardners probably had to interact in day-to-day life with their white neighbors, the family was not emotionally close enough to them actually or imaginatively to include them among the images of their most intimate community. It is impossible to tell if this was solely dependent on race, but the absence is provocative and leaves us no way to see the Gardners as part of Rondo's multiracial community.

The Gardner photos indicate that, as the city's residential areas were becoming increasingly segregated by race, the minds (if not the daily lives) of the residents were undergoing a parallel segregation. Causality aside, the two events must be considered in tandem. Yet in a handful of images, the family members appear alongside children who appear to be white, and the white subject is not marginalized in any of these pictures. Five of the photos depict a young girl identified as Dorothy Ohme (or sometimes as Dorothy Ochme, Dorothy O., or D.O.), whose close familiarity with the family seems certain but whose identity is a mystery. All that is left of her is her name, written underneath a few of photographs in Gladys Gardner's photo album.[33] In those images she appears to be young and fair-skinned with wavy hair and ringlets, and she is pictured in intimate photographs alongside young Dorothy Gardner. The two girls are viewed through the lens in the same way, and the lack of explanatory notes about Dorothy O. suggests that none were necessary for the family photograph compiler.

The connection between the Gardners and Dorothy O. was not fleeting. In the collection's first image of her, labeled "Dorothy G. Dorothy Ohme," taken when she and Dorothy Gardner are perhaps three or four years old, the two round-faced girls are standing side by side on a neighborhood side-walk (fig. 10).[34] Importantly, the photograph's formal elements and setting match those in numerous images of the Gardner siblings over the course of two decades. The assumption that this young girl is an intimate of the family is supported by the fact that there is obviously a rapport between her and the photographer. Like the Gardner children in similar photos, she appears to be relaxed and spontaneous and faces the camera straight on. In two photographs apparently taken on the same day a few years after the first one, both Dorothys look on as Dorothy Gardner's mother and aunt tend to what appears to be the garden at Ella's home around the corner, a recurring setting in a decade's worth of family photographs. Neither child is posed. In one image, Dorothy O. observes the women's work while she eats an ice cream cone. In another image, both girls stand with their hands on their hips watching the activity at hand. Neither appears to be particu-larly aware of the camera, and both seem to be generally comfortable in their surroundings. Dorothy O. is positioned in the picture frame neither as an addition (that is, marginalized on the edge of the frame) nor as the central feature. Instead, she is unremarkably positioned as an intimate, an equal, standing in the midst of the family's everyday life.

This integration and familiarity consistently appear in the remaining few photographs of Dorothy O. and Dorothy Gardner together in the garden, that day. In one, the two girls, seated outdoors on small chairs, peer at each other around the sides of a large plant. Their grins indicate a genuine fondness for one another, while their almost identical appearances and positioning within the picture frame indicate that the photographer saw them as a pair. In a final photograph, the two girls (now perhaps six or seven years old) are posed one in front of the other, as if they have stopped in play to have their camaraderie recorded (fig. 11).[35] Their fondness for one another seems to be natural, integral to their relationship, and built over a period of regular interaction. Was Dorothy O. a fairer-skinned relative? Was she somehow connected to Ella and Billy Williams? Was she a neighborhood child? It is tempting to assume that the affection between Dorothy Gardner and her playmate indicates an alternative reading of the Gardner family's relationship with its white neighbors, one that matches Wilkins's recollections of the era. This may be possible, even likely, given the number of renters, both black and white, in the neighborhood. Perhaps Dorothy O.'s family moved elsewhere after a few years. However, without knowing where she lived, and without any later images of her in the collection, one cannot draw any conclusion other than the possibility that personal intimacy negated strict demographic-based modes of determining the bounds of community.

Though Dorothy O.'s inclusion in the collection remains a mystery, another photograph depicting white children does not. It records a confirmation at St. Peter Claver Catholic Church, a diocesan parish established in 1888 by Archbishop John Ireland to serve the African American Catholic community of St. Paul. While initially organized as a mission parish primarily for St. Paul's African American population, the parish was, from the beginning, an interracial parish, even though it remained dedicated to serving the needs of African American residents. The church was only a few minutes' walk from the Gardners' home, and the photograph, taken in about 1905, depicts two boys and six girls, including one of the Gardner daughters (fig. 12).[36] All the girls are dressed in nearly identical white dresses and have flowers in their hair. The children in this confirmation class sit together at a table with a priest standing at the head. Except for Carrie Gardner, all members of the class appear to be white. They look appropriately solemn as they stare intently at the camera on this important day. Carrie, second from the right on the right side of the table, is virtually indistinguishable from her fellow classmates except for the darker tone of her skin. She appears to be the only black child in the photograph, but she does not appear to be marginalized.

The photograph suggests that, in this historically African American institution, the issue of race was minimized for the Gardners—particularly for the generation coming of age in the first two decades of the century. Most likely this was linked to their active involvement in parish life, which gave them a sense of ownership in the space and its rituals. Although none of the family's photographs depicts the church building itself, the deliberate inclusion of this image in the collection corroborates other sources indicating that the people of St. Peter Claver had shaped the family's experience and definition of community.[37] Yet this assumption must not be taken too far. After all, while the confirmation photograph apparently includes white children and thus promotes a vision of the parish as an institution that may be able to radically transform the experience of community in black and white St. Paul, none of the white figures in the image appear anywhere else in the collection. Much like the lack of images of white Rondo residents, by limiting the St. Peter Claver whites to formal depictions (and thus formal interactions), the collection as a whole challenges a reading of this photograph as an indicator that the Gardners were part of an extensive interracial intimate community and highlights the church's ultimate impotence in fostering such an experience. Although it provided an institutional link between white and black St. Paul Catholics, St. Peter Claver appears to have been less successful as a mechanism for establishing significant emotional or reciprocal ties among them.

The church also seems to have failed to completely unite black St. Paulites from different economic classes or professional groups. While the city's black Catholic community was small, its members cut across class lines. They included, for instance, Frederick McGhee, a nationally renowned figure, who was the city's premier black attorney and one of its wealthiest black residents. McGhee was more than a Catholic in name. His faith was a prominent element of his identity, and he was regularly involved in the goings-on at St. Peter Claver.[38] It seems likely that the Gardners would have met and interacted with McGhee in the context of parish life. Yet even though he was a member of the institutional community of their church and lived in the spatial community of Rondo, neither he nor any other upper-class black communicant appears in the Gardner photographs.[39] In effect, his absence serves as a cautionary tale for those who presume that the black community was unified. While few cities of the urban North had a large-enough black population to support completely separate communities based on class, many of them, including St. Paul, had populations that, by the 1910s, were at least partially stratified by class, with street address, occupation, or type of employment serving as a point of division. The Gardner photographs underscore this point.[40]

In sum, while it seems that race was generally a limiting factor in the Gardner family's experience of secular community in St. Paul, exceptions did exist—driven, for instance, by the emotional needs and friendship of a young child, the presence (perhaps) of a white neighbor, the force of the family's Catholic faith, and even the obstacles of class status. But while the last of these exceptions was a secondary consideration for most black St. Paulites, whose economic mobility was largely limited by structural barriers, it was increasingly central to the communal identity of the city's white population, as one can see in the collected photographs of John W. G. Dunn, a white contemporary of William Gardner, who lived with his family less than three miles away.

Although the two collections share similar subject matter (family and home), the Dunn collection is dramatically different from the Gardner photographs, for it was shaped by the technical skills and pointed artistic aims of its creator. Dunn composed, shot (with a large and cumbersome Graflex camera), and printed his own photographs in a deliberate attempt to emulate the popular pictorialist aesthetic of the time.[41] In contrast to the snapshots that fill the Gardner collection, the Dunn photographs include few spur-of the moment images.[42] Rather, they reveal a sophisticated understanding of arrangement and dramatic lighting and a familiarity with developing techniques and practices. Like most pictorialist photographs, the images exude an artistic quality intended to provoke thought and feeling. Pictorialists hoped to prove to the public and the artistic community that photography, like the traditional visual arts, could duplicate "the certain something . . . personal, human, emotional . . . in work done by the unaided union of brain, hand and eye."[43]

Thus, they possess a greater degree of intentionality than the Gardners' do. The Dunn photographs record the photographer's idealized view of his subjects, and their formal components offer direct evidence of how he imagined his community, including who was and was not central to it.[44]

Dunn was an up-and-coming insurance agent, and the main subjects of his grand albums are his immediate family members. The vast majority of the images record his children's activities in and around their St. Paul home and garden over the course of two decades.[45] But as with the Gardner collection, the exceptions to this rule tell us most about the nature and limits of Dunn's definition of community in the St. Paul that existed beyond the boundaries of his property. The two collections' most telling similarities are the degree to which they reinforce the idea that St. Paulites were active participants in creating their own narrow communities and the importance of class status in that undertaking. Although formal and structural forces were at play in Dunn's work, he also used the lens to select, shape, and record a specific set of intimates as well as a related spatial referent. Together, they worked to define, imaginatively and materially, the family's community.[46]

The first image of Dunn's St. Paul appears in an album titled *Minnesota 1897–8, 1902–4,* which holds eighteen landscape photos of the city's Lake Phalen. But these images of St. Paul are anomalies, for his focus quickly shifts away from his city's natural spaces. He begins to compile a collection of St. Paul photographs taken in and around the neighborhoods and streets where his family resides. The city makes its next appearance in a photo titled "The Holland," which depicts an apartment building where Dunn and his wife, Alice, lived between 1899 and 1902. Alice poses in the window as if to prove that they belong to it and it to them. With this photograph and its caption, Dunn establishes the importance of home in his work. As a whole, his pictures are much more explicit than the Gardners' are about a prevailing sense of pride in a specific place.

The next two photographs emphasize this point. Affixed to the same page as "The Holland" are two pictures of the couple's new home at 1033 Lincoln Avenue, which the photos show as still under construction.[47] The importance of the structure to Dunn's sense of identity is reinforced later in the same album. When arranging of a series of photos taken immediately after the completion of the home, Dunn frequently chose to highlight the house over his wife who, while often named in his photo captions, in more than one photograph seems to be dwarfed by the house command-ing the picture frame. See, for instance, figure 13.[48]

The final pages of this first album record interior decorations and feature Alice and the couple's new baby in a series of photographs taken inside the Lincoln home and in the backyard, front yard, and garden. In subject and form, they exemplify two tropes that appear repeatedly in Dunn's St. Paul photographs during the next decade. The first is a fascina-tion with capturing family members interacting outdoors with the house or its land (fig. 14).[49] The second, which gave him a chance to sharpen his pictorialist skills, is an interest in shooting interior shots of his sons in the same places and poses over time.

The first album that focuses primarily on the Dunn family's life in Minnesota is titled *A Nice Boy and His Home 1903–1904;* and, true to the title, the images track the growth and development of Jack, the eldest child, born in 1903, and the new home his parents were creating for him on their large lot on Lincoln Avenue. The album opens with a photograph of the infant Jack propped up on pillows, an image that also appears in the previous album (fig. 15).[50] More repeat photographs follow this one, but eventually Dunn began pasting in new compositions. In the first of these, "Lincoln," Alice pulls Jack in a sled down their street, and in the second she poses in front of their own house (fig. 16).[51] The vastness of a snowy landscape is broken only by the presence of houses in the distance, proof that the area is beginning to flourish. The Dunns appear here as early settlers of sorts. Alice's dark coat and hat provide a sharp contrast to the whiteness of the ground and the whiteness of her son's sled and blankets. Here, unlike other images, the photograph clearly articulates Alice's com-manding presence in the landscape, and the composition reflects her (and, by extension, their) ownership of the land and the house.[52]

These images of Alice with a child outside prove to be almost as anom-alous as the Lake Phalen photos of the first album. As Dunn continued to photograph his family, images of her became rarer; those that exist tend to be interior shots like the ones that appeared next in the second album. His focus on the relationship among his family, their land, and what he saw as their grand house is reflected in a series of images that capture family members gazing out of windows; for instance, see figure 17.[53] Taken in December 1904, it depicts Alice and Jack at the window. Jack's white gown blends almost completely into the white light outside, and the folds of the gown mirror the folds of the sheer curtains that frame the window. Alice, in contrast to her obvious presence in figure 16, seems to be little more than a prop in this image, her face obscured and her dark clothes blending into the left side of the frame. In keeping with this pattern, she appears less often in the later albums, while the couple's sons remain central.

The next albums—*St. Paul 1904–07, A Nice Boy and His Home 1905–06*, and *The Nice Boys 1907–08*—follow the family as Jack grows and another son, Monfort, is born (in 1907). These romantic images, some of them re-creating photographs from the earlier album, capture the boys in reflective poses at the windows and the piano. The window shots appear often: over the years Dunn returned again and again to photograph his sons in front of the same window in which young Jack had sat cradled in his mother's arms. In these images the boys' bodies are bathed in light coming from outside. The security of the family home appears to wrap itself around them, as a parent's arms in a middle-class American family of the time might.

Dunn also created images of his sons, both alone and with him, as they worked in the garden of the expansive yard behind their home; see, for instance, figure 18.[54] These photographs portray the male members of the family as both of the earth and masters of the land. By including himself in many of the images, Dunn underscored the fact that his family was a secure nuclear family, the middle-class ideal of the early twentieth century.

In 1912, the family welcomed a third son, James, and Dunn's chronicle continues, showing images of the gardens and the house as they are transformed over time.[55] Here, it is helpful to note that, despite the formal differences between the Gardner and Dunn images, the collections share a similar, narrow subject focus. Likewise, in both, the few exceptions that do appear are instructive. In Dunn's case, they reveal the impact that class status had on his experience of community and ground speculations about the way in which that status (and the related residential organization of St. Paul) might have factored into the Gardners' images.

In this context, none of Dunn's photos are more illuminating than the four that capture activities of the exclusive Oxford Skating Club.[56] Unlike the vast majority of his images, these are primarily a visual record of the club's location and successes rather than artistic renditions of either the site or the skaters. The photographs, all attached to a single page in the album, display little obvious manipulation of composition or concern about artistic printing methods. The page includes the simple notation

"Oxford Rink Jan. 1917." One representative photo depicts a group of skaters, primarily children, who have stopped to face the camera (fig. 19).[57] Behind them stands the club's warming house as it appeared in the winter of 1917 (perhaps on the eve of that year's winter carnival, as some of the skating costumes suggest). While the caption does not identify the skaters by name, the sign on the warming house offers clues about their identities. The words "Oxford Club" appear in small letters in the upper left corner while the main portion of the sign is filled with "PRIVATE RINK" in lettering more than twice the size of the club's name.

Incorporated in 1916 by three well-to-do area businessmen, the Oxford Club aimed to promote "social intercourse among its members and educate its members as to the benefits which may be derived from physical exercise of all kinds."[58] Membership was five dollars per family, and care was taken to ensure that non-members did not sneak onto the rink. According to club records, the approximately five hundred members were drawn from surrounding residential streets extending perhaps a half-mile.[59] In other words, the Oxford Skating Club was a segregated community. Poor families would have found the membership fee prohibitive, while the rink's location effectively restricted membership to people who lived within a reasonable walking distance. In St. Paul, as in most urban locations by 1920, residential areas were increasingly shaped by class status; thus, "reasonable walking distance" also meant reasonable wealth and shared social standing.[60] The recollections of James, the Dunns' youngest son, support this reading of the club. He later recalled that the names recorded year after year in his father's black membership books included the families of "all the kids in the area" as well as some of the "Summit Avenue wealthy."[61]

As chapter 3 will explore, in St. Paul, associational communities based on economic status and class position were both encouraged and enforced by the growing relationship between neighborhood and class status. Because class status was often also tied to racial, immigrant, or ethnic identity, members of the white, often native-born, middle and upper classes were able to gather socially within their own neighborhoods without having to intentionally exclude others. This phenomenon helped residents create and reinforce a sense of connection with people who shared key demographic, occupational, and financial attributes without forcing them to abandon an imagined sense of belonging to a community that encompassed the city as a whole.

Institutional structures such as the Oxford Club, which were linked to both neighborhood and class, demonstrate how the idea of a place-based community (in which the city was understood as a shared place) could coexist with more limited experiences of community. Because the Oxford Club controlled membership by structural means—location and fees—that could be dismissed as arbitrary rather than by more explicit mechanisms or criteria, club members and leaders could easily overlook its exclusivity and race- and class-based nature. In other words, people such as the Dunns could hold on to an imagined place-based community that encompassed all of St. Paul while experiencing, even creating, a much narrower community. Their life in St. Paul seems very similar to Carol Kennicott's in *Main Street*.

In many ways the Oxford Club was a symbol of the relationship among class, geography, shared leisure interests, and communal identity that was increasingly shaping the lives of St. Paulites. Dunn's inclusion of these photos in his family albums makes its import clear. He took a hands-on approach to the club: almost daily, he tracked its membership and activities. His sense of responsibility for and to this club and its members seems to have gone beyond any official requirement. He deeply cared about its success. In addition to photographing the place and its members, he inserted these images into his intimate family photo albums—an almost sacred place where few other such images appeared. In so doing he signaled that he saw the club and its members as an extension of his family and thus as part of his most personal experience of community.[62]

By identifying the importance of class status and its geographic referent within the Dunns' experience of community, one can extrapolate on the complex ways in which race, class, ethnicity, and geography overlapped and interacted in the Gardners' photographs and lives. Although the two collections represent only a fraction of those that existed in St. Paul in the early twentieth century, they are, in style and subject, representative of family photographs in this time and place. Both collections repeatedly suggest that race and class were critical factors in a family's understanding of its intimate community. Simultaneously, they raise questions about the role that the city's distinct neighborhood demographics played in fostering such distinctions. Regardless of a photographer's racial or ethnic identity, gender, photographic expertise, or technical style, geography and the way in which it was linked to class and race shaped the spatial and human boundaries of intimate communities. In the narratives of the family photo albums, such tension and divisions are sometimes reproduced. Even more significant is how both of these collections reveal the power of individual St. Paulites to shape, present, and re-present their understandings and experiences of communal relationships despite the structural forces at play. Without denying the limits that the Gardner family faced in a time of class- and race-based divisiveness, one can see that both families had some control over where and with whom to forge communal relationships.

Photographs were both a means to gain this control and proof of its existence. By choosing to record only a select portion of all the people and places that made up the physical entity that was St. Paul, each photographer was able to actively shape the real and imaginative boundaries of his own St. Paul. Implicit in this action, however, was a message of exclusion. Although neither Dunn nor Gardner created images that indicated explicit exclusion, the albums' silences tell this story. The experience of community for St. Paul families was circumscribed by class, race, and an increasingly exclusive geographic divide.

Family photographs were not the only photographs making this point during the opening decades of the century, and they did not capture all nuances of communal life in St. Paul. Equally telling were the images disseminated by some of the city's social reformers. These photographs worked to not only record and reinforce the lines that divided St. Paulites into distinct communities but create them as well. Whereas family photographs focused on identifying, depicting, and recording those who were seen as members of the photographer's own community, and only implicitly spoke to those who were not, the reform photographs printed and disseminated in the Wilder Charity's Housing Survey report of 1917 delineated the contours of community in St. Paul in precisely the opposite fashion. The goal was to gather support from middle- and upper-class St. Paulites who would be willing and able to finance social reform. To do this required establishing the distance between those who would be reformers and those who needed to be reformed. Photographs were well suited for this task, and in the Wilder report they were used to create the image of a separate and unified community of the needy and to position that community imaginatively within the middle class's perceived realm of responsibility. By so doing, they allowed middle-class viewers to maintain their distinct class-based communal identity.

Social reformers had been proving their proficiency at identifying and exploiting the power of publicly disseminated photographs since the 1890s, thanks to the work of Jacob Riis, a New York newspaper reporter and photographer. His images of the New York City poor helped spark action on the part of that city's reform groups. In the first decade of the twentieth century, Lewis Hine began to add his images of the nation's poor and destitute workers (especially children) to the visual record of growing economic disparity, the ill-effects of the industrial growth of the Gilded Age, and that growth's impact on life in what was to be known as the Progressive Era. Although distinct in style, the photographs of both men helped construct a vocabulary for reform photography and establish the medium as a powerful tool available to those who advocated specific and dramatic social change.[63]

Wilder Charity was St. Paul's leading reform organization; and when its administrators set out to survey and report on the city's housing conditions, they made sure that photographs would play a central role. The resulting report, "Housing Conditions in the City of St. Paul," included a number of photographs that, like the images in Riis's and Hine's work, reflected the goals of the project's initiators: to scientifically record the housing situation in the city and to draw support for proposed changes in legislation and zoning. The two types of photographs in the report helped to further one or the other goal. Yet at the same time the photographs also serve a third, presumably unintended, purpose: to establish and reinforce a class-based division in the city. The survey photographers (who remain unknown) achieved this end by foregrounding the structural-physical elements of the housing problem and by isolating and dehumanizing the citizens who inhabited the places they photographed.[64]

In 1917, the St. Paul Association of Commerce (later the St. Paul Area Chamber of Commerce) asked Dr. Carol Aronovici, a sociologist and the new head of Wilder Charity, to undertake a study of the city's housing conditions. By the end of that year, he had compiled a 120-page report aimed at "revealing the public sanitary conditions that may be a menace to the health of the residents of the poorer sections of the city, [and] . . . stimulating more efficient service on the part of the municipality in the control of the existing evils."[65] Aronovici hoped that the report would spur powerful citizens and city leaders to enact legislative measures to create a citywide housing policy "of a constructive character."[66] These goals, though grand in scope, were similar to those that were fueling social reform work across the nation and that had inspired Hine's and Riis's work.[67]

Alongside textual accounts that offer poignant descriptions of life and conditions in St. Paul's most impoverished areas, the photos scattered throughout the report construct a narrative about the unsanitary living conditions present in St. Paul and thus helped to establish a visible yet generalized underclass around whom the city's reform-minded individuals and groups could mobilize. One of the greatest differences between the Wilder survey and the work of either Hines or Riis lies in the fact that nearly 65 percent of the report's forty-three photographs depict no human subjects at all. Granted, the report is focused on housing conditions, but this alone does not account for such a noticeable absence. Neither Riis nor Hine seemed to think that human subjects would distract from their interest in capturing humans' living conditions. On the contrary, both photographers hoped to elicit public support and empathy by means of photographing human inhabitants of the "places" they photographed, either by articulating the plight of individuals (Hine) or exposing the degree to which poverty posed a threat to the foundations of American civil life (Riis). In contrast, the majority of the Wilder photographs focus on inanimate objects—yards, basements, streets, kitchens, bedrooms— without a human subject in sight. Presumably, these areas were inhabited, but there is little evidence, either pictorial or textual, to confirm this assumption.

The report's designers apparently had reason to believe that they could make an impact on readers without focusing on images of human subjects. This might seem improbable, yet there is clear evidence in family photographs that middle- and upper-class citizens linked their homes, neighborhoods, and material possessions directly to self-construction. Their identities were bound up in the trappings of an increasingly consumer-oriented culture, and those structures and possessions helped them define themselves and the group to which they belonged. Thus, if the middle- and upper-class viewers of the report did not see structures or neighborhoods that they recognized as their own, they could theoretically separate themselves from the imagined inhabitants of those other places.

This idea had precedent as well, for the ability to create a visual record of "us" and "other" had been important in the success of a nineteenth-century campaign to clear the slums of the English city of Leeds. In that case, a series of photographs recorded the built structures and public areas that were the "homes" of the residents of these blighted sections. Viewers saw in these photographs cluttered, unsanitary spaces without the healthful benefits or elements of middle-class existence. Consequently, as John Tagg has argued, the camera was able to "operat[e] across the gulf dividing here from there, the eye from the real, the seer from the seen."[68] In Leeds the camera's ability to record and "make real" perceived differences became a liability for the residents of the slum areas. The photographs made "these points [of separation] seem irreversibly fixed, and rendered transparent what held them together and apart."[69]

St. Paul avoided this outcome, thanks to an early twentieth-century social reform agenda that held that the middle class had the power to amend identified problems. However, the Wilder report used similar formal techniques to draw support, and its images also paid homage to Riis's formal tropes, which attempted to expound on the moral decay imbedded in the physical spaces of his photographs. The images of structures and living conditions in the report capture a variety of places, yet all are alike in their focus on filth and blight. For instance, two that appear in different sections of the report, captioned "Rear View of Butcher Shop. Bad Condition of Repair" and "Rooming House Shack in Midway District," emphasize structural decay and shortcomings. Both focus on crumbling, peeling ceilings, though only portions of the rooms are in the frame. Both highlight the absence of outside light (and, by association, ventilation). In "Rear View of Butcher Shop," the room is unnaturally illuminated, even though there is no indication of electricity, and the open door clearly does not lead outdoors. "Rooming House Shack in Midway District" is dark, despite the presence of two windows (fig. 20).[70] Neither photo attempts to tell the stories of the people who use or inhabit the spaces. The beds are empty, and the shop has no proprietor. The structural elements of the spaces are paramount.

This de-emphasis, this inability to narrate anything about the people whose lives are lived in the locations that are being photographed, is affirmed again and again throughout the report in images full of such empty and deteriorating spaces. Yet this is not the only method by which the photographs create distance between viewer and viewed. They also appropriate one of Riis's tactics: creating images that are crowded and slightly unrecognizable. In images such as Riis's well-known "Hebrew Master," the clutter keeps the viewer from identifying any subjectivity in the photo, despite the human subject. Likewise, the clutter in the report's "Junk Yard surrounded by Dwellings" doubly erases the presence of the unpictured people who must work or live there (fig. 21).[71] In this image, as in Riis's, the viewer's eye is drawn from place to place, hardly settling on any one item or spot before moving on to the next. The disordered nature of the frame, filled from corner to corner, makes it hard for a viewer to imagine the space as suitable for human habitation. Such a reaction may have prompted middle-class residents of St. Paul to identify it as a site in need of their assistance.

Many of the Wilder landscape images record and reproduce intimate, even taboo spaces. For instance, in addition to a number of bedroom photographs, viewers see toilet facilities, spaces generally considered too private for inclusion in photographs of middle-class family homes. (There are none in the Gardner and Dunn collections.) The eleven-page-long section on toilets and baths includes thirteen photographs, a ratio that was in keeping with other sections of the report. Apparently, the report editors were not concerned about offending or embarrassing the residents who used those facilities.

Bathrooms and bedrooms, basements and kitchens, front yards, backyards, abandoned yards: all were photographed, ostensibly to illustrate the accompanying textual descriptions of the city's housing and sanitation conditions. Any middle-class St. Paulites who flipped through the report would have been unable to avoid noticing that these physical spaces called *home* were significantly different from their own. In this way, the report organizers implicitly helped viewers distance themselves from the subjects of the investigation and reaffirmed existing class distinctions. Whether intended or not, the strategy served the Wilder Charity's ultimate ends. By assuring viewers that they were outside the purview of the poor, the photographs helped to mobilize the reform impulses of an already established liberal middle class who, like Carol Kennicott in the St. Paul of *Main Street,* believed that they had the right and the duty to oversee the alleviation of social ills, particularly those that plagued the poor.

The sixteen human photographs included in the report emphasize the social distance and disconnect between the viewers and the viewed. Many earlier social reform photographs, especially Hine's, aimed to give their subjects human dignity. In contrast, the people who appear in the Wilder photographs do little more than add human-like figures to what still appear to be generally uninhabited spaces. They are regularly dwarfed by their surroundings and are never identified. Though they are composed differently from Riis's, these images, like his, offer their human subjects little dignity or autonomy. People are posed in the picture frame to clarify what the landscape photos only hint at: that humans do inhabit these places and that their humanity is in jeopardy.

The first human subjects appear in the report's opening photograph, "Rear Lot Homes," which occupies in the middle of the second page and marks the end of Aronovici's introduction (fig. 22).[72] Two adults—one male, one female—and ten young children stand near or sit on the front stoop of a wooden building. There is no legend identifying the individuals or their relationship to one another, and the odd wording of the caption negates the very existence of the people depicted. Notably, while the humans are centered in the frame, the photograph was shot from a distance, so that their faces and therefore their unique identities are difficult to distinguish. Their humanness is reduced to a general sense of belonging to a nameless group of people who, in their poverty, stand in for any number of St. Paul residents who are part and parcel (and perhaps victims) of the city's slums. Moreover, even though their curvilinear forms stand out against the starkly linear arrangement of houses and utility poles in the background, the caption focuses the viewer's attention away from the people and toward the landscape. Together, the photograph and the caption blur the distinction between the human and non-human elements of St. Paul's poor while visually situating the people of "Rear Lot Homes" squarely at the center of the housing problem. The stylistic and descriptive themes of "Rear Lot Homes" reappear in images such as "Artesian Well, Upper Levee," "Typical rear view of old type of single dwelling," "Shack Occupied by family with 10 children," and "Junk dealer's store and home." In each instance, structures, debris, and dirt fill most of the frame while shadowy human figures, too small to identify clearly, appear in their midst. The inhabitants of the homes seem to be an organic part of the structures themselves; they are absorbed by their surroundings.

Yet, in several other images that include human figures, the goal seems to be different. The report appeals to the emotional world of middle-class readers and supporters by suggesting, visually and textually, the ways in which accepted middle-class white "American" norms are being degraded in these physical spaces. The most obvious example is "Flat Building. One Toilet and water in basement used by six families" (fig. 23).[73] Here, the subjects can be interpreted as members of a family, though the caption offers no clue about their relationship. The viewer's eye is quickly drawn to an adult woman standing on the building's upper balcony. On the roof to her right is an adult male who appears to be engaged in some kind of work there. Next to the woman stands a young boy, and on the steps below her are two girls. The subjects may be members of a family unit. They may not be. Viewers have no way of knowing. The arrangement of the image exploits and recalls the family portraits of middle-class families in front of their own homes. In so doing, it works to elicit viewers' empathy. With some assistance, one thinks, this "family" might be able to ascend to the moral and material life of the middle class.

The report also uses another type of persuasive imagery: the parentless child motif. Such photos show individuals or groups of children standing close together, as if for safety, in unsanitary environments and without any adult nearby. Are they orphans? Perhaps; perhaps not. But the facts are irrelevant. The idea that they *could* be parentless is enough. "Rear of Cody Block. Garbage and Waste Infested with Rats" is a good example of this type of image (fig. 24).[74] It offers viewers a close-up of a young unidentified boy centered in the middle of the frame. The foreground is filled with trash and waste extending to the edges of the image. The child sits calmly against a wooden wall, eating a piece of fruit and gazing intently at the camera. Compositionally, the image is not only one of the most sophisticated in the report but also recalls, in a sharp departure from the rest of the photographs, the work of Lewis Hine. The photographer obviously composed the shot to capture an innocent alone and at risk in his own backyard.

In a report that is explicitly about structures, the human figures remind viewers of a moral imperative: that action is necessary because human beings, not only buildings and land, are part of the world of "Rear Lot

Homes." The report does not necessarily use this sense of shared humanity to promote the idea of a unified St. Paul community; more often the images articulate just the opposite. Yet, ironically, this strategy was effective in drumming up middle-class support for reform agendas. After its completion the report was disseminated to Wilder Charity's board of directors as well to members of the commission that had funded it and to St. Paul's city government. Each of these recipients was an established member of the middle or upper class, but there is no indication that the people depicted in the report ever saw it.[75] Accordingly, the images and the people in them became objects on display for people who were already set apart by virtue of class and social status. Viewing these images reinforced that distance because it gave one group of St. Paulites intimate access to the lives of other city residents without the opportunity for reciprocity.

This opportunity to gaze upon another's image, one that in many ways dehumanized or aggregated the lives of the people pictured, reinforced the idea that two distinct communities existed in St. Paul. The first community was made up of the poor, a unified mass of human beings whose unidentified images, indiscriminately mixed with those of garbage, toilets, and decrepit structures, peered from the pages of the report. Viewers might have assumed that these varied subjects inherently shared some fundamental similarity. Because their differences aren't emphasized in the report, what other conclusion could be reached? The second community comprised the people who were viewing the images. Because the report includes no photographs of *their* homes, friends, neighborhoods, toilets, or baths, they were allowed to imagine themselves as fundamentally different and separate from the people and places they saw on the page.

In her study of Hine's *Pittsburgh Survey,* Maren Stange argues that it "linked the documentary photographic style to the ever-increasing cultural authority of social expertise . . . by providing a theory of benign social engineering that helped to mask the facts of class exploitation."[76] This argument seems applicable to the Wilder survey, for in the end its combination of stylistic decisions, caption and textual choices, and modes of dissemination reinforced the idea of two distinct communities in St. Paul: (1) a united and generalized community of those without agency who deserve pity and need assistance: that is, the people in the pictures; and (2) a separate community of those whose individual collective agency and actions could understand and address that plight: that is, the absent viewer whose social status was such that his or her face, home, and neighborhood were safe from the reformer-photographer's gaze. Its creators managed to illuminate the degree to which the impact of reform photography in the city was linked to already established class divisions in a particular locale and was also, perhaps even more centrally, an active force in establishing and reinforcing the specific contours of those divisions in real and imagined ways.

Reform photography was not the only type of public photography that worked to create and shore up city-based unions or divisions, and the city's poor were not the only subjects who could be used to this end. As reproduction techniques improved in the late nineteenth and early twentieth centuries, even local and regional newspapers were able to include more and better-quality photographic images alongside their news stories. Consequently, the more well-to-do citizens in St. Paul and elsewhere frequently saw their own pictures and those of their intimates in the local papers, while residents without access to political, economic, or traditional social capital did not. The circulation of newspaper photographs, then, underscored the class- and race-based divisions, both imaginative and real, that were also on display in the Wilder report and the family albums. They even indicated some of the ways in which gender shaped notions of community. By predominately reproducing images of white middle- and upper-class St. Paulites—those residents most centrally positioned within the economic and social power structures of a modernizing American city—these local papers helped members of that group imagine that the municipality known as St. Paul was synonymous with community in general. After all, the city they saw in the papers looked more like their own intimate communities than not.

Although halftone production techniques had been possible in the late nineteenth century, newspapers did not begin printing photographs with any regularity until the early years of the twentieth century. In St. Paul and elsewhere in the nation in the early 1900s, they led the way among all forms of cultural production in circulating images to the general public. As a result, most St. Paulites looked to local newspapers for photographic representations of their city, and the images presented there had an outsized impact on shaping a visual reference point for place-based community.[77] Three major white dailies were published in St. Paul during the early twentieth century: the *Pioneer Press,* the *Dispatch,* and the *Daily News.* The city was also the publication point for an important African American paper, the *Appeal.*[78] Circulation figures for any of these papers are difficult to determine, but there was a large-enough readership in the city to support all four, albeit at different levels, and the images chosen by and printed in these papers had significant cultural power and influence.[79]

All of the editors and publishers had particular agendas that fueled their editorial practices and shaped their news and photographic coverage. The *Pioneer Press* and the *Dispatch* were morning and evening versions of the same paper; they were owned by the same man and were closely tied to the Democratic Party. The *Daily News* was under separate ownership, but otherwise its most significant departure from the *Pioneer Press* and the *Dispatch* was its specific, self-conscious focus on local events. It, too, had Democratic leanings. In contrast, the *Appeal,* which had a local, regional, and national reach, was staunchly Republican and, for obvious reasons, emphasized the concerns and struggles of African Americans.[80] But in spite of their differences, the four papers offered St. Paulites remarkably similar images of themselves and their city.

An analysis of the images printed in the three major white newspapers reveals that the St. Paul of their photos was made up primarily of white middle-class men and their concerns. While women's photos did appear, their volume and locations were different, thereby adding a gendered component to the imagined St. Paul community. In addition, in both cases, the printed photographs allowed many St. Paulites to imagine themselves as part of communities that, because of necessity or desire, transcended the city limits.

In the first decade of the century, photographs in all three white-owned papers were limited mostly to reproductions of portrait or studio images of the city's leading citizens. Often they appear on pages containing articles about recent promotions or hires or the professional activities of local doctors, lawyers, and businessmen. A random selection from December 1904 and January 1905 editions of the *Pioneer Press* demonstrates that, while there are very few photographs in any of those issues, the vast majority fit into this category. "Men Prominent in the Church Work," "Four of the Macalester [College] Orators," and "Samuel G. Strickland newly appointed superintendent of the Chicago, St. Paul, Minneapolis and Omaha Railroad" are typical captions.[81] Each of these images features a well-to-do, white, male citizen.

A survey of *Dispatch* images during the same period yields strikingly similar findings. Furthermore, a study of the images in the two papers reveals no significant changes during the first two decades of the century.[82] Although larger candid photographs were replacing the earlier small oval studio portraits, the range of subjects remains constant, differing only in including more images of events and people outside of St. Paul.[83] In April 1910, the *Dispatch* printed local photographs of Reverend G. Arvid Hagstrom, the white male pastor of the First Swedish Baptist Church; two portraits of the white male "Officials of New Hotel"; and images of "Miss Williams and Mr. Welch," two white residents slated to perform in a production of *Professor Napolean* at the City Auditorium.[84] Editions from September 1914 show images of the Elizabethan Club of St. Paul, made up of young white men and women, including a youthful F. Scott Fitzgerald, and Miss Marcelle Visby, a white aspiring actress described in the caption as "one of the most attractive younger girls of St. Paul."[85] The caption informs readers that Miss Visby lives at 1907 Marshall Avenue, an address that places her squarely in the midst of up-and-coming St. Paulites. The *Dispatch* also printed the winners of the weekly Kodak photo contest, chosen from area submissions. These photographs, taken apparently by amateur pictorialists (à la Dunn), are almost exclusively pictures of white children and families from the middle- and upper-class sections of the city.[86]

While the newspapers did not completely exclude photographs of women, their scant representation in the hard-news sections of the papers did not reflect their numbers within the general population. As in most newspapers of the time, images and stories about and for women most often appeared in the social and society pages.[87] For instance, a photo of "Miss Alice Michaud" commands the top left corner of page 3 of the January 21, 1917, "Society" section of the *Pioneer Press*. Billed as covering "Society, Clubs, Drama, Movies and Music," this section was the only one in which women's images were more common than men's. The photo is accompanied by a typical society-page caption, telling us that "Miss Alice Michaud has gone to Seabreeze, Fla. She was accompanied by her mother Mrs. A. E. Michaud 797 Linwood place" (fig. 25).[88] The society pages of the

Dispatch are similar, focusing on white women's roles as travelers, event goers, and brides.[89] The relative paucity of women's photographs in the papers' general sections suggests the limits of women's place within an imagined St. Paul community. Yet, ironically, by segregating these images into a visual and textual space in which women were the central actors, newspapers here and elsewhere offered white middle- and upper-class female readers a vision of themselves as an affinity group separate from, though folded into, representations of the expanding city.[90]

Other individuals and groups were excluded almost entirely from the *Dispatch* and the *Pioneer Press*—most obviously, St. Paul's working-class and African American citizens. These absences are particularly telling, given the working class's large numerical presence in the city and the prominence of many of St. Paul's African American residents. The papers also steered away from publishing photographs of neighborhoods that were known to house the very poor, the non-white, or the identifiably foreign-born. In short, they failed to depict the sections and people who figured so prominently in Aronovici's survey.[91] Part of the explanation is that both papers were attempting to offer a broad range of news and information to their readers. They divided their efforts between local news and events at the national and international levels. Thus, the number of local photographs published in any one edition was necessarily limited. Nonetheless, over a twenty-year period, there seems to be a consistent absence of St. Paulites who were not white, native-born, or wealthy, a fact that challenges any argument based on coincidence or lack of opportunity.

Further challenging any easy explanation for the exclusivity of the *Pioneer Press* and the *Dispatch* is the overwhelming similarity between the images in both of these newspapers and in those that appeared in the *Daily News*. While all of these papers' publishers and editors were cognizant of their civic duties, the *Daily News* had billed itself from the beginning (it was founded in March 1900) as "The People's Paper—Independent, but not neutral." The *Daily News* took local news as its primary focus.[92] Because this paper was able to focus its energy on the people and events in and around St. Paul, it seems likely that if public sentiment had proven amenable to an inclusive representation of St. Paul such an image would have been more likely to find its way into *Daily News* than into its competitors. Yet its images reflect the same gender, racial, and economic biases.[93]

For the city's poor, immigrant, black, and (to some degree) female residents, the public community represented and embraced by the city's major white-owned newspapers did not include them. What seem to have been at play in these exclusions were the market and political forces that drove the era's newspaper business. Creating and sustaining an audience (and attracting advertisers) meant capitulating to actual or potential audiences. At times, this strategy reinforced social structures and, at other times, transformed them.[94]

The white-owned dailies were not alone in creating a visual world of St. Paul that was exclusive and limited. While photographs in the *Appeal* did include both white and black subjects, images of women and the poor were scarce. The *Appeal* was edited by John Quincy Adams, a proudly Republican African American leader who had come to St. Paul in 1881 to take charge of the fledgling newspaper, then called the *Western Appeal,* and worked there until his untimely death in 1922. In addition to its politics, the paper had a few key differences from the white dailies. Of particular note was its relatively small number of printed photographs: an average edition had between a quarter and a half as many as a comparable edition of the *Pioneer Press,* the *Dispatch,* or the *Daily News* had. Thus, each photo that *was* included—especially those depicting St. Paul residents—carried a bit more weight. In addition, while the *Appeal* was headquartered in St. Paul and published a dedicated local edition, it aimed to be a voice for black Americans in the Midwest and beyond, so its main articles were broad in scope. Nonetheless, its advertisers were local businesses (the paper often urged readers to frequent those advertisers), and it published a standing column about events, activities, and concerns in St. Paul.[95]

Despite these differences, photographs in the *Appeal* share similarities with those in the city's other papers. The vast majority depict white men or women, even when the articles are discussing Minnesota or St. Paul. It included a significantly higher percentage of photographs of black Americans in general; but unlike the Gardner collection, it did not create a visual image of a black majority in the city. By limiting its images of black St. Paulites to a percentage that was only slightly higher than the city's black population, the *Appeal* underscored the perception that St. Paul was primarily white. Moreover, like the white dailies, it also portrayed the city as primarily male.

Importantly, the *Appeal*'s photographic practices also constructed an image of community that was linked closely to class status. By the early 1900s St. Paul had an established black professional class whose members were the leaders of the black community, not just locally but often regionally or nationally. Near the top of the list was Adams himself, along with lawyers McGhee and W .T. Francis as well as doctors, teachers, spiritual leaders, and a powerful group of businessmen and women who made up what was increasingly identifiable as a black elite, though the financial distance among subsets of African Americans in St. Paul was never as sharp as it was elsewhere.[96] As a result, in the paper's presentation of a community that included black men and women, there seemed to be even deeper divisions based on occupation and attendant class status. For instance, the portraits in the *Appeal* are almost all captioned with names from the city's or the nation's black elite. Doctors, pastors, lawyers, scholars, businessmen, entertainers—they were the black community that was reflected in the press. Members of the working and even of the lower middle classes, such as the Gardners, are not readily visible in this pictorial community.

Also telling is the limited nature of the photographs printed in two special issues of the *Appeal*: a 1910 issue celebrating its twenty-fifth anniversary and a 1911 issue marking Adams's twenty-five years as editor. In each instance the paper focused unprecedented photographic attention on St. Paul and its African American residents. The nearly one hundred photographs printed in both the September 24, 1910, and October 28, 1911, issues underscore the ways in which the images tell stories about the groups linked by and through access to the press. The result is a public-facing yet exclusionary photographic narrative of black life in St. Paul, circulated for thousands or more to see. In its content the *Appeal* spoke to and addressed the concerns of a wide swath of the city's and the nation's black community, but the images reproduced in these celebratory issues presents a narrower picture. In page after page, the paper offered portraits of almost all of the city's leading black citizens alongside their kind words about the paper and Adams. As "Residence of J. Q. Adams, 527 St. Anthony Avenue, St. Paul" (fig. 26) and "Residence of F. L. McGhee, 665 W. University Avenue, St. Paul" (fig. 27) demonstrate, there are also pages of photographs and captions identifying their homes and businesses, often including street addresses.[97] In an era in which poverty, education, lack of professional training, and low class status were beginning to subtly divide the African American residents of St. Paul, such photographs underscored some of the complex ideas about race, identity, geography, and community boundaries that the Gardner family captured in their private photographs.[98]

In the end, every element of these various photographic records offers consistent evidence about the different ways in which community was negotiated, defined, experienced, and represented in the city between 1900 and 1920. Again and again photographs seem to divorce experiential community from a definition based on the geopolitical boundaries of the city itself, in some cases even celebrating an imagined place-based unity. At the same time they affirm the power of photographs and photographers to shape understandings and experiences of community that are tied to a range of variables both narrower and broader than city borders. Although family albums generally presented a St. Paul community that looked like the family to whom it belonged, the boundaries of these communities were at least partially linked to race and class—a version of community that the photographer had some control in creating. Likewise, social reform photographs created a sense of division between the community of the poor (who were being viewed) and that of their benefactors (who were doing the viewing) by underscoring the material differences between the lives of the two groups. As they dehumanized the subjects of their photographs, reformers exploited a sense of shared humanity to solicit the support of the viewers. The difference between these images and those in family collections was a matter of degree. Finally, the city's newspapers, by consistently failing to print images that reflected the diversity of the city's populace, promoted a definition of an imagined St. Paul community that was primarily white, male, and well-off. Even the *Appeal's* images, while offering greater racial diversity, created a visual record that was limited in terms of gender and class.

But in spite of these similarities, the strongest link among the various types of photographs is what they do *not* show. That is, regardless of which type of photograph is studied, the actual municipal boundaries of St. Paul are irrelevant. Small-scale places such as neighborhoods or residences or decrepit buildings are depicted, but there is no grand bird's-eye view of the city. Nowhere is there an image that rivals Carol Kennicott's sweeping, universal view in *Main Street*. Photographers might have imagined that a communal feeling existed among all St. Paul residents, and some might even have felt that way themselves, but the communities they chose to capture were communities linked to and driven by narrow, shared affinities within the city's boundaries. Simultaneously, they suggested possibilities for connections based on affinity and status that might reach beyond the borders.

CHAPTER 3

DESIGNING FOR COMMUNITY

Solidarity and Exclusion
through Architecture

I n the waning days of the nineteenth century an orator stood before a crowd inside the state capitol in St. Paul, poised to deliver a celebratory address on the occasion of the city's semi-centennial. But instead of speaking of the city's founding fathers, Samuel Smith spoke of the significance of the city's many public buildings. He urged his audience to recognize that "a building is not chiefly brick and mortar." Rather, its "essential facts" were in "the thought of the builder, the adaptation of the materials, and the organized utility for which it stands."[1] The built environment, he argued, both influenced and was influenced by life in a municipality, a state, a democracy.

Sinclair Lewis would no doubt have agreed. When he published *Main Street* nearly thirty years later, he pressed into service St. Paul's built environment to help describe both the city and Carol's experience of her place in it. Standing on the bluffs above the Mississippi River, she looks down over a sweeping St. Paul that is united in her mind but visually divided by elements of the architectural landscape. The city's buildings, from the cathedral on the highest peak to the shacks lining the river, not only mark the various boundaries of her hometown but also reflect its diversity.

Lewis's description reflects a very real phenomenon in St. Paul during the 1910s. From their grand civic buildings to the details of their private

homes, modernizing St. Paulites marked their places in the social structure
of the city and the nation through the edifices they erected or occupied.
In the process they created visual reminders of an increasingly differentiated citizenry who were, more and more, only imaginatively understood to be a unified whole and who, more and more, only imaginatively
understood themselves as such. St. Paulites were not the only Americans
who were focusing on the uses and implications of urban architecture. By
1920, reformers and planners everywhere were united in the belief that the
built environment possessed redemptive qualities and had the power to
reshape definitions and experiences of a city's community.

Between 1870 and 1910, the population of the United States increased
by a factor of two and a half, and the ratio of city dwellers to rural dwellers shifted dramatically from 28 to 45 percent.[2] With these changes came
attendant shifts in the ethnic and racial makeup of American cities, and St.
Paul was no exception. Immigration from eastern and southern Europe,
among other places, was increasing the foreign-born population and
introducing cultures, languages, and peoples who were identifiably different from native-born Americans. More African Americans, especially
young men, were leaving the South in hopes that the industrial centers
of the urban North would provide better lives and steadier work.[3] The
United States was becoming a nation predominated by cities and city life.
As concerns about these new venues grew, individuals and organizations
initiated a variety of reform programs intended to stop what they saw as
the erosion of both morality and community.

By the 1880s, two different strategies for urban moral reform had developed. One supported the repression of vice through coercive law-and-
order methods, while the other advocated lifting up the moral character
of city dwellers by improving their physical and cultural environments.[4]
The second approach captured the imaginations and spurred the actions
of a great many urban reformers, for there was a growing belief that
the built environment often lay at the heart of unhealthy and undesirable civic life and could be manipulated to create idealized, productive
urban spaces, both domestic and public. While reformers in various cities debated about exactly what constituted *improvement*, they consistently
believed that the physical environment would be a vital element in effective reform and should be mobilized to that end. That belief also began to

shape the ideas and actions of artists of all sorts, spurring what has been called the American Renaissance.[5] The ideas of both artists and activists found their most powerful articulation in the visions of architects, whose craft served as the central element of a powerful cultural triumvirate that also included landscape architecture and city planning and imposed on the physical world the strong moral and reform impulses that pervaded the modernizing era.

These new approaches to city building and reform coalesced around the 1893 World's Columbian Exposition in Chicago. The exposition's White City displayed, on a grand scale, the order and rationality that could be applied to city building. In time, newer forms would augment the classicism that marked the buildings of the White City; but as the twentieth century dawned, it served as a landmark and a model.[6] Its neoclassical white architecture and model green spaces were, in many ways, all that American cities of the late nineteenth century were not, and "wondering visitors came to admire [the White City] and returned home to imitate [it]."[7] This was especially true in the cities of the Middle West, where Cleveland led the charge. In 1899 its mayor assembled a committee to plan and arrange a grouping of civic buildings that would blend harmoniously and exemplify order and reserve. The city's leaders concluded that the final product was, for their city, "what the [exposition's] Court of Honor of 1893 was for the entire country."[8]

By the early twentieth century, then, the impact of the Columbian Exposition and the broader understandings of the role of architecture, landscape architecture, and city planning had begun, in conjunction with growing reform impulses, to transform the physical landscapes of American cities in much the same way that immigration and urban growth had begun to shape their social, demographic, and economic landscapes. Sometimes unwittingly, sometimes consciously, builders and financiers of both civic improvement projects and private edifices were helping to shape the communal identities of those who would see and use the new structures. Cities across the nation became backdrops against which architects and city planners could erect monuments in stone and brick to American idealism and civilization. In particular, the designers, architects, and reformers saw the built environment as a way to bring order to a social world that, especially in cities, was understood to be chaotic and thus potentially immoral. To reverse this trend, they took a multifaceted approach. With the goal of shoring up civic unity, city leaders across the nation began to raise public buildings with a fervor never before seen. Additionally, as a way to improve the moral and physical condition of the nation's poorest residents, housing reformers called for the elimination of slum housing and an increase in small, simple, single-family homes.[9]

In St. Paul, this fervor took hold in the 1900s and 1910s and was made manifest in the city's numerous plans for civic improvement and civic unity, many of which relied on buildings for their effect.[10] Yet reformers and planners were designing buildings in an environment in which an older understanding of the built environment's power to create or affirm communal boundaries already existed. For decades St. Paulites had used ecclesiastical buildings and domestic architecture to find and define their positions in the physical and mental space of the city. By visually dividing the city into distinct, often discreet sections linked to class, race, ethnicity, and religion, in each instance wood, brick, stone and mortar combined to create tangible evidence of divisions and connections.[11]

In the early twentieth century, political and business leaders tried valiantly to reverse this trend, promote the idea of citywide community, and unite a diverse and divided citizenry around shared place of residence through the erection of new civic buildings. A series of such projects—notably, the construction of the City Auditorium—were designed with this goal in mind. In the end, these projects were unsuccessful. That is, given the ideological shift toward affinity-based communities and the pervasiveness of race and class prejudice, they did not make *city* and *community* synonymous in the lives or minds of all residents. At the same time, however, the new buildings reflected, renegotiated, and brought into being a more complex and multifaceted conception of community. By 1920, St. Paul's built environment announced to society near and far both "the place held by each of its members" and the connections or distance among various groups of the same.[12]

Any visitor to St. Paul in the 1910s would have been struck by the vast number of church steeples piercing the skyline. By 1920, the city had nearly two hundred churches, and their ubiquitous spires combined to create a regular pattern across the city, one that might have prompted a casual observer to assume a citywide unity of belief or at least a united experience of faith as a tenet of daily life. In fact, while the latter assumption was in many ways true, the former was certainly not. Although many residents did belong to churches and participated regularly in their activities and services, the superficially interchangeable steeples were attached to buildings that were used not to celebrate civic unity but to mark the separate spatial and ideological ground of numerous faith-based communities. In addition, in a world in which locality was competing with affinity as a foundation for personal identity and group solidarity, the buildings were identifiable physical places with which both narrower and more expansive communities could identify.

The placement and ownership of the various churches in the city reveal that faith-based communities challenged notions of the city as community even as they offered alternatives to familiar race- and class-based divisions. A building to call its own was a critical element of any faith-based group's journey toward self-identity and public recognition. By constructing individual churches, different denominations marked their presence in the city. Yet a structure might also indicate the presence of a particular ethnic or racial subset within a given faith-based community, thereby complicating a simple understanding of faith as a foundation of communal bonds. The St. Paul Cathedral became the most powerful manifestation of these complications, standing as a symbol of Catholic unity and of the relationship between the Catholic community and the city's larger political community even as it failed to transcend divisions within the Catholic population. In other words, church buildings themselves highlighted the complicated webs of community and faith.

The role of church buildings in establishing images and announcing the identity of St. Paulites goes back to the early days of the first permanent European American settlement at this bend in the Mississippi. One of the first structures erected at the site was the Chapel of St. Paul, built in 1841 by Father Lucien Galtier and thirteen Catholic families. As the city grew during the nineteenth century, church buildings became increasingly numerous.[13] By 1903, there were close to 160 churches in the city, representing about twenty different denominations and traditions; by 1920, there were 185 churches representing twenty-five.[14] By the end of the second decade of the twentieth century, it was difficult to cross the city without glimpsing a steeple or a church façade.[15] To St. Paulites, these structures signaled the tenacity of religiously based communities and the presence of those people and groups who saw metaphysical beliefs as sufficient grounds upon which to identify and congregate. Scattered throughout the city—from elite neighborhoods to some of the poorest— the churches made a statement about the desirability of faith-based community affiliation, even on the verge of the modern era.[16]

The city's churches reminded St. Paulites of the presence of alternatives to the class- and race-based divisions that other elements of the built environment suggested. But the sheer number of churches tempered religion's ability to transcend these divisive factors. Deciding which faith community to join required more than simply matching one's religious affiliation to a church because almost every denomination in the city was represented by more than one. Certainly, place of residence could be a driving force in determining church membership, but the influences of race, class, and ethnicity were more central—and they were often related to place.[17]

In general, communicants wanted to worship with people who looked, sounded, and acted like them, as much as they wanted to worship with people who believed like them. The history of the Lutheran and Catholic parishes in St. Paul provides telling examples of this phenomenon. More than half of the Lutheran congregations listed in the 1920 *City Directory* were identified by ethnic affiliation: either by their name alone (for instance, "First Swedish Evangelical Church") or by a parenthetical note after the name (as in "St. John Evangelical [German]"). Significant numbers of the Catholic population were also self-conscious about identifying themselves as members of particular ethnic Catholic communities. Assumption and St. Bernard parishes were identified as "German," while Holy Redeemer was "Italian," St. Louis "French," and St. Casmir and St. Adalbert "Polish." Compared to their Lutheran counterparts, fewer Catholic churches listed their ethnic affiliations in the *City Directory*. Still, the fact that there were some such listings at all is revealing.

The relative importance of ethnic identity and faith-based communities was not a constant among all St. Paulites. Some ethnic Catholic parishes, for example, were frequented by a variety of individuals who were not part of that particular ethnic group.[18] However, such parishes did maintain and create connections along ethnic and linguistic lines, and congregants pressed for ethnic parishes and for ethnic priests to serve in them. In 1856, the German Catholics in St. Paul intentionally split off from the sole (therefore heterogeneous) cathedral parish to organize Assumption Church. The French soon followed, establishing St. Louis Parish in 1868. Eastern European Catholics created St. Stanislaus in the 1870s to serve Bohemian and Polish immigrants. And when the number of Polish communicants reached a critical mass, St. Stanislaus gave birth to St. Adalbert, a specifically Polish parish. The most pressing concern among Catholics in the late nineteenth century was finding and assigning priests who had the same ethnic and linguistic background as their parishioners. Across the United States, thousands of men from all ethnic backgrounds formed a multiethnic pool of priests who, in turn, helped create a network of strongly ethnic parishes within the Catholic church.[19] St. Paul's parishes were part of this network.[20]

The history of church building provides evidence of the motivations of parishioners across a variety of denominations. In early twentieth-century St. Paul, the conscious construction of ethnic parishes reflected an understanding that "[church] architecture [could] serve as a medium for the conscious public expression of [ethnic] identity."[21] More than a quarter of the churches erected between 1900 and 1920 belonged to ethnic congregations.[22] Residents who worked to finance and build, for instance, the Swedish Evangelical Free Church, the St. Volodymyr and St. Olga Ukrainian Orthodox Church, and the St. Louis King of France Church were actively expressing their desire for physical spaces in which to celebrate their faith and their heritage. They were articulating the degree to which ethnicity was essential to their understanding and experience of communities of faith in particular and to community in general.

Thus, the poor and working-class Italians who lived in Swede Hollow had a parish (St. Ambrose) that met their needs as Italians, first and foremost. Having this place allowed them, in some ways, to escape from the designation *poor* and identify with an ethnic community. Residents throughout St. Paul also saw St. Ambrose as an Italian parish. In a 1912 report of the St. Paul Chapter of the Guild of Catholic Women, the guild members, discussing "Our Italian Friends," emphasized the ethnicity of the communicants at St. Ambrose separately from their poverty: "The number of Italians in the East Seventh district was found to be so great that they could not be accommodated at the nearest church and we rejoiced when it was decided to provide a place of worship on Bradley Street close to the homes of a large number of Italian people. We see there every Sunday a congregation that more than fills every available seat and a group of children who have grown to love their church."[23] Yet even in this instance there was a clear and intricate relationship between ethnicity and class. Among communicants themselves, the two were often compressed into component parts of a single identity: parishioners at St. Ambrose.

The architecture of another St. Paul church built at the turn of the twentieth century demonstrates the ways in which church buildings were used to define and announce complex intersections of personal identities and communal affiliations. St. Agnes, located north of University Avenue and constructed between 1909 and 1912 as a parish for German immigrants and their families, is notable for its baroque design. The style was familiar to the parishioners, many of whom had immigrated from southern Germany and the Austro-Hungarian Empire and who hired a German-born architect to carry out their ambitious plan.[24] St. Agnes was unusually explicit in linking architectural style to ethnicity, but more than a dozen other city churches built in these years had unambiguous architectural links to the European origins of their congregants—what has been called a "larger, region-wide trend toward ethnic self-expression."[25]

The most complex examples of the intersection of religious and racial or ethnic identities involve the churches that served St. Paul's black population. Although statistically small, this segment was religiously diverse; and by 1920 there were three self-described black churches in the city, each with its own building. This fact alone raises questions about the wisdom of assuming that race-based community is an uncomplicated concept. Pilgrim Baptist, St. James African Methodist Episcopal, and St. Peter Claver formed the triumvirate, and the membership of each drew from across the ranks of the city's black population. None had an exclusive hold on a certain class-based subset of the larger racial group. Nor did residential proximity appear to be a significant factor in determining church membership.[26] Religious belief was the essential factor affecting affiliation with one or another of these churches. During the late nineteenth and early twentieth centuries, these parishes evolved to meet the various spiritual needs of black residents. Regardless of whether parishioners from any given congregation interacted with or formed other communities outside of their church ones, on Sundays each set constituted a community of its own, marked and surrounded by the façade in which its members worshiped.

Yet the existence of faith-based communities did not erase the issue of race in the experiences of the city's black residents, as the locations of the churches suggest. By 1903, all three parishes had physical presences in neighborhoods that were becoming identifiably black. Pilgrim Baptist was situated in the capitol approach area while St. Peter Claver and St. James AME were at the eastern end of the Rondo district.[27] Like white ethnic parishes, they were geographically isolated. But the black churches were often also institutionally isolated. For instance, Pilgrim Baptist was rarely involved in larger denominational affairs in the city. On the rare occasion when a representative did participate in citywide Baptist concerns, his or her comments were often dismissed as having coming from the "colored" parish.[28] Even more dramatic was the situation involving the Ministers' Union, a regular assembly of pastors from most of the city's Protestant churches, which did not invite participation from either Pilgrim Baptist or St. James AME.[29]

The story of the Catholic parish of St. Peter Claver offers a telling example of the conflicting and complicated definitions of community that arose from the combination of religion and race. Tied in different ways to St. Paul's black population, its Catholic hierarchy, and its white, Protestant, social elite, the parish challenged and exposed the city's class- and race-based experiences of community in the city and brought them all to the fore.

Begun in 1888 as a mission for St. Paul's African American Catholics, who had previously attended mass at other churches, St. Peter Claver received parish status in 1892. Fundraising efforts by the laypeople of the parish funded purchase of land and construction, and before the year was out a church had been consecrated. The structure was a tangible, physical space that the city's black Catholics could claim within a powerful local and global institution. Individually and as a group, Catholics and the Catholic church in St. Paul had a great deal of political capital.[30]

At their center was Archbishop John Ireland, who had the ear of the city's politicians and social elite, including James J. Hill, the "Empire Builder," the city's wealthiest resident, the executive of a group of railroads headed by the Great Northern, and a nationally significant financial, cultural, and political figure of the late nineteenth century. Ireland was known nationally not only as a powerful Catholic figure but as an integrationist who was working toward the full participation of black Catholics in the Catholic church as a whole. In one of his many speeches on the topic, he declared that "color is a mere incident . . . and . . . against this ridiculous [racial] prejudice Catholics are banded to protest most strenuously and continuously." Although Ireland may have overstated the point when he claimed that "wherever the Catholic Church has sway this prejudice has been wiped out," it does seem that, at least in St. Paul, St. Peter Claver offered a tangible symbol of integrationist possibilities.[31] To be affiliated with the institutional church in any way may have given African American Catholics a sense of belonging within the civil society of the city.

There can be no doubt this redefinition of a united Catholic community was linked to the fact that the parishioners at St. Peter Claver were not exclusively black. In fact, although it had been established as a mission parish to evangelize and serve African Americans, by 1921 the black press was describing it as "mostly white."[32] Such a statistic could be interpreted as an indication of black marginalization within their own parish, but this does not seem to have been the case. The parish offered an integrated environment in which some black and white residents (the latter generally drawn from the surrounding working-class multiethnic neighborhood) could come together, linked by their shared belief in the tenets of the Catholic church. It was also a place where black residents could participate in decision making in an integrated environment. St. Peter Claver was a parish not only led by a black priest for portions of the era between 1910 and 1920 but also one in which "the two races work[ed] together in apparent unity."[33]

For a number of years prior to his untimely death in 1912, Frederick McGhee, the city's leading black attorney and a national figure in the fight for racial equality, was a leading congregant at St. Peter Claver, having been cosignatory with Archbishop Ireland on the parish's 1892 charter documents.[34] Yet even though he believed "it is mainly owing to . . . St. Peter Claver that the rights of my people are coming to be recognized in [St. Paul]," the mere existence of a black parish did not translate into automatic membership in the St. Paul community at large or in the city's white-dominated Catholic community.[35] The editors of the *Pioneer Press,* for example, publicly questioned the validity of using diocesan funds for what they called the purchase of a church "for the Negroes."[36] While this editorial view did not reflect the opinion of every white St. Paulite, neither was it unrepresentative. Even within the Catholic community, St. Peter Claver was marginalized. Although almost every ethnic parish in the city was represented in the St. Paul chapter of the Guild of Catholic Women, no one represented St. Peter Claver. And despite the fact that the guild was working to increase its membership throughout the 1910s, the parish never had an active chapter of that nationally recognized organization.[37] The same held true for the Society of St. Vincent de Paul, the guild's male counterpart.[38]

The parish's existence also raised the ire of some non-Catholic African Americans in the city. Although Archbishop Ireland was outspoken about eliminating racial segregation within the Catholic community, some members of the city's more traditionally black denominations saw the creation of St. Peter Claver as a ploy to couch segregation in integrationist rhetoric. One of the most outspoken of these critics was Reverend J. M. Henderson of St. James AME, who viewed the establishment of a separate black Catholic congregation as a way to keep blacks from attending services at the cathedral downtown. The archdiocese countered this attack by claiming that it was merely sparing black Catholics the expense of renting a pew at the cathedral. More to the point, officials argued that, because the archdiocese had established churches for other specific cultural groups in the city (and here they enumerated the ethnic parishes), they were simply giving African American Catholics the same consideration.[39]

The situation at St. Peter Claver, then, highlighted much of the ambiguity that all faithful St. Paulites felt. Each was actively trying to negotiate a variety of intersecting and divergent communal options at the intimate local level and within more universal conceptions of communion and community in a Christian denomination. Adding to this ambiguity was the relative lack of architectural differentiation among church buildings in the city (with some notable exceptions, such as St. Agnes and St. Bernard).[40] Congregants may have seen their own church building as a symbol of their particular group's claim to some of the city's space and resources, but a casual observer was unlikely to notice that difference. For the most part the city's churches were built with relatively similar massing and tall spires or projections announcing their status as houses of worship; most of the architecture provided little evidence to the casual passerby of the ethnic or racial or even denominational affiliation of the communicants who claimed it as their spiritual home.[41] The architectural similarity of the buildings no doubt diminished their power to offer significant help to any group hoping to assert its importance and presence in the larger civic community of St. Paul. Yet that uniformity might have helped to eliminate at least one way of categorizing—and thus eliminating—groups from a larger community of believers. To a noticeable degree, the generalized architectural style that seemed to dominate ecclesiastical building across the United States during this period might have softened overt images of ethnically or racially based communities while reinforcing the idea of communities based on faith alone.

This uniformity did not satisfy everyone. John Ireland, for one, believed that architectural grandiosity might be the key to uniting disparate members of his faith community. To this end, he conceived of and promoted the idea of a grand cathedral in St. Paul, a building that would stand out architecturally from all other ecclesiastical buildings in the city while bringing all local Catholics into communion and connecting them to a worldwide community of faith. At the same time, the building's location and design in relation to the Minnesota State Capitol would offer a visual metaphor for the overlapping, even concentric notions of community that St. Paulites were coming to recognize and internalize.

More than any other Christian denomination represented in St. Paul, the Catholic church was universal in both name and spirit. Yet the significant number of small parishes in the city, each catering to the needs and desires of a particular subset of Catholics, was indicative of a larger trend in faith-based communities in this and other American cities. Construction on St. Paul's massive new cathedral began in 1907, and the church held its first mass in 1915. In Ireland's moving 1905 appeal to raise construction funds, the archbishop relied heavily on a theme of unity:

> The Cathedral is the Diocese. It is the Bishop's Church, holding within its walls the Cathedra, or chair of episcopal authority. It is the spiritual home of the Catholics of the whole Diocese; as its Cathedra commands and guides the whole flock, so its altars and shrines give

forth invocation for all, and welcome all to love and prayer in the oneness of one flock around the one spiritual shepherd. This truth is well understood by Catholics who are intelligent of their faith and loyal to its promptings. Each local Catholic community has its pastor and its church. But the very essence of Catholic life and action is Catholic collectivity. No Catholic is isolated from his fellow-Catholics in faith and charity; no parish is isolated from other parishes. . . . All are members of one body; all are branches from one tree. . . . The Cathedral, it has been said, is the diocese—its rallying point; its symbol, the scene of its specific life and work. To the Cathedral then, Catholics of all parishes must turn; in the Cathedral all must find the expression of their common faith and obedience.[42]

The French architect E. L. Masqueray was called upon to make this unifying rhetoric manifest in a material way. He was selected to design the cathedral from among a talented field of applicants, including the renowned firm McKim, Mead, and White as well as Cass Gilbert, who had recently designed the new state capitol. No doubt Masqueray's universal vision factored into the judges' final decision as much as his impeccable credentials did.[43] He approached architecture as an artist; and for the cathedral design, he invoked his beaux-arts training while drawing on the image and form of French Romanesque churches, a Renaissance floor plan, and the newly erected capitol (opened in 1905), which was situated on a facing hill just east of the proposed cathedral site. The building he envisioned and designed took on the shape of a Greek cross, with a dome over the intersection of the nave and the transept (fig. 28).[44] This arrangement, an apparent nod to St. Peter's in Rome, seemed to serve as a symbol of Catholicism. But his decision to appropriate and include other historical forms and to modify the scale of some elements resulted in a slightly more modern-looking building, one that could stand up to its neighbor, the capitol. The pediment sculptures were ancient Greek, the rose windows gothic, the cartouches baroque. Masqueray intentionally designed the transepts to be wider and the nave shorter than traditional medieval or Renaissance proportions called for. The dome itself was oversized, and the interior was intended to facilitate communicants' sight and hearing.

The cathedral's classical allusions were not as clean or monolithic as the capitol's, whose dome was modeled on the Vatican's St. Peter's Basilica, but the buildings' striking profiles reinforced one another and would soon become the most identifiable elements of the city skyline. In the first decades of century, the two profoundly transformed St. Paul's visual contours, participating in and reinforcing the renegotiation of community. Together and separately, they signaled some of the concentric and intersecting conceptions of community that were everywhere marking residents' daily lives.[45]

For St. Paulites, the capitol was a material reminder that they existed within a nested set of geopolitical entities. They were residents of St. Paul, yes, but they were also part of a more abstract and overarching community called Minnesota. Just as the capitol was a symbol of the presence of an imagined community of the state, the cathedral was a symbol of spiritual unity and communion. In addition, the church building visually and materially narrowed the divide. With its eclectic design elements it crossed the line separating the ecclesiastical from the secular. Thus, it was possible to see the cathedral as a symbolic insertion of the Catholic church into the city's—maybe the state's—daily and political life.[46] Masqueray had intended this symbolism. In the words of a cathedral historian, he had "proposed to create a grand and serene edifice which would also be representative of the democratic . . . society in which it was located."[47]

Ireland recognized the relationship between the two buildings. In fact, he had always hoped that the cathedral, like the capitol, would be both a building and a symbol; and he believed his role included the integration of the Catholic church, particularly its immigrant communicants, into the social and political fabric of modern America.[48] In position and power, then, he believed that his spiritual home should rival any legislative one; and to meet this goal, he could not have picked a more perfect site: the city's highest point, a hilltop lot at the east end of fashionable Summit Avenue that had previously held one of the city's most elegant private homes. After designating the spot he proclaimed, "Let there be in Minnesota, a monument grand and sublime, to proclaim that the Cathedral Church is not merely a memory of a glorious and honored past, that it lives and reigns. . . . The Cathedral of St. Paul, towering high over the City's highest hill, arresting the eye of every traveler winding his way east towards Minnesota's Capital, will be the monument of the Catholic

Church in Minnesota."[49] Contemporary chroniclers of the Catholic church in the western United States underscored this assessment. The St. Paul Cathedral, they wrote, "will stand on an eminence fairer, higher even than the new Capitol's site. Its dome will be a rival landmark; its stones will last as long; its ruins will be sketched alike by the artist of some remote after-age."[50]

The idea that a Catholic cathedral should mirror, even rival, the design of a state house was no surprise to anyone familiar with the workings of St. Paul society and politics. Ireland and the city's Catholics (especially the Irish Catholics) had long been key players in the local political world. Individual Catholics, especially those who were not Irish, saw the project as a way to shore up their own cultural and political presence and prominence. Funding for the cathedral, as for other building projects in the diocese, came in large part from the parishioners of the various Catholic churches in the city, indicating that there was widespread support for this monument to Catholic unity. Yet neither this financial support nor the image of Catholic unity and civic presence had a dramatic impact on the day-to-day experiences of more localized Catholic communities in the city. While the cathedral symbolized the possibilities of a universal faith-based definition and experience of community, it did not diminish the vibrancy of the numerous small ethnic parishes that were flourishing in its shadow.[51] In this and other ways, it was a visible reminder that no mere design or monument could transcend the power of ethnic and racial identity to shape and define community.

Given the universality of Catholicism, the dynamic tension between the cathedral and the city's smaller parishes exemplified the power and limits of faith to unite people in St. Paul while connecting them to fellow Minnesotans and imagined communicants around the globe. Yet variations of this story were repeated across many denominational lines in the city. The very existence of numerous church buildings, most of them catering to at least somewhat homogeneous congregations, indicates that faith alone was not the defining element of parishioners' ideas of community. For many, what seemed to be a clear-cut identification with a given faith community was, in reality, mediated by each individual's other intimate communities. The presence of so many unique and specialized church buildings provided reassurance of a given group's established place within the city. The proliferation of churches of all denominations between 1900 and 1920 reveals a fairly consistent story. Not only did they offer semi-public spaces that could and, at times, did bring together disparate groups, but they also served as tangible reminders of the smaller, narrower, and competing communities within the city.

Churches were only one of several building types that were reinforcing and encouraging particular forms of affinity-based community within and beyond the city's boundaries. While the link to a parish was strong, so was the link to a neighborhood or residential area whose distinctions were reinforced visually by domestic architectural styles therein. Houses, whether or not they were designed specifically for the current owner, whether or not they were the product of an architect's unique project or mass-market specimens, generally reflected and shaped some aspect of how residents imagined and viewed themselves in relation to others in the social order of their city and nation.[52] Certain sizes, designs, and locations marked a homeowner as belonging to a particular segment of the population. Individuals and social classes recognized the power of domestic architecture to signal their position in the social fabric of the city, both positively and negatively. Therefore, differences in their design, size, and relative newness in different areas of the city can be read as self-conscious displays of a family's real or perceived experience of intimate community. These homes indicated to residents and visitors that there were not only different experiences of life in St. Paul but that that there were different St. Pauls altogether.

The photographs in the Dunn collection and the *Appeal* photographs of the homes of the city's black elite demonstrate the importance of the single-family home in creating and solidifying a sense of self and community. In both sets of images, houses appear to describe residents' relationship to the city's power structures and social circles. As public displays of wealth, taste, and success and as indicators of the residents' relationship to the ideal or to modern efficiency and culture, private homes could be read as markers of a family's place in the citywide community, a place whose boundaries were influenced by racial, class, or ethnic identities and affiliations.

By the turn of the twentieth century, St. Paul had moved far from its territorial roots as a small settlement of scattered houses on the banks of the Mississippi. Now it was made up of a series of distinct neighborhoods fanning in all directions from the original settlement site.[53] This growth was related to sharp increases in population and the continuing land speculation and building activities that had begun in the 1880s and 1890s. Much like church architecture, domestic architecture in St. Paul was generally unified; the vast majority of homes were variations on the single-family, detached, wood-frame dwellings that characterized most urban housing across the nation, especially in the booming Middle West. Because of this citywide emphasis on single-family homes, the boundaries of most St. Paul neighborhoods were quite malleable as late as 1900. As a result, the city never developed neighborhoods that were as distinct and exclusive as those in Chicago or even Minneapolis.[54] Yet this malleability and uniformity were relative, as evidenced by the eclecticism of some residential districts and the formal similarities among many of the individual structures in others. By 1900, the architectural map of the city revealed a series of identifiable regions that told the story of residents' positions in the St. Paul community.

As the twentieth century dawned, some neighborhoods continued to mix architectural styles and classes of people. In others, however, that mixture had given way to separate areas marked by distinct housing styles.[55] This transition meant that, at times, surface similarities combined with nuanced variations in architectural choices, complicating experiences and ideas about community solidarity. In some cases a casual observer would have been able to distinguish differences among areas of the city and their residents; in other cases those distinctions would have been much subtler. In other words, St. Paul's domestic architecture allowed observers to make assumptions about the people who lived in a given house, but those assumptions might be that it was difficult to make assumptions. At the same time, residents themselves were often quick to note or internalize subtle but crucial indicators of status and group differentiation in housing styles, provenance, and ownership.

There were few chances to misread or misunderstand the social worlds or imagined communities of the city's wealthiest residents during the modernizing era. The years between 1885 and 1917 have long been recognized as the golden era of the Hill district, a section of the city on the bluffs above the Mississippi's eastern bank and centrally located along the city's east-west meridian. In this period the area matured and expanded, first slowly and then more rapidly, from Ramsey Hill westward and northward, forming a progression of house styles that reflected the shift from established elite families at the eastern end to newer middle-class professionals at the western end. As a whole, the housing constructed in the district between 1890 and 1910 was grand. Ward statistics for residential building permits indicate that the real estate values on the Hill were greater than in any other area of the city, except for the central business core.[56]

By 1900 the easternmost end of the district had been established as the home of most of the city's wealthiest residents. During the next twenty years the trend continued, and by 1920 the majority of the St. Paul names in the *Dual City Blue Book* (a biannual publication listing the names of "the best families" in St. Paul and Minneapolis) were paired with addresses in this area.[57] Between 1890 and 1920 residents were generally American-born; the Hill district had a smaller percentage of foreign-born residents than most other areas of the city, a fact that established a set of demographic-based similarities, which, in turn, reinforced visual and architectural similarities.[58] Nonetheless, there were three relatively distinct sections of the district: Summit Avenue, Crocus Hill, and the neighborhoods north of Summit and west of Victoria. Each boasted a particular architectural style that tended to correspond to and indicate the relative economic and social worlds of its residents.

The far-eastern edge of the Hill district (the section on the bluffs overlooking downtown) was developed first, and in the latter half of the nineteenth century it became home to the grand mansions that, by the opening of the twentieth century, snaked along Summit Avenue, the grand boulevard winding along the top of Ramsey Hill. Wealthy St. Paulites who had made their money early on in the railroads and breweries or in the financial, trade, or commercial realms were attracted by the area's geography.[59] It was largely undeveloped, unlike the older "good" neighborhoods of Irvine Park and Lower Town (which were becoming increasingly marked by commercial development) or even the very westerly suburban developments of Merriam Park, Lake Iris, and Macalester Park. Consequently, opportunities abounded for those who wished to build extremely large, architect-designed, single-family homes on impressive expanses of land. They were also drawn to its isolation. Sitting high above the city's core, the section was somewhat protected from the commercial district and from the lower-class residences lining the riverbanks and downtown areas below.[60]

At the center of this area, literally and imaginatively, was Summit Avenue. By 1900, it was already the grande dame of the city. As St. Paul's foremost residential boulevard, it was lined with Victorian houses along a stretch that would eventually extend to the Mississippi River on the western end of the city. Many of the structures had been built in the 1870s and 1880s, when houses were seen as expressions of artistic achievement, individual taste, and personal identity.[61] In their uniqueness and individualized detailing, these houses articulated owners' personal tastes, ideals, and status. In this way they reflected the assertions of the well-known nineteenth-century preacher Henry Ward Beecher, who argued that "a house is the shape which a man's thought takes when he imagines how he should like to live. . . . It interprets, in material form, his ideas of home, of friendship, and of comfort."[62]

In this case, however, the ideal was not just to design any type of home. Owners wanted a house that, in its design, detailing, and interior decoration, articulated the increasingly powerful social forces of comfort—what the economist and sociologist Thorstein Veblen labeled "conspicuous consumption."[63] They began building homes that elaborated on the already popular Queen Anne, Eastlake, and French Second Empire styles, adding more ornate detailing and combining elements of each to create sometimes absurd but always highly individualized homes. As the twentieth century approached, members of the highest echelon of society inflated this middle-class ideal to an even grander scale. Their newly built homes reflected their belief that personal residences should make public statements about the owners' independence and wealth, and the performative acts of these massive domiciles helped position the residents as members of a regional, national, even international elite.[64] As Abigail Van Slyck has argued, American elites of the late nineteenth and early twentieth century were interested in "translating economic capital into cultural and social capital," and their grand homes participated in this endeavor.[65]

In St. Paul, Summit Avenue was where such homes predominated. The best-known and most prominent of these houses belonged to James J. Hill and his family. Their residence at 240 Summit Avenue was an impressive Romanesque house built to the owner's specifications and completed in 1891 (fig. 29).[66] At a time when many other well-to-do St. Paulites were using local architects, Hill hired the Boston firm of Peabody and Stearns, and he made no compromises in the design, construction, or furnishing of his 36,000-square-foot dream home. When complete, it was the largest and most expensive house in Minnesota, costing its owner slightly more than $900,000. It boasted thirteen bathrooms, twenty-two fireplaces, sixteen crystal chandeliers, a two-story sky-lit art gallery, a nearly one-hundred-foot reception hall, and incredible amounts of hand-carved mahogany woodwork.[67] Although it was built before 1900, it remained St. Paul's resident "castle" throughout the twentieth century.

In its grandness the Hill house approximated the homes of other Gilded Age financiers and entrepreneurs. Like the Vanderbilts and the Carnegies, the Hills understood that their home was a public symbol of their wealth and their social, financial, and political connections. Its opulence (scaled down to a midwestern size and form) proclaimed the family's social standing, both locally and beyond. There has been much written about Hill's national prominence and the extensive social and business networks of his fellow Gilded Age entrepreneurs. As Van Slyck writes, "for American aristocrats, class status was a complicated process that had spatial components," and it is easy to see how the Hill home helped establish the magnate and his wife, Mary, as members of the intimate community of the nation's elite.[68] Hill's decision to hire Boston's premier architects was an important part of this work. By 1891, that firm had worked on numerous grand houses, including The Breakers, the Newport, Rhode Island, mansion that the Vanderbilts had purchased in 1885. Likewise, when the Hills requested a house in the American Romanesque style, which the architect H. H. Richardson had made famous in his design for Boston's Trinity Church, they were, like many other midwestern elites, linking themselves materially and imaginatively to their counterparts on the East Coast and beyond.[69]

Yet the scale of St. Paul, the Hills' standing as the city's only magnate family, and the couple's modest immigrant backgrounds meant that their mansion was also a signifier in the city's social, economic, and political world. What was the relationship between the Hills and their fellow St. Paulites, none of whom would ever build such a grand home? And how did architecture work to mark their social world in their hometown even as it reaffirmed a more expansive set of relationships that also shaped the their life? In general, the relationship between the Hills and their fellow St. Paulites seems to have been one of permissive association made manifest in the structure itself and in the human interactions it inspired and housed. Because there were no comparable homes in St. Paul and thus no truly comparable aristocracy to entertain, the Hills were not bound to associate with a narrow group of elite intimates as they might have done had they lived in a larger American city. They were free to form relationships with residents drawn fairly widely from the ranks of the upper classes.

For instance, as one would expect, Mary Hill's social circle included a host of women from other well-to-do families. According to her diary, most of them lived on Summit Avenue, in Crocus Hill, and in the wealthier parts of the Lexington-Victoria area to the west.[70] But she was the daughter of poor Irish-Catholic immigrants, and her records reveal that she continued to keep up intimate relationships with residents on the margins of the city's social elite.[71] The same was true of her husband, a Canadian immigrant who found his way to the St. Paul docks as a teenager seeking work and a future. While Hill famously filled his mansion with European artworks that rivaled those in most private collections, he also famously eschewed a narrow definition of his social class. Throughout his life he maintained close friendships with the modestly successful local entrepreneurs he had met when he was still a man on the rise in St. Paul.[72]

To some extent, then, the individualized, eclectic designs of expensive architect-designed homes were visible symbols of such communal latitude. The relatively understated magnificence of the Hills' home (as compared to the homes of their eastern counterparts) announced such willingness and interest.[73] Nonetheless, the couple still resided in the city's most exclusive neighborhood, a place where architecture signified a great deal. And it is clear that the residents of Summit Avenue believed that the architectural integrity of their avenue was an important part of their collective identity. In 1915, they took advantage of brand-new state legislation for creating residential districts and collectively voted to ban the erection of any apartment buildings on the street. Four such structures had already been built, and now the residents made it clear that they wanted to keep such anomalies to a minimum. Notably, this particular resolution did not ban commercial buildings, schools, or churches. Rather, for the majority of Summit Avenue's residents, it was residential architecture that had the power to visually define them and their neighborhood. Apartment buildings housed people whose lives, goals, and qualities were not obviously compatible with the vision of community as understood by those who lived on Summit.[74]

Just to the south of the avenue was an insular neighborhood known as Crocus Hill, and just north and west was the Lexington-Victoria neighborhood. Both had been built up in the late nineteenth century with residences that housed many of the city's well-to-do newcomers, people with aspirations who did not yet possess the bankrolls of the Summit Avenue mansion owners. The boundaries of Crocus Hill were more geographically visible, thanks to the cliff running alongside it, but by 1900 both sections had been architecturally marked as highly desirable neighborhoods. Most of the residences were large-scale, wood-frame homes with elegant and sometimes elaborate detailing, in keeping with the aesthetics that had inspired Summit's Victorian mansions. In the early twentieth century, classical and historical revival elements began appearing on some homes in these areas, but in general they featured gables, turrets, and uniform trim details.[75]

A sense of architectural connection linked these homes and those on Summit Avenue. Likewise, their social worlds often overlapped. As mentioned, Mary Hill's intimates included women who lived in both of these areas. Yet distinctions remained, and even slight differences could mark the limits of intimate circles among those who strove for inclusion. The novelist F. Scott Fitzgerald grew up in the district, in the area just north of Summit, living in a series of rented homes that were architecturally similar to those of Crocus Hill. He played with some of the city's well-to-do children and later recalled attending dancing school with the offspring of Summit Avenue millionaires. Yet an excruciating sense of class division pervades Fitzgerald's chronicle of his boyhood. He may have danced among the Summit elite, but his family's precarious financial circumstances put high-status home ownership out of reach, and he felt that his place in this community was tenuous at best.[76] The recollections of his contemporaries support this impression, though some of them were inclined to view the subtle class distinctions as a powerful means of unifying the residents of smaller neighborhood groups.[77]

In their individuality and grandeur, then, the Summit Avenue mansions (and, to some extent, the homes of Crocus Hill) helped to establish
their residents as wealthy members of an elite social circle. By the early
twentieth century, as housing styles began to change, they also marked
their owners as members of an older guard whose housing style demonstrated that they had already arrived at the top.[78] As such, they were free
from the pressures of creating a legacy or proving their right to move in
any particular social circle in the city. This work was taken up by many
of the up-and-coming St. Paul businessmen and young professionals who
were building newer, more modern homes on the city's western edge.

In the 1900s and 1910s, anyone traveling westward from the grandest
homes on Summit Avenue would have seen prolific construction. Although
these slightly less grand houses were not as opulent as those on Summit or
Crocus Hill, they reflected the taste and aspirations of a new group of St.
Paulites who were self-consciously carving out a social and architectural
niche in the city. Most of these men were middle-class professionals (lawyers, doctors, and so on) and white-collar workers employed in St. Paul's sizable publishing, financial, wholesale, and transportation industries. Building
in this area occurred rapidly, and by 1920 a nearly uninterrupted swath of
solid frame homes stretched along the streets immediately south of Summit
Avenue to the area just west of Lexington Parkway.[79] Almost all of these
houses were slightly smaller and more conservative than their Summit
counterparts, suggesting that their owners had not yet reached the status
of the city's wealthiest citizens. Even the homes being built on the western
reaches of Summit Avenue were generally simplified, rectilinear versions
of the eastern end's Victorian styles.[80] Yet simplicity and smaller size did
more than hint that the residents were a step down on the economic ladder.
These attributes demonstrated that the owners appreciated and adhered to
a more modern, more minimalist ideal of the middle-class home, thus separating this group of St. Paulites in ideology and lifestyle from their wealthier
Summit counterparts while solidifying their shared middle-class values and
related material trappings.[81]

The home that the Dunn family built at 1033 Lincoln Avenue in 1903
illustrates this pattern. The brick house was a foursquare design with
colonial revival elements. Although slightly larger and more elaborate
than other middle-class homes of the era, it was remarkably similar to

styles that home design companies and catalogs popularized around the nation at the turn of the century. The Dunns were obviously interested in presenting themselves as members of the new and fashionable generation of twentieth-century American professionals—an interest that is reflected in their home's similarities to its neighboring houses, which were generally owned by men of similar vocational and social status.[82] Photographic evidence makes this clear.[83] Although the ornamentation of each home was often unique (some had Queen Anne styling; some had shingles; some were colonial revivals) and the size varied from plot to plot, the general look remained the same. Many were two- or two-and-a-half-story rectilinear structures with peaked roofs, an aesthetic that was increasingly common throughout the nation in the 1910s. In St. Paul as elsewhere, such uniformity reflected an increasing reliance on standard house designs that were usually constructed by local carpenters and contractors.[84]

Another commonality was their newness. Unlike the mansions of Summit Avenue, the buildings in this area housed a group of people who represented the new middle class. These men and women were marking their membership in this particular community by constructing houses that reflected a newer vision of the ideal home, and they were surrounded by residences that were transmitting the same message. Thus, the potential for neighborhood-based definitions of community was great. Especially in the western part of the Hill district, the social world of these newly middle-class residents with their new middle-class houses was often linked to the geographic area in which they lived. These members of St. Paul's second tier understood themselves to be part of a community made up of those who lived in the surrounding area—people who ostensibly shared many of the same ideological, professional, familial, economic, and social characteristics. So it is not surprising that the members of Dunn's beloved Oxford Skating Club generally lived in the 900, 1000, and 1100 blocks of Laurel, Osceola, St. Clair, Goodrich, Ashland, Portland, North Victoria, Fairmount, Summit, and Oxford streets—most a brief walk from the Dunns.[85]

Although it was not the only factor at play, the architectural uniformity of these homes helped these middle-class residents identify and solidify their position in the social world of the city. As Kevin Lynch argues in *The Image of the City*, urban dwellers often use identifiable markers such as neighborhoods and special-interest areas of a city to orient themselves within that municipality.[86] In St. Paul, the location and design of homes in the Hill district—whether at the elite east end or the middle-class west end—were tangible markers of the social world, real or imagined, of its residents. But if architectural uniformity was a way to unify the residents of a neighborhood, what effect did architectural eclecticism have? The answer to this question is multilayered, as the stories of two other residential areas make clear.

The Dunn's neighborhood was not the only area of the city that experienced a housing boom in the early twentieth century. On the other side of town, high on the bluffs overlooking the Mississippi on the city's eastern edge, houses were also going up in record numbers.[87] In 1900 the new housing in this section of town, known as Dayton's Bluff, looked a great deal like that in western sections of the Hill district; the typical home was a foursquare with limited ornamentation and a pattern-book look.[88] Even when new residences retained some of the basic elements of older styles (Queen Anne and the like), excessive ornamentation such as elaborate gingerbread trim was replaced by simpler elements, reflecting the trend toward the classical and colonial revival styles. Simpler columns, rooflines, and porches predominated.[89]

What differentiated Dayton's Bluff from the Hill district was the fact that these homes were mixed among larger and smaller, grander and simpler homes on every block. The area's earliest homes had been large mansions along the edge of bluff itself; but beginning with the first housing boom of the 1880s, the area's new construction had consistently matched the class diversity of the area. Dayton's Bluff was known as a place in which laborers and middle managers lived side by side, in some cases just a few house lots away from some of the city's more prominent men and women. In 1909 the Dayton's Bluff Commercial Club even publicized this aspect of the neighborhood, using it as a selling point to lure potential residents and commercial enterprises to the area. "There is no particular . . . class that predominates on Dayton's Bluff," the pamphlet declared, "It is a section of a city strictly metropolitan and cosmopolitan in its residents. All nationalities and all classes are represented."[90]

In this neighborhood, architectural integration seemed to match class integration; the steady construction of two-story rectilinear homes next door to small workers' cottages and not far from the grand old mansions helped promote this image. Whether or not the social world of the area was as integrated across class lines as the blocks themselves were, by the late nineteenth century the area's visual diversity (much like the unifying design of the cathedral) promoted the possibility of establishing intimate communities across identifiable class lines—even of imagining a geographically referenced community that would encompass a range of residents with a variety of class and ethnic backgrounds.

The ascendancy of a more uniform type of new housing structure may have helped promote this vision. Beginning in 1903, a large number of foursquare pattern-book homes were erected in the shadow of one of the wealthier estates on Dayton's Bluff. After this point, new homes in the area became more uniform; residential growth was targeted "not [to] those who desire to live surrounded by great luxury and display, but those who desire health, comfort, quiet and convenience."[91] The neoclassical predilections of the era appeared everywhere in these new houses, whose most noteworthy characteristic was their lack of distinction or individuality. Although newcomers to Dayton's Bluff continued to be a mixed economic lot, the availability of similar-style homes in almost every price range made it increasingly difficult to immediately distinguish among the homes of laborers and middle managers. The result was a visual leveling of the field.

This is not to say that architectural differentiation ceased to exist on Dayton's Bluff. But the differentiation between the homes of the middle class and the laborers was less often made manifest in the particular size or overall design of the structure and more often apparent in smaller details, aesthetic accoutrements, and decorative elements such as dormer size and degree of exterior trim or elaboration. The upshot by 1920 was a residential area that architecturally did not obviously reveal any working- or middle-class sub-neighborhoods.[92] In many ways this visual appearance mirrored the area's ethnic and class diversity: it had been populated for decades by immigrants (especially German), and both workers and business owners were living there by 1920. Because bonds of ethnic and immigrant status united residents both actually and imaginatively, architecture's ability to unite or divide may have been reduced. Dayton's Bluff serves as a reminder of the renegotiation of community and the various ways in which cultural production and individual identities intersected in the era to complicate any uniform understanding of community or place-based unity. In particular, it suggests the limits of architecture in making public the nuances of a neighborhood's story—a critical lesson for those who study the Rondo neighborhood.

By 1920 Rondo was home to a majority of the city's African American residents. Only a short walk away from the Hill district, it was an ethnically, racially, and economically mixed neighborhood in which residents formed intimate communities that were not always predictably configured. While its domestic architecture offers some clues about the nature of these relationships, it is less instructive here than in other sections of the city. Rondo extended north and south from University to Marshall streets and east and west from Rice to Lexington streets. Residents were an eclectic mix of new immigrants and black and white working- and middle-class families as well as some of the nation's African American elite. The residential area was marked by many shady streets and had both its own commercial center and fairly easy access to the business center of St. Paul.[93] Architecturally, it was far removed from images of racially segregated neighborhoods of the sort that Riis had depicted in New York City. Some portions of the area had been settled at about the same time and by same types of people who had settled Crocus Hill in the late 1800s, and the large Victorian homes of these prosperous whites remained even after their original owners began abandoning the area for newer, more fashionable residences and developments to the west.[94] Not surprisingly, this exodus came at about the same time that the black population began moving up the hill from downtown and settling near Rondo Avenue.[95]

A significant portion of the homes in Rondo were smaller and less ornate, more in keeping with the architectural trends of an area known as Frogtown, just north of the eastern portion of the neighborhood. Both Rondo and Frogtown had a number of small frame houses irregularly arranged on their lots.[96] They were similar to the two-story rectangles in the newer areas of the city, albeit often with less ornamentation. Some were new construction, but many more were older and less uniform, reflecting an older aesthetic linked to the Victorian era, as seen background of the Gardner photographs.[97] These two styles formed the general architectural trend in Rondo, and for some residents this visual integration both reflected and helped foster a sense of racial integration.

Writing about his childhood among the "tree-lined lanes" that surrounded his family's "little cottage," the NAACP leader Roy Wilkins asserted that "the men who owned the tidy frame houses in my neighborhood were white: Swedes & Norwegians, Poles, Germans, and Irish—first-and-second-generation immigrants. They worked as carpenters, patching up boxcars in the nearby yards of the Northern Pacific, or as laborers and janitors, watchmen, policemen, and firemen."[98] Residents' interracial sense of neighborhood-based community arose partly from the fact that, as Wilkins would later put it, "everyone around us, white and Negro alike, was struggling to support a middle-class outlook on a poor man's income."[99] If the ticket into the imagined St. Paul community was to be perceived as part of the middle class, Rondo was a place where people could theoretically take the first steps toward that end. Because the homes were quite similar, class divisions could be masked fairly easily—at least from the outside. Furthermore, the neighborhood was a place in which working-class people could stake a claim to middle-class values and ornamentation, regardless of their race or ethnicity, even if that status did not extend outside the district.[100] Thanks to declining property values (as the white middle class began to leave), homes whose design reflected a late nineteenth-century ideal of middle-class housing became available for rent or purchase. In an era in which community building was part of a process of embourgeoisement, attaining the trappings of some version of that middle-class life, even an outdated one, could offer hope to those who were marginalized in other ways.[101]

Wilkins's memories notwithstanding, this continuity in home design did not guarantee the existence of a neighborhood-wide sense of community in Rondo. Nor, as the adults in Wilkins's world experienced, was its relative similarity to the architecture of other areas of the city enough to overshadow racial and class divisions between Rondo residents and middle-class residents elsewhere in St. Paul. In a number of ways the architecture in the neighborhood could be as divisive as it was cohesive. On the most basic level, some members of the Rondo community lived in homes that were far grander than the simple frame houses of Wilkins's memory. Delia Cheney, a white woman, an amateur photographer, and a Rondo resident, captured this reality in a number of photographs she took shortly after the turn of the century. One image, for instance, taken not far from her own extremely modest home, shows older-era houses that were larger and more ornate. These discrepancies were publicized when the *Appeal* chose to print photographs of select neighborhood homes in its 1911 anniversary tribute to John Quincy Adams. While images of more modest homes did appear in the paper, the vast majority were grander than the "tidy frame houses" of Wilkins's memory. In particular, the homes of Adams and Frederick McGhee stand out as symbols of wealth and status. Adams's home had elaborate exterior ornamentation, and its sizable interior included four rooms and a reception room downstairs and five bedrooms upstairs.[102] Even more than Adams's, McGhee's house marked his financial security and his position at the top of the black community's social ladder. Adams's daughter Adina remarked decades later that "[Mr. McGhee] made money and he had a fine home on University Avenue, a big place. And it was a very, very, nice home."[103]

Such homes and their photographs proved to owners and neighborhood residents was that there *were* class- and status-based distinctions in Rondo. These distinctions were not new in 1911. Although slow to become deeply ensconced and not fully realized until the 1930s, they had been a long time in the making. When blacks first began settling in Rondo in the 1890s, the eastern ends of Rondo, St. Anthony, Central, and Carroll streets were the principal avenues of residential life. By 1920, the more affluent black families had moved westward, often along Rondo and St. Anthony avenues, toward Lexington Parkway. By the early 1920s, the area's black residents colloquially referred to Lower Rondo (the area below Dale Street) as "Cornmeal Valley" and Upper Rondo (above, or west of, Dale) as "Oatmeal Hill."[104] Further east the homes generally became smaller and less ornate, and apartment buildings and rooming houses figured into the landscape more frequently. According to city reformers, in 1917 the areas on the extreme lower end of Rondo abutted one of the city's most decrepit districts. (It is worth noting, however, that a 1937 survey of the city made patently clear that the area was not a slum).[105] In contrast, many of Rondo's prominent black families lived in the area west of Dale along Iglehart, Carroll, Rondo, St. Anthony, and Central avenues. While residents of both areas might have belonged to the same churches and shared a racial identity, by the late 1910s the split between the eastern and the western ends of Rondo had begun to widen. The fact that such labels as "Oatmeal Hill" and "Cornmeal Valley" existed at all underscored the presence of at least a psychic division among the area's black residents.[106]

Class divisions were not the only divisions in the social fabric of Rondo. Despite Wilkins's childhood memories of interracial neighborliness, racial divisions also existed in Rondo, and they were much harder to link to the area's physical structure. The photographs of the Gardner family speak of the degree to which race shaped intimate communities for at least some Rondo residents—apparently despite their shared location in the city or their mutual status as working class. Furthermore, an undercurrent of structural racism undoubtedly shaped the communal experiences of Rondo residents. After all, white ethnics could eventually rise in social standing and move to newer, more fashionable, more middle-class parts of the city. But restrictive real estate practices, similar to those in force across the urban North, severely limited black access to more desirable areas.[107]

As far back as the 1870s, exclusionary practices had shaped St. Paul's real estate market, and they had not been much altered by the coming of the new century. In 1910, the *Appeal* ran the following ad targeting current and potential St. Paulites: "If you wish to rent a house or a room call at the Afro-American Renting Agency. . . . We have a list of houses and rooms that Afro-Americans can rent. Don't spend unnecessary car fare and time and subject yourself to embarrassment, come to see us, we will tell you where they are."[108] Five years later the *Twin City Star,* one of Minneapolis's black papers, reasserted the same issue in an ad repeated nearly weekly under the headline "The Housing Problem." "Where can I get a good apartment? Is a serious question among us today," it read. "There are many restrictions against Negroes as tenants in desirable places and many places undesirable for respectable Negro tenants. There are many strangers coming to our city, and they are unable to get decent locations."[109]

This racial dividing line was particularly obvious for members of the black elite in St. Paul. Men such as Adams and McGhee, who were influential within the black community, not only in St. Paul but also nationwide, and were generally respected among white St. Paulites, all lived in Rondo. True, their homes were arguably nicer than most of the others in the neighborhood, but they were still relegated to life in a neighborhood that many successful white citizens saw as undesirable. Members of Rondo's black elite might have been able to move between the black and white business and professional communities of St. Paul in their working lives: Adams's office was in the middle of the downtown, and the Gardners' relative and neighbor Billy Williams served for decades as the assistant to the governor in the state capitol. But in their most private moments and places, they were identified primarily as black. The experience of residential life in Rondo indicates that racial identity and identification bound people to residential areas as much as, perhaps more than, economic status or citywide prestige did.[110]

Most homes in Rondo were variations of the two-story rectilinear structures built by middle-class Americans in the later years of the Victorian era and the opening years of the twentieth century. While some retained ornate architectural elements, many more were closer in style to the newer homes of the Lexington-Victoria or Dayton's Bluff neighborhoods. As in those white neighborhoods, the homes in Rondo tended toward uniformity. But because of the diversity of the residents, the architectural evidence does not confirm the link between architecture and community building. Rather, the complicated and often unpredictable social world of Rondo underscored the limitations of architecture to significantly reorganize or reestablish communal relations in the face of deep-seated convictions about the role of race, class, or ethnicity in the social order. Among other things, Rondo's built environment reinforced what Dayton's Bluff's only hinted at: that architecture can mask divisions as much as reveal or create them.

Perhaps no sections of the city were more clearly marked as separate than those areas that housed the city's poorest residents, most of whom lived relatively close to the old city core or the river.[111] The homes in these areas were easily identifiable because they were vastly different from the tidy frame homes of Rondo, the new construction of the expanding western neighborhoods, and the elegant mansions of the Hill district. Yet even within this general grouping of poor areas, Swede Hollow stood out. The neighborhood was not only architecturally poorer than the middle-class neighborhoods, but it was also geographically isolated from almost all of the others. Its dilapidated structures marked the residents as members of social circles and intimate communities that were distinct from any others in St. Paul. In other words, here, too, a residential neighborhood closely resembled an intimate community—although in this case the conflation of geography and intimacy was built on the basis of poverty and ethnic solidarity.

Swede Hollow was an evolving settlement in a 150-foot-wide ravine cut by Phalen Creek in the northeastern section of the city. First settled by Swedish immigrants in the mid-nineteenth century, it had become by 1900 a primarily Italian immigrant enclave hidden from the rest of the city by the high bluffs (nearly seventy feet tall at some points) that reached up to the city's east side. By the early 1900s, some of the original shacks had been reconfigured into small homes, a few even with porches. Nonetheless, by 1903 the hollow was still scattered with shanties that extended haphazardly toward Sixth Street.[112] A photograph from around the turn of the century shows small one- or one-and-a-half-story houses throughout the hollow (fig. 30).[113] By 1918 the area was marked most notably by the fact that it had the highest percentage of poor-quality housing anywhere in the city.[114] Nonetheless, acquiring one of these homes was the goal of most Swede Hollow families.

Despite the transient nature of life in the hollow, the area's isolation helped it become a reciprocal, intimate community unto itself. Gentille Yarusso, a former resident and its most prolific chronicler, has asserted that "very few people participated in outside neighborhood activities." Calling Swede Hollow "our little community," he recalled that the residents were "happy" people who "dressed the same, spoke the same language, [and] ate practically the same kinds of food."[115] This unity of experience helped the impoverished residents raise the $2,700 in 1918 to purchase the nearby St. Ambrose Catholic Church.[116] Yet that unity, like Rondo's, appears to have come at the expense of integration into the city as a whole. Although many Swede Hollow residents worked as laborers on the nearby railroads or at the Hamm brewing plant, thereby functioning as the economic base of the city, city leaders usually left them to fend for themselves. No matter that they paid the city $5 a month as rent for use of the land: the city left maintenance of the neighborhood to its residents.[117] When snow blocked the only road leading into or out of the hollow, trapped residents were forced to survive on their own stores of food. From the late 1800s onward, there were numerous complaints about the lack of a neighborhood sewage system, but city leaders dismissed the problem, claiming that the cost of building one was prohibitive.[118] Thus, in a slightly different way than was the case in Rondo, the Swede Hollow example indicates that isolation from others could lead to an experience of community as much as geographic proximity could.

Ultimately, the shape of St. Paul's domestic architecture and its neighborhood development helped mark St. Paulites' relation to and distance from the professional and middle classes and thus to imagined notions of a united city community. While some residents could actively manipulate or construct homes to visually position themselves within this community, the structural limitations of race and class kept others at the mercy of the messages implicit in the types of homes to which they had access. These deep-seated divisions and a range of narrower and broader allegiances were also evident in the most explicitly universal public building erected in St. Paul in the early twentieth century: the City Auditorium. As a secular version of the cathedral's story, its creation illustrates both the potential and the limits of architecture to build or promote municipal unity in modernizing cities where the meaning of community was complex and evolving.

Completed in 1907, the City Auditorium was the first of two major public building erected in St. Paul during the century's opening two decades. A group of interested business and professional men had formed a committee to stir up support for the project, and they solicited money from residents to construct a building that would rectify what they saw as a serious municipal problem: the city's lack of a public exhibition or performance hall. In 1893, St. Paul had built a primitive auditorium on Eighth Street to host a celebration marking the completion of the Great Northern Railway's transcontinental line, but the all-wood structure (erected in just a month and never painted) was little more than an oversized shed and was torn down in 1903.[119] City boosters believed that a new auditorium was essential, and they also argued that it needed to be multipurpose— able to house large public gatherings, support the needs of stage and hippodrome performances, and host both grand operatic performances and small intimate concerts. The seating capacity, they declared, had to match that of New York City's Metropolitan Opera House.[120]

City leaders asked for a great deal, and they found architects who could deliver: Charles Reed and Allen Stern, who would go on to design New

York City's Grand Central Station. The duo's plans for the auditorium proved wildly successful. When complete, the structure was on par with many of the nation's greatest public buildings. With its movable interior walls and seating, the space could be configured in a number of different ways. More importantly, its exterior worked to reinforce its democratic purposes. Taking into consideration the era's emphasis on historical elements in the design of public buildings, Reed and Stern used the tropes of classical architecture to project an image of unity and universalism. The Fourth Street façade was designed in Renaissance revival style and constructed of brick with terracotta trim. This pattern was repeated on the First Street side, which was also decorated with medallions and plaques as well as classically pedimented windows.

Funding for the auditorium came from an impressive array of city groups and individuals. In fact, average citizens donated close to half of the total, mostly in small sums. Through a systematic canvass, members of the auditorium committee drummed up more than $200,000 from what they claimed was "a city aroused . . . as it had never been before," one in which "every citizen was bent upon doing his best for the advance of the public welfare."[121] Such rhetoric suggesting the auditorium's role as a promoter of public welfare and unity was in part tied to the auditorium's physicality. As one member of the committee wrote, "nothing appeals more to the local spirit and pride of a city of the character of St. Paul than something which can be seen for all time."[122] In other words, the project's tangible nature was purportedly behind its ability to unify citizens and win their support (financial or otherwise).

There is ample evidence that a large percentage of the city's population flocked to the auditorium for activities and entertainment. Sensitive to the needs and rights of the city's working-class citizens, the fundraising committee followed up its invitation-only grand-opening fête with a series of popular shows at reasonable prices that had, according one newspaper report, "the definite aim of affording to those who could not attend the opening concert and ball an opportunity to see the building while it is brand new."[123] Clearly, the intent was to create a "Monument to the People" that "belong[ed] to the people of St. Paul."[124] Even after the opening celebrations were over, the committee continued to advocate for periodic free events, noting that those offered in the first years of the auditorium's life had drawn so many citizens that they had tested the limits of its seating capacity.

But which people was the building designed to serve? Apparently, being white was a prerequisite. It would overstate the point to say that the city's black residents did not identify at all with the "people of St. Paul" for whom the monument was supposedly erected. But while each of the white newspapers devoted the better part of three pages to events surrounding the auditorium's 1907 opening (even though the other big news story of the day was James J. Hill's retirement as president of the Great Northern), the *Appeal* did not make a single mention of the festivities.[125] Given that paper's policy of reporting on the social activities of its readers, particularly its prominent ones, its silence is noteworthy and raises questions about de jure, if not de facto, segregation at the auditorium. There is no doubt that, in 1909, the black press was focused on a major anniversary, the founding of two national African American benevolent societies (the United Brothers of Friendship and the Sisters of the Mysterious Ten), and that a reception and ball for local and visiting black Americans was held at the auditorium. Yet evidence suggests that this was an anomaly in early twentieth-century St. Paul.[126]

The *Appeal's* silence about the auditorium's celebrations makes sense when considered in light of the other exclusions and humiliations that the city's African American citizens faced when they tried to access public venues during the period. Whether or not the rhetoric of city leaders acknowledged the existence of racial segregation in their hometown, the black community had often felt its effects; and in the years following the auditorium's opening, such exclusions continued to affect their lives in other so-called public spaces.[127] In these same years, St. Paul's African Americans were working to raise money for Union Hall, a structure intended to provide a space for black lodge members to gather and the city's black residents to hold public events. Although it did not open until 1915, its planning and construction were a long time in the making, and the limits placed on black use of the auditorium likely factored into its creation.

The other limitation of the auditorium, despite its supporters' plans to make events available to the city's working-class citizens, was its association with the center of the city's business world. True, turn-of-the-century city plans generally placed civic buildings in city centers. But in St. Paul, rather than erecting the auditorium on a neutral, specially designated site for civic buildings (as was done in Cleveland), the funders chose to erect it in the heart of the established commercial core. In so doing, they implicitly linked it and the idea of St. Paul not only to the everyday world of the middle-class professionals whose work and economic status and daily lives directly shaped that part of the city but also to the drivers, mechanisms, and institutions of industrial capitalism and economic progress—a link to be discussed in detail in chapter 5.

In sum, the built environment of St. Paul in the opening years of the twentieth century offered residents substantial evidence of the lines that divided, defined, extended, and sometimes complicated ideas about and experiences of community within the city limits. Despite the attempts of city leaders to erect public buildings that would unite residents, these divisions, renegotiations, and allegiances, which residential architecture and the city's many churches signaled and reinforced, highlighted an experience of community that, by the 1910s, included daily experiences of community tied to affinity of one sort or another. Time and again St. Paulites found that their intimate communities were related to the shape and structure of the world in which they struggled to come into being. For many, this was a world in which intersecting identities challenged the primacy of place as synonymous with community. Those who could also imagine a unified community of St. Paul that was tied to shared city residence in addition to narrower (or broader) affinities tended to be those for whom the city's public or "universal" buildings served members of the affinity-based communities with which they identified.

CHAPTER 4

COMMUNITY AND OPEN SPACE

Parks and Playgrounds in St. Paul

B eginning in the late nineteenth century, the leaders of the St. Paul Park Board, like their counterparts elsewhere in the United States, sought to reconfigure and expand the municipal park system to create symbols of citywide unity. In their vision, a well-planned series of parks would provide spaces and opportunities for St. Paulites to come together as members of a single community, one that transcended the bonds of neighborhoods, class, race, and ethnicity. St. Paul's grand parks became tangible examples of this noble intent. More than any other cultural product in the city, they were successful in promoting an inclusive definition of community. But the *experience* of community that these parks promoted never quite matched the definition. Even though the possibility of chance encounters and the mixing of social classes was possible in the largest venues, cross-class, cross-race communal interactions were rare. In fact, given the proliferation of neighborhood parks after the turn of the century, established divisions were actually reinforced by the overall park scheme. By 1920 the park and playground system, like those in many of the nation's urban areas, encouraged and reflected—rather than challenged—the reality of affinity-based experiences of community coexisting alongside the idea of city as community in modern America.

Nineteenth-century advocates and practitioners of landscape design were behind the idea of intentionally placing open green space in U.S.

cities. Both Frederick Law Olmstead and his lesser known but equally influential contemporary H. W. S. Cleveland believed that properly landscaped parks could counteract the stress and moral failings of city dwellers.[1] In Olmstead's mind, a key element of these afflictions was the "erosion of the social bond," which he believed could be alleviated by a well-planned park.[2] From the mid-nineteenth century on, many Americans agreed with him; and by the time of the 1893 World's Fair, most reformers and public officials were convinced that green spaces, as potentially redemptive sites of communal values and experiences, were important components of any cityscape.

But just what these green spaces should look like was up for debate. Olmstead and Cleveland had focused on developing elegant, open, carefully landscaped parks, and in the late nineteenth century many City Beautiful adherents picked up and expanded on this approach, believing that parks could and would exert influence primarily based on their aesthetic value. The movement's advocates produced the first comprehensive formulation of a theory of the organic city, thereby creating a framework within which other city planners could operate. While such ideas were petering out by 1909, a focus on the importance of green space in cities remained, pervading Progressive Era thought and activities under the cloak of a more utilitarian exterior.[3] In some ways, this marriage of practicality and reform was similar to the initial goals of Olmstead or Cleveland. The era's city planners and reformers felt that an improved environment would instill "a wider social consciousness, a heartier spirit of cooperation, [and] a keener sense of responsibility to the future."[4] Like their City Beautiful predecessors, these "city practical" proponents believed that the creation of municipal parks and playgrounds would help them reach such goals, even as they emphasized utility and recreation rather than aesthetics.[5]

In St. Paul, the divisions between City Beautiful and City Practical were less pronounced than they were on the national scene, and the city's park system became a hybrid of the two approaches. Work on the system began in the mid-nineteenth century with a few small green spaces in the downtown area, but by the eve of World War I the city had four large parks—Como, Phalen, Riverside Boulevard, and Indian Mounds—and numerous smaller ones scattered throughout the neighborhoods. For years the system's growth had been stunted by the common council's penny pinching, and the voters had routinely denied it funding. Now, however, it offered residents a variety of options; in fact, the parks proved to be so popular that city boosters claimed in 1915 that they had gained "national reputations[s]."[6] The system as a whole made a significant amount of city acreage available for public, "present[ing] an assemblage of diversified beauties which would seem to be adapted to every mood of the lovers of nature and to the satisfaction of every variety of tastes."[7]

Two men shaped the vision of the St. Paul park system: Frederick Nussbaumer, who was the park superintendent from 1891 to his retirement in 1922, and Joseph A. Wheelock, who was the president of the Board of Park Commissioners from 1893 until his death in 1906.[8] Their writings indicate that they shared an ideal of a park system that had a broad constituency in mind. They hoped to offer the public at large some of the niceties that wealthy residents enjoyed in private settings and to provide activities that the middle and working classes specifically desired. Again and again they asserted their beliefs that the park system needed to serve the average citizen. Nussbaumer, in particular, provided a voice for the vast majority of the city's working people and, early in the era, helped create public spaces that on some level challenged the pervasive neighborhood bonds reinforced by the city's layout and its residential architecture.

The city's two largest parks, Como and Phalen, gave city residents the best opportunity to shrug off the confines of class-based, race-based, or ethnicity-based divisions in the city and imagine themselves as members of a St. Paul community writ large. Located in the northwestern and northeastern corners of the city, they were originally designed in the late nineteenth-century pleasure-grounds style: as large, outlying green spaces with informal landscape designs and plenty of open ground for recreation. Yet after the turn of the twentieth century, the city began adding to them recreational opportunities of the sort that were common to *reform parks*— that is, to parks that were designed for organized activities—ultimately positioning the parks somewhere between the pleasure-grounds and the reform style. The latter type of park became popular between 1900 and 1930 as urban planners came to believe that the masses were inept at designing their own recreation.[9]

Como was the older of the two. Established in the 1870s, it was, from its inception, intended to highlight flora and fauna. There were places to stroll, picnic, and otherwise engage with nature in a genteel manner. The park was initially aimed toward the needs and interests of the cultivated elite, and part of the original argument in favor of the 1874 land purchase had been based on the claim that "public parks are . . . for the cultivation of the love of the beautiful in nature, for the opportunities they afford for the social cominglings and innocent amusements of which we have too few." The advocate continued, "They should be diligently used for the social and kindly purpose of which parks are an invaluable aid, Public parks belong to the category of art galleries, public libraries and open air concerts and things of like character which are everywhere recognized as potent agencies in elevating and refining popular taste and promoting a high form of civilization."[10]

But a park that met the needs and reflected the ideals of a ruling class of Victorian elites was far from a symbol of citywide solidarity. While the city government did not seem concerned about this issue, by 1895 a group of St. Paulites had become vocal about their beliefs that the parks should have a broader and perhaps nobler purpose. The city's park board, a group of unpaid middle-class citizens, began to make their position known, and in his president's address in that year's annual report, Wheelock argued that parks needed to be more than leisure sites for the well-off. Sounding much like H. W. S Cleveland had during an 1872 speech he'd given in St. Paul, Wheelock noted that, in addition to playing an "important part in the physical and moral sanitation of the city [parks] . . . are the pleasure grounds and playgrounds of the people. . . . They are not for ornament, except as ornament is subsidiary to the noblest and most necessary of human uses, to give enjoyment, health, rest, recreation to the multitudes whose circumstances deprive them of other opportunities for these essentials of well-being." More importantly, "parks are . . . especially for the people who cannot afford the costlier pleasures of rustication, which are always at the command of the well to do. . . . On ground consecrated to the public enjoyment—the common property of all—there should be no distinction between rich and poor in this best use of parks for the common good of all."[11] In this way Wheelock set the tone for a number of park board decisions that followed over the next two and a half decades, decisions that focused on making the system as attractive and accessible as possible to the largest number of people.

This reality was hindered in St. Paul until the 1890s, when the city finally began offering reliable, affordable transportation to the parks. Previously, only people with horses and buggies could easily access them. Cleveland noted this problem in his 1872 speech.[12] Yet despite his warning as well as the pleas of concerned residents, nothing was done for years.[13] Finally, on July 8, 1893, the city began offering streetcar service to Como, much to the delight of the park board members, who noted the flurry of "enormous crowds" visiting the park every day. In the years that followed, the streetcar system expanded rapidly, and by 1900 many St. Paulites could get to Como at relatively low cost. By 1915 the city's complex streetcar system was transporting residents to the park from virtually every corner of the city.[14]

But accessibility was not the only concern of park planners. They were convinced that the grand parks needed to provide activities that would attract the broadest possible group of visitors. Thus, as they worked to develop Como, they paid particular attention to creating recreations such as boating, pony rides, concerts, and a carousel, each of which, the board members argued, should be free or at least affordable for an average working-class individual or family.[15] As the twentieth century dawned, Como continued to expand its offerings. The board added tennis courts and baseball diamonds, constructed pathways, built wading pools and playgrounds, designed an appropriate entrance to the park's Japanese garden, and built a public conservatory to house and exhibit a variety of botanical specimens.[16]

At the heart of these improvements was a fervent belief that neither economic status nor social position should be a barrier to park visitation or enjoyment. Nussbaumer wrote in 1902,

> Nothing should be introduced, and nothing permitted which would have a tendency to lessen its value and usefulness as a recreation ground for all classes of people: a safe and decorous place, within easy reach of the people, of a city by trolley car, at reasonable rates of fare, or other modes of conveyance, where families with children, sick or convalescent persons, the nature-loving enthusiast and the frugal workman alike may find a visit to it refreshing, restful, profitable and beneficial to soul and body.[17]

The board made a concerted effort to turn this goal into a reality. Its members tried, whenever possible, to structure park offerings in ways that would allow workers to enjoy them in their limited free time. To this end, they were adamant about making concerts free and keeping fees for other activities as low as possible.[18] In addition, as late as 1917, Nussbaumer pushed for year-round hours at the Como conservatory. The plants and flowers, he argued, provided a "delightful and educational recreation . . . [for] the plain people."[19]

By this time the board had also undertaken major projects to transform long-neglected Phalen Park into a site of multiple recreational opportunities in the northeastern corner of the city. According to planners' grand scheme, each of the city's major parks was to complement the others. In contrast to Como, characterized as a "park wherein the enjoyment of floral beauty and plant beauty of a special character is liberally provided for," Phalen would be a "large park, the character of which is strictly and distinctively aquatic," with a "triple lake expanse, and primitive wildness [on] its woodland border."[20] Although it had been established in 1894, Phalen (identified in 1912 as "one of the most favorite spots of the masses for picnics and recreation") did not really get off the ground until the beginning of the twentieth century. Then its development was swift, and by 1920 the aquatic haven included 240 acres of land and a 247-acre lake. Its recreational facilities included a beach, a diving tower, canoe docks, a boat launch, ball fields, a pavilion, and a bandstand.[21] There was also a public golf course, which Nussbaumer believed would draw a more diverse group of visitors and provide "other forms of outdoor exercise for grown-up folks."[22] He was so convinced that a golf course was necessary that he strongly recommended that the city purchase a large tract of land expressly for that purpose. When the links were completed in 1917, more than 7,000 players "crowded the workmen off the course," thus more than justifying Nussbaumer's push.[23] By the following year the golf course was reported to be hosting tens of thousands of people annually.[24] As with Como, the 1905 extension of the streetcar line to Phalen increased accessibility, and all of the recreational facilities and activities were kept as inexpensive as possible.[25]

By combining popular attractions with the beautiful open green spaces of Phalen and Como, the board persistently promoted a vision of parks that went beyond both the traditional ideas of landscape architecture purists and the recommendations of contemporary social reformers. Nussbaumer's and Wheelock's creations underwent a singular test: did they meet the needs of the masses? Driven by a firm understanding that the residents of the city—all of them—were paying for the parks, Nussbaumer repeatedly prioritized the desires of the working class over the desires of the elites.[26] In so doing he worked to balance nineteenth- and twentieth-century ideals and seemed to suggest that, if a city were to be a community, it needed to care for all of its members, especially the least among them.

In the early twentieth-century United States, reform park ideology was the prevailing trend, but Nussbaumer recognized that St. Paulites still longed for places of natural recreation that were free from too much organization and structure. Thus, by 1917 he was recommending that, while the playground facilities at both Como and Phalen should be extended, no playground teachers should be assigned to them. Rather, they would "furnish a supplement to recreation" and offer children a park experience more in line with the older late nineteenth-century image of the pleasure ground, while making available some elements of the playground movement.[27]

The debate about the flower displays at Como Park is an equally telling example of his orientation. At the end of the nineteenth century, some St. Paul residents began complaining that the many colorful flowers adorning Como's grounds somehow offended the purist school of landscape architecture. Both Nussbaumer and Wheelock held fast to their belief in the value of such displays. Nussbaumer argued that "a correct rural landscape, distinctly adapted to stimulate a poetic sensibility" did not meet the needs of the urban masses flocking to the parks looking for more than just serene, contemplative vistas. The urban visitor, he asserted, had needs that were best met when parks provided shelter buildings, refectories, music pavilions, restrooms, picnic grounds, drinking fountains, park benches, boat houses, and even floral displays. He expressed this philosophy in a 1902 article that underscored the greater importance of the desires of the average person over those of the elite aesthete. The gardens of the rich, he wrote, had inspired the "creation of parks for the common people in recognition of their common right to the enjoyment of God's pure air and the beauties of nature." In a discussion of the traditional "ideal garden," he described key elements: a tranquil rural setting with gently rolling hills, an occasional stream or lake, groves of trees and open green spaces, drives and walks in harmony with the terrain's native plants. But such landscape designs, he argued, did not meet the needs of the majority of residents who were visiting St. Paul's parks. Rather, "a successful or ideal park must provide facilities for recreation and, to a certain degree, objects of attractiveness in horticultural displays—especially so in the high northern latitudes where, on account of the long, bleak winters the floral decorations in public parks excite special admiration. . . . [For] the great mass of the people enjoy flowers."[28]

In 1903 Wheelock expounded upon this even more forcefully in his President's Address:

> [The park's] main purpose is to make the beauties of nature minister to the creation and enjoyment of the people at large—of the plain people whose pleasure grounds they are and to whose use and benefit they are dedicated. To them the flowers in Como Park are one of the most prized attractions. They would have but little patience with a park manager who had no feeling for the delicate charm of flowers, and who could find no room and no suitable places for them in the wide expanse of its rural landscape.

To make his point clearer, he invoked the longstanding rivalry between St. Paul and Minneapolis in his closing comment: "That the flowers in Como Park are a potent element in its remarkable popularity there is no question. Its visitors count about 1,300,000 during the park season. Large numbers of them come from the neighboring city of Minneapolis, whose flowerless parks, the late president of the Minneapolis park board ruefully complains, are poorly patronized by the public."[29]

In addition to the development of the two large parks, the board also pushed for a comprehensive parkway system that would link the city's main residential areas to the big parks and the parks to one another through a series of scenic drives. At least symbolically this design would have united the various districts of the city and, by proxy, their inhabitants.[30] However, as late as 1920 the proposed links were only partially completed; they would remain so for some years to come.[31] All told, the park board's activities underscored its willingness to create spaces in St.

Paul that could be, in both reality and theory, truly public. The leadership team worked hard to meet the needs of a majority of St. Paul's citizens and entice as many of them as possible to partake of what the parks had to offer, regardless of race, ethnicity, class, creed, or gender.[32] Although daunting, this goal seems to have been successful. Anecdotal evidence in numerous annual reports indicate that there were increasingly large crowds at both Como and Phalen, and almost annually there was a call for new structures and facilities at one or the other to meet the growing demands of park visitors. General accounts cite annual-use numbers topping 1 million.[33] And these crowds were diverse. "The rich do go to Como in their chaises, propelled now by gasoline," one official report conceded in 1915, but "it is a safe hazard, judging from what one may observe at Como every summer, that there are at least fifty poor people and those of the middle class financially who patronize Como, to one who goes there in an automobile or carriage."[34]

The records of individuals, families, and clubs also indicate that park visitors were as diverse as Wheelock and Nussbaumer had hoped they would be. A number of existing photographs from the early twentieth century depict wealthy whites as well as working- and middle-class black and white St. Paul families in and around the parks on outings with relatives and friends. Not surprisingly, white middle-class residents were most often represented; photographs of Como and Phalen appear again and again in the albums of such families, and the published images of park visitors depict visitors who fit this demographic profile.[35] But importantly, there is also evidence that St. Paul's black residents visited the parks.

In *The Politics of Park Design,* Galen Crantz writes, "in theory the pleasure ground brought all different sectors of society, presumably including its various racial and ethnic components, together, [yet] the practice of racial segregation was so unquestioned that officials did not need to call attention to it in any way."[36] In St. Paul, however, working-class African American families such as the Gardners appear to have made the parks a destination for family outings, which suggests that for at least some black St. Paulites the parks were both accessible and desirable.[37] In addition, they were the site of numerous events and special meetings ranging from athletic clubs to women's church societies and reflecting both white and black St. Paul.[38] In short, many residents, black and white, male and female, wealthy and working-class, found solace and recreation in the city's two major parks, spots that one chronicler called "communal property of all the people for the purposes of rest and recreation."[39]

Although the goal of creating a sense of citywide ownership was noble, it was not the park board's only one. Additionally, St. Paul's park leadership imagined that the parks might help visitors redefine their understanding of community as a limited, intimate experience linking to kin and neighbor. In 1895 planners articulated their hope, much as Olmstead had done several decades before, that the parks would not only attract large crowds but also foster "a sympathetic bond of fellowship in the concourse of visitors."[40] This goal proved more elusive than they had expected. The fact that the park visitors were, in general, a heterogeneous group does not imply that visiting the park led to transformative experiences of intimate community. As scholars have noted, in locales marked by a heterogeneous populations, residents may have difficulty making connections with others in public because they are usually unable to identify those who share a background or an interest.[41] In other words, the very openness and popularity of the parks probably hindered such intergroup community building.

For instance, there was no way to know whether fellow visitors were St. Paul residents or not. Although Minneapolis had its own highly developed park system, its citizens regularly visited Como and Phalen, assisted in part by the streetcar system linking the two cities. Thus, there was no guarantee that park contact would involve St. Paulites whose resulting relationship might strengthen the idea of the city as a material rather than an abstract community. Moreover, the parks' spaciousness and the diversity of their activities hindered cohesive intergroup social interactions. Visitors could boat or fish or swim or skate or walk or sit contemplatively. They could attend a concert, eat a snack, paddle a canoe, visit the conservatory, or nap in the shade. In short, Como and Phalen actually encouraged visitors to enjoy themselves in exclusive, highly individualized ways.[42] Finally, the evidence that reveals diversity among park visitors also indicates the degree to which they saw the parks as places for socializing with people they already knew (clubs, families, friends) rather than as places for expanding their intimate communities.

While some members of the park board may have continued to believe that the parks could unite diverse groups and individuals, no mention of that goal appears in any official report after the statement of 1895. Instead, they increasingly focused on drawing a variety of people to the city's largest parks and showed less concern about what was happening once those visitors arrived. Year after year, the annual reports emphasized linking various areas of the city via parkways, but they made no explicit mention of a need to link people. By the second decade of the twentieth century the board appears to have begun to accept that there were established intimate communities in the city that resisted alteration.

It would not be fair to say that Como and Phalen failed in their mission to unite St. Paul residents. Beyond being sources of civic pride, they functioned as symbols of an ideal that equated community with municipal residence. Yet their presence in the city did not dramatically reshape the experience of living in St. Paul. Communal relations persisted among residents who shared more limited connections, and those links were shored up by the simultaneous expansion of a second type of recreational area in the city: neighborhood parks and playgrounds.[43]

The city's network of neighborhood parks grew rapidly in the early years of the twentieth century, but St. Paulites were already familiar with the concept. In fact, park planning had begun in the mid-nineteenth century with a series of neighborhood parks established on donated land in the Lowertown area, where residential growth was then most significant. As the city grew and Lowertown became more commercial, planners shifted their attention toward building Como and Phalen on the city's outer limits. Yet private citizens continued to donate small tracts of land in various sections of town and, in so doing, added more neighborhood parks to the system.

This somewhat haphazard expansion continued into the 1900s. For example, between 1907 and 1909 well-to-do and interested residents purchased five tracts of parkland in five different sections of the city without assistance from the park fund.[44] By donating or actively working to acquire such spaces, these residents made it clear that they were experiencing community in neighborhood spaces and through neighborhood-based relationships and that they wanted recreational facilities that would serve those particular communities that contained elements of both shared affinity and shared geography. Nussbaumer and Wheelock noted this trend, even as they worked feverishly to make Como and Phalen sites of citywide unity, and began a concerted effort to provide neighborhood-based recreation for all city residents.

By 1900 the city had forty-eight improved and unimproved neighborhood parks unequally distributed throughout the city.[45] Wards 7 and 10, which comprised the older wealthier sections of St. Paul, shared twenty park spaces between them, while each of the remaining ten wards had five parks or less.[46] Nussbaumer was concerned that "most of the other residence districts of the city are destitute of these small neighborhood parks."[47] Accordingly, he and Wheelock turned their attention to rectifying the inequity. "The attention of the board has heretofore been directed mainly to the acquisition and improvement of our larger parks, such as attract or will attract multitudes from all parts of the city," wrote Wheelock in the president's report portion of the 1901 annual report. But "it is highly important to acquire, as soon as possible, . . . small tracts of land, each embracing at least a square or more, for neighborhood parks and playgrounds in the residence districts of the city." He continued, "The lack of [more small parks] is but little felt, or not felt at all, now, when such large areas of unoccupied spaces characterize the newer residence districts . . . [but] as these districts become filled up with a denser population, it will be regretted that the present opportunity was not improved to set apart frequent breathing places for the adornment and enjoyment of these compactly built-up neighborhoods of the future."[48] Four years later, the call came again. In 1905, this time quoting Chicago reformers in his annual report, Nussbaumer reminded St. Paulites that "wage earners are most in need of park service."[49]

While the situation improved somewhat, by the 1910s some neighborhoods still did not have parks, and others, particularly in newly developing western areas, had woefully inadequate ones. In 1911 a concerned resident wrote to the park board asking for immediate action to improve the park just west of the Smith Avenue High Bridge.[50] Without responding to this request directly, the board continued to voice concerns, but little changed quickly.

Almost two decades after his first plea, Nussbaumer was still complaining that "no new areas were added to the park system during the past year, which is to be very much regretted as considerable property should be acquired to round out our park system." He had three specific recommendations. First, he wished to acquire a new park in southwestern St. Paul, "where none exists, except [for] two small tracts." He was eyeing property "bounded on the north by Randolph Street, on the south by Montreal Avenue, on the west by Edgecombe Road, and on the east by Lexington and Pleasant Avenues." The 115 acres inside this boundary would not only "make a fine recreation ground" but "would . . . serve the people of that section of the city with adequate park facilities." Second, he called for the creation of a park in the Midway district that would be "large enough in extent to care for all kinds of recreation." He warned that this park should be acquired soon, for it would quickly become a "necessity . . . on account of the thousands of laborers employed in that industrial district."[51] Third, despite his lack of interest in highly organized activities at Como and Phelan, he wanted to establish playgrounds in every district of the city.[52] Local advocates of social reform agreed with him. For instance, Carol Aronovici noted in his 1917 housing report that the city would be wise to appropriate some of the unused land in these congested neighborhoods (which amounted to 27 percent of the total area in his survey) for playgrounds. Such facilities, he believed, were desperately needed.[53]

Eventually, the board's persistence about the importance of the neighborhood park system paid off. By the late 1910s the vast majority of the city's parks were located in residential areas, providing accessible recreational spaces and opportunities for people who lived or attended school in the surrounding neighborhoods. In many ways this accomplishment reflected the ascendancy of the board's philosophy of democratic park planning. After all, the push for neighborhood parks was fueled by the same democratizing ideal that had shaped the larger park projects. But while the large parks were aimed at fostering civic unity, the smaller ones were never intended to play such a role. Consequently, they never did. Rather, they strengthened bonds among members of preexisting groups, for logic as well as comfort drove residents to those that were geographically closest. In fact, the push for more parks was itself premised on the reality that residents in industrial or working-class areas would not otherwise have enough access to them. To borrow Aronovici's words: because there were "marked differences in the character of various unit areas which form distinct social and economic strata," the interactions in neighborhood parks and playgrounds generally involved members of more homogeneous crowds than one would find at Como or Phelan.[54] These small recreational areas limited interactions among members of dissimilar groups while encouraging the formation of communal bonds among neighborhood visitors. Events such as sporting competitions between children from different playgrounds increased this identification with a particular district and its residents.[55]

The development of neighborhood parks was not intended to destroy broader experiences or definitions of community.[56] After all, Nussbaumer continued to develop and tout the large parks. Furthermore, presumably he believed, as did many of the era's thinkers and reformers, that the root of large-scale solidarity, if not community, lay in establishing smaller neighborhood-based ties, a need that local parks could meet.[57] Although the development of both large and small parks was fueled by a desire to better equalize life in St. Paul, the small ones provided an alternative rendering of community and a more limited image of the public. Tied to the economic and demographic realities of modernizing America, they encouraged and supported ideas and experiences of community that were narrower than the city's population as a whole. They also encouraged and reinforced the formation of intimate communities based on neighborhood affiliations, which were often based on shared ethnicity, race, or class. By emphasizing the creation of small parks without also laying out explicit strategies for using them to unite a diverse city, the park board tacitly acknowledged that St. Paulites' lived social reality and thus their experiences of community were closely tied to their residential districts. The success and proliferation of neighborhood parks reflect a growing realization that an experience of citywide community was less real than ideal. Unlike the large parks, which forced citizens to confront the heterogeneous nature of their city community, the neighborhood parks assured them that, even in a diverse city, intimate, reciprocal communities were possible—as long as they were defined in a limited way.

In the process of shaping a park system, the board reinforced and in some ways produced messages that had been implicit in other cultural products. Along with the parks, the stories of the City Auditorium, Union Hall, ethnic parishes, and architectural choices all reveal the shifting and increasingly multifaceted ideas about and experiences of community that coexisted in the lives of urban Americans on the eve of World War I. The previous decade and a half had demonstrated that the idea of a place-based community continued to fuel public and private efforts even as other forces and individuals' daily lives supported, created, and reflected narrower experiences. Yet it was becoming apparent that access to an imagined community of St. Paul was more readily available to those with power in the city—economic, political, or otherwise.

FIGURE I. Christmas at 369 Jay Street, St. Paul, 1912. Ralph, Dorothy, and William Gardner. William J. Gardner Photograph Collection. Courtesy of the Minnesota Historical Society.

FIGURE 2. William J. Gardner, Ida Gardner and their three youngest children Ralph, William, and Dorothy (1912). Courtesy of Evelyn Hill and Rosella Limon.

FIGURE 3. "Ida, Mildred, Marie, 1920." Courtesy of Evelyn Hill and Rosella Limon.

FIGURE 4. In the photo album, this photograph from 1912 is accompanied by a caption that reads: "Important steps in the family." All but the two eldest daughters appear in this photo. From left to right: Marie, Ethel, Ida, Mildred, Agnes, Gladys, William, Jr. (Bill), Ralph. Dorothy is in front of Ethel. William J. Gardner Photograph Collection. Courtesy of the Minnesota Historical Society.

FIGURE 5. Carrie Gardner Williams and Ethel Gardner Sheets, standing near the family home at 369 Jay Street and St. Anthony, St. Paul, circa 1910. William J. Gardner Photograph Collection. Courtesy of the Minnesota Historical Society.

FIGURE 6. Photo labeled "Gladys, Ralph, Uncle Bill, Dorothy," circa 1920. The bounty of this backyard garden at the home of Gardener relative William F. Williams and his sister Ella at the corner of Jay and W. Central Streets is on display in a number of images in the collection. William J. Gardner Photograph Collection. Courtesy of the Minnesota Historical Society.

FIGURE 7. Some of the Garner family children while on a family outing at Como Park in 1912. Courtesy of Evelyn Hill and Rosella Limon.

FIGURE 8. William, Jr. and Ralph Gardner, 1916. According to a label accompanying the photo, the brothers are standing at 260 W. 3rd Street, below a tunnel. William J. Gardner Photograph Collection. Courtesy of the Minnesota Historical Society.

FIGURE 9. William, Jr. and Ralph Gardner shoveling snow in front of the family home on Jay Street (now Galtier), St. Paul, 1912. William J. Gardner Photograph Collection. Courtesy of the Minnesota Historical Society.

FIGURE 10. "Dorothy G. Dorothy Ohme," circa 1915. Courtesy of Evelyn Hill and Rosella Limon.

FIGURE 11. "Dorothy Gardner, Dorothy Ohme, 1918." Courtesy of Evelyn Hill and Rosella Limon.

FIGURE 12. Confirmation at St. Peter Claver. Carrie Gardner is the second from the right. This photo was likely taken circa 1905, given Carrie's age here. William J. Gardner Photograph Collection. Courtesy of the Minnesota Historical Society.

FIGURE 13. Alice Dunn in front of 1033 Lincoln Avenue, St. Paul. Photo by J. W. G. Dunn. Courtesy of the Minnesota Historical Society.

FIGURE 14. Alice Dunn and Jack in yard of 1033 Lincoln Avenue, September 1903. Photo by J. W. G. Dunn. Courtesy of the Minnesota Historical Society.

FIGURE 16. Alice Dunn pulling Jack near 1033 Lincoln Avenue. Photo by J. W. G. Dunn. Courtesy of the Minnesota Historical Society.

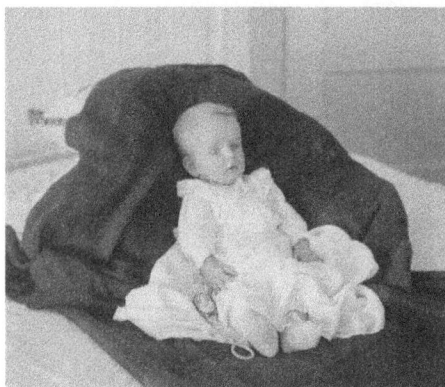

FIGURE 15. Jack Dunn, March 1904. Photo by J. W. G. Dunn. Courtesy of the Minnesota Historical Society.

FIGURE 17. Alice Dunn and Jack Dunn looking out of a window at 1033 Lincoln Avenue, December 1904. Photo by J. W. G. Dunn. Courtesy of the Minnesota Historical Society.

FIGURE 18. This is one of a number of photographs in the Dunn collection depicting the Dunn sons working (sometimes with their father) in the garden. This photo is labeled simply "The Garden, St. Paul, 1918." Photo by J. W. G. Dunn. Courtesy of the Minnesota Historical Society.

FIGURE 19. One of the four photos on a single album page depicting the Oxford Club skating rink in January 1917. Photo by J. W. G. Dunn. Courtesy of the Minnesota Historical Society.

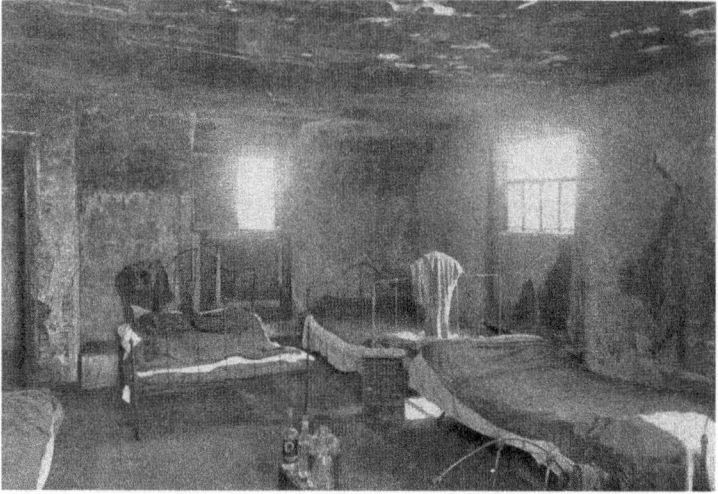

FIGURE 20. "Rooming House Shack in Midway District," in Carol Aronovici, *Housing Conditions in the City of Saint Paul* (1917). Courtesy of the Minnesota Historical Society.

FIGURE 21. "Junk Yard surrounded by Dwellings," in Carol Aronovici, *Housing Conditions in the City of Saint Paul* (1917). Courtesy of the Minnesota Historical Society.

FIGURE 22. "Rear Lot Homes," in Carol Aronovici, *Housing Conditions in the City of Saint Paul* (1917). Courtesy of the Minnesota Historical Society.

FIGURE 23. "Flat Building. One Toilet and water in basement used by six families," in Carol Aronovici, *Housing Conditions in the City of Saint Paul* (1917). Courtesy of the Minnesota Historical Society.

Figure 24. "Rear of Cody Block. Garbage and Waste Infested with Rats," in Carol Aronovici, *Housing Conditions in the City of Saint Paul* (1917). Courtesy of the Minnesota Historical Society.

FIGURE 25. "Miss Alice Michaud has gone to Seabreeze, Fla. She was accompanied by her mother Mrs. A. E. Michaud 797 Linwood place," *Pioneer Press*, January 21, 1917. Courtesy of the Minnesota Historical Society.

FIGURE 26. The home of J. Q. Adams, 527 St. Anthony Avenue, St. Paul. Published in the *Appeal*, September 24, 1910, and October 28, 1911. Courtesy of the Minnesota Historical Society.

FIGURE 27. The home of Frederick McGhee, 665 W. University Avenue, St. Paul. Published in the *Appeal*, September 24, 1910, and October 28, 1911. Courtesy of the Minnesota Historical Society.

FIGURE 28. Cathedral of St. Paul, Summit and Dayton, St. Paul, circa 1915. Courtesy of the Minnesota Historical Society.

FIGURE 29. James J. Hill residence, 240 Summit Avenue, St. Paul, circa 1905. Courtesy of the Minnesota Historical Society.

FIGURE 30. Swede Hollow, Phalen Creek, 6th Street Bridge, circa 1900. Courtesy of the Minnesota Historical Society.

FIGURE 31. Image of King Boreas and his "attendants" inside the throne room during a pre-Winter Carnival pageant in 1917. This image appeared in an album produced for the Sports Carnival Association by the Camera Art Company, which took official photographs of the 1917 pageants. Courtesy of the Minnesota Historical Society.

FIGURE 32. This image (on left), which includes two African American "attendants," appeared on the front page above the fold in the January 2, 1917, issue of the *Pioneer Press*, nearly a month in advance of the 1917 Winter Carnival. The headline read "King Boreas II and Some Members of His Court in Country Club Pageant," and the caption above the photograph read "The picture at the left shows King Boreas with Louis Newman of Great Falls, Mont., 'King of the Smelter,' at his right, approaching the throne room, with his attendants." This photograph (and others like it) was taken during the publicity-generating pageants at Como Park and the Town and Country Club in the days prior to its publication. Courtesy of the Minnesota Historical Society.

FIGURE 33. This photograph was taken during the pre-carnival pageant staged at the Town and Country Club on January 20, 1917, whose stated goal was to help attract visitors to the carnival. The image appeared in the multi-page winter carnival supplement to the *Pioneer Press* on January 21, 1917. The accompanying caption read "Boreas Rex, ruler of the carnival (James Ridler), and his attendants who will accompany him throughout the week's festivities." Note that this image appeared in the in the same issue of the *Pioneer Press* as figure 34. Courtesy of the Minnesota Historical Society.

FIGURE 34. This photo accompanied a story headlined "Minneapolis Ku Klux Clansmen Coming in Force," in the *Pioneer Press*, January 21, 1917. The caption above the photo read: "More than thousand expect to be in St. Paul afternoon and evening of February 21 automobile men plan at dinner." (Note: The February 21 date is a typographical error. The date was February 2). Courtesy of the Minnesota Historical Society.

CHAPTER 5

"MAKING IT A HOT ONE" FOR SOME

The Winter Carnivals of 1916 and 1917

As the calendar flipped from 1915 to 1916, Louis W. Hill, son of the railroad magnate James J. Hill and a chief executive of the Northern Pacific Railroad, was overseeing the final arrangements for the St. Paul Outdoor Sports Carnival. Sponsored by business and civic leaders, it was scheduled to begin on January 27 and run until February 5. It had been ten years since the city had hosted a grand winter celebration, and residents' excitement was palpable. The city was full of people who, like the fictional St. Paulite Harry Bellamy in F. Scott Fitzgerald's 1920 short story "The Ice Palace," were gushing, "It'll be slick. . . . There'll be skating and skiing and tobogganing and sleigh-riding, and all sorts of torchlight parades on snow-shoes. They haven't had [a carnival] for years, so they're going to make it a knock-out."[1]

While the event was not exactly like the carnival that Harry describes, the spectacle was indeed fantastic. The city was thronged with costumed revelers enjoying parades, pageants, sporting competitions, and even a staged battle between two rival "kings"—complete with an ice palace under attack. Organizers were so pleased with the outcome of the 1916 event that they decided to incorporate the St. Paul Outdoor Sports Carnival Association and host another festival in 1917. This second carnival included many of the events of the previous year and was expanded to include a celebrated sled-dog race from Winnipeg to St. Paul.

Ostensibly, business leaders had revived the carnival to rekindle what they saw as waning civic unity. Tensions between labor and business had been growing, and those with a vested interest in maintaining the peace hoped the festive mood of the carnival would act as a salve.[2] The organizers believed mightily in their ability to erase class-based divisions, thereby reinvigorating a spirit of place-based community and the sense of reciprocity that came with it. In their official summation of the 1916 event, they boasted that the resulting "new spirit of civic pride" pleased them more than "all of the advertising and boosting which [the host city had] received in the eyes of the world."[3] Yet as the summation suggested, civic pride had not been the planners' only goal; a great deal of boosterism was also involved in the carnival design. From their inception the carnivals were intended to highlight the unique and healthful aspects of St. Paul, especially in the winter. The whole city was to become a showcase, a stage set on which planners could dramatize life in St. Paul and, they hoped, increase trade and tourism.

Celebrations and rituals are important ways to understand the collective psyche of a group. As the anthropologist Clifford Geertz has written, they uncover "a series of overt values that the community recognizes as essential to its ideology and world view, to its social identity."[4] The St. Paul winter carnivals serve as particularly rich texts through which to explore the transformation of ideas about community that marked the nation in the early years of the twentieth century. In fashioning their spaces, events, and publicity, the organizers presented an image of the community of St. Paul that had something to do with residence and something to do with the affinity-based connections that were daily shaping the lives of all the men and women who called the city home.

When designing the carnivals, Louis Hill and his colleagues in the civic and business elite of St. Paul understood the extent to which they would draw attention to the city and perhaps bring outside money to its business establishments, and they were not shy about celebrating this fact publicly.[5] Yet these leaders and the white newspapers that largely served their interests continued to assert that the most important goal of the carnivals was an "Awakening of Civic Spirit." As a 1916 *Pioneer Press* article put it, "the business world of St. Paul [would] profit," but residents would be "awakened to a civic spirit that is bound to result in even a greater gain than the monetary one."[6]

However, St. Paulites were neither as naïve nor as passive as their leaders might have imagined. Before the 1916 carnival even ended, they were calling the leadership's sincerity into question in a manner that suggests that the notion of a place-based community was only one understanding among many. The most powerful, well off, and best-connected citizens might wish for and be able to imagine such a manifestation, but others could not. In a letter to the organizers, one angry resident declared that, in his mind, the shape of the carnival was shoring up a thought "that now arises in the minds of a great many citizens of St. Paul that the whole Carnival is a graft and that they are the innocent bystanders who get stung."[7] Exactly how many St. Paulites shared his discontent remains unclear. But the letter writer's message was direct, and it had some support. The carnivals failed to unite citizens who did not see themselves as connected to and responsible for everyone who lived in the municipality. Rather, such residents had shifted their sense of responsibility to and for individuals and groups who shared their desires and experiences, whether or not those people lived in St. Paul.

Despite their attempts to promote the old ideal, the carnival organizers could not hide the reality of this new understanding and experience of community. The perceived success of the carnivals derived largely from the planners' appeal to individuals and groups who fulfilled the criteria that Louis Hill had set forth in the early days of the 1916 carnival. On that carnival's second day he had proclaimed to a group of city business leaders who were gathered at the fashionable St. Paul Hotel that "men who cannot forget their business and get out and take part in the winter carnival are not the kind of men we want in St. Paul."[8] He then reassured them that they were just the group of revelers the carnival committee wanted. There is no way of knowing if these men subsequently rushed out to join the festivities, but Hill's words had made it clear that the carnival was more than simply a respite from the winter cold. It was aimed at solidifying a national community of businessmen and middle-class professionals. In short, Hill was accentuating the idea of community as Americans were coming to understand it (as both wider and narrower than place of residence), even as he was holding onto (and promoting for financial gain) the idea of an imagined community based on place of residence.

In making his plug for participation, Hill indicated that the carnival would attract those who shared a particular set of attributes: they would be professionals, members of the middle or upper class, and have disposable time and income. Although all of his listeners seem to have been St. Paulites, he made no reference to the necessity of residence in the city, nor did he hint at excluding anyone who might live elsewhere. His emphasis was on identifying the shared experiences that would link carnivalgoers—many of whom he hoped would be visitors from out of town. As the carnivals themselves would prove, the men who made up Hill's audience that day were able to embrace his notion of affinity-based communities, even in the midst of a place-based spectacle. Such willingness was not a dramatic break from the recent past but an indication of how St. Paulites had come to experience and discuss community in this increasingly diverse city.

The carnivals attempted to re-create place-based unity but succeeded in announcing its growing obsolescence. As the events and their related controversies demonstrated, they were public venues in which various groups of residents asserted their understandings of the relevance or irrelevance of place within their experiences of community. The public support for the carnivals indicates that many St. Paulites desired an experience of local unity, but the shape of the events revealed deep-seated divisions that were more powerful than a desire for change. Not even the liminal time and place of the carnivals could contain these tensions. Nor could they contain the expansive and varied ways in which residents of cities were understanding community by the end of the 1910s. The carnivals both created and reflected a renegotiation of the concept.

The organizers had hoped that their carnivals would reunite the factions that, in their view, were threatening the economic success of the city. But they had not considered that the carnivals might reveal the deep roots of those splinters and highlight the numerous other barriers to place-based community that, by the late 1910s, were shaping daily life in St. Paul. Worker-owner relations eased somewhat during the carnival days but were not erased permanently; and the events highlighted other sources of division, especially those based on race. The carnivals of 1916 and 1917 served to announce the shift underway in the meaning, experience, and structure of community in modern America; the addition of affinity to place-based ideas was on display.

Affinity-based experiences of community require the exclusion of some subset of the home city's residents while also asserting translocal connections. St. Paul's winter carnivals highlighted the places and people of the professional and upper classes and thus excluded certain groups of residents who did not share the attributes of Hill's desirable carnivalgoer. At the same time, the organizers worked to attract all business leaders, civic leaders, and middle- and upper-class Americans, whether or not they resided in St. Paul. In this way, they reinforced the divisions below the city's veneer of unity, mutuality, and reciprocity.

But the carnivals also revealed the renegotiation that was well under-way by the end of the 1910s. Even as the civic and business elite tried to make the carnivals an affirmation of place-based community, they and other groups had already complicated that idea by embracing and rein-forcing an additional affinity-based model that both overlay and under-girded shared location. The winter carnivals were supposed to show off St. Paul as a more or less homogeneous city-as-community. Instead, they showed off a St. Paul that, like Carol Kennicott's in *Main Street*, was diverse, tribal, and full of more or less autonomous subcultures that shared some connection to a geographic referent but also defined community in ways that were not geographical. Yet because the carnival leaders were white and middle class, they were able, like Carol, to imagine that the city was united in the ways they hoped it might be.

Fueling this shift was the growth of the market and its resulting impact on the society and culture of life in St. Paul. Communal relationships grew up around the various ways that people entered and interacted with the market. By the early twentieth century both the market and the capitalist ethos that fueled it had created sets of relationships that many people have identified as strictly instrumental or rational. Relationships created through commerce or interactions in the commercial sphere are often deemed inher-ently noncommunal. This has led scholars to seek and, ultimately, to see community in modern urban America in places and with people other than those who are linked to the functioning of the market. Time and time again, critics indict the market for bifurcating communal relationships from those supposedly utilitarian relationships that shape the public realm. According to this argument, commerce and consumption might link people or bring them together in some superficial way, but they fail to evoke or nurture com-munal interactions. Even Thomas Bender has concluded that the "market and community [constitute] alternative and competing patterns of order."[9]

Yet in fact, the market played another role in modernizing America. Commerce—the way in which one enters the market—can both accentuate and ease the stress of bifurcation. The St. Paul carnivals displayed the market's power to create, transform, mold, and define communal relations, just as activities in the cultural realm reinforced or challenged the same. The ways in which individual St. Paulites entered the world of commerce was critical to determining their position in relation to the community that was being celebrated in the carnivals. Whether they were uniting businessmen from across the nation or highlighting the way in which a lack of money or access to capital could disqualify a person from a given community, the festivities reflected and reinforced the dominance of affinity-based communities. By the close of the second carnival in early February 1917, many St. Paulites seem to have recognized that their ideas of community were multifaceted and that their experiences of it had little to do with place except in an abstract sense and a great deal to do with the demographic and cultural markers that had shaped their lives. In the end, the development of a small business community and an industrial-commercial elite in St. Paul and beyond did not simply erode community, substituting a cash nexus for other bonds. Instead it helped transform the very definition and experience of community; it was an essential vehicle for creating and exposing the growing presence of transgeographic affinity networks, sometimes based on generating business, sometimes on shared interests, associations, class, training, and worldviews. Importantly, the winter carnivals, then, reveal not only the tensions within and between St. Paulites but also the increasingly unattainable ideal of a community that was defined by emotions and mutuality yet was still synonymous with a specific urban municipality.

Promotion of the carnival events in St. Paul began weeks before their official opening. Sites such as the official carnival slides began to appear across the city, and some even had official christening ceremonies. Work on the 1916 ice fort on Harriet Island began long before any outside visitors had arrived.[10] In these early days, the carnival spirit was reserved for residents, who watched daily as downtown shop windows filled with merchandise designed in the red, green, and white carnival colors. They saw the smiling face of the official carnival girl appear on posters in hotel windows across the city. As the first snow fell, they began flooding empty lots for skating and hauling out their toboggans for sledding. Press coverage suggested that a vast majority of St. Paulites were involved in preparations for the event, and articles projected that they would be equally as involved once the carnival had officially opened.[11] In other words, in these early days of 1916, the carnival was actually, not just theoretically, accessible to many citizens and to few others outside the city.

In 1917 the advance image of civic unity was even more dramatic. The carnival association began its planning in October 1916 so that it could orchestrate and film multiple pre-carnival events for advertising. On December 31, King Boreas, his retinue, and 3,000 costumed revelers paraded around Como Park accompanied by multiple drum corps. According to the *Pioneer Press,* the king held court and reviewed a fancy skating exhibition while movie cameras "ground away." The following day, in front of a well-equipped camera crew at the Town and Country Club, 6,000 costumed "subjects" tobogganed, held blanket bouncing and skijoring demonstrations, marched, passed in review, and took part in carnival pageantry.[12] And for good measure, just a week before the start of the carnival, more than 15,000 costumed revelers braved deep snow and a bitter wind to descend onto the grounds of the Town and Country Club for yet another pageant, which included abbreviated versions of nearly all the carnival events. The pageant was filmed by six major motion-picture companies specifically in order to "secur[e] motion picture publicity for the city and the Carnival." Although not shown as far and wide as the boosters originally touted—"throughout the civilized world," as they claimed—these publicity films were circulated around the country.[13]

Evidence from these pre-carnival weeks supports the image of a citizenry that was generally invested in the events. Pleased with such a response, organizers shaped many carnival activities to maintain this strong local participation. Tobogganing was a highlight; in both years, organizers set up and helped subsidize toboggan slides across the city that drew throngs of revelers each day. They also offered a number of other events to draw as many citizen-participants as possible. Hockey, curling, skating, snowshoeing, skiing, and horse trotting filled many of the festival days, as did less familiar but equally participatory activities such as basketball on skates, pushball on ice, and motor-sled racing. To underscore the idea of full civic participation, the organizers did not clutter the sporting events with professionals. The goal was for average citizens to take part.[14]

According to most published accounts, the festival events attracted a significant number of St. Paulites who might otherwise not have come into contact. A newspaper reporter for the *Pioneer Press* asserted that the playground atmosphere in the city was breaking down established boundaries: "Staid and Dignified businessmen, gentlemen of the cloth, elderly matrons and even those whose daily routine of duties rarely carry them out-of-doors have surrendered to [the carnival's] influence. Artisans have laid down their tools, bookworms their books and clerks their yard-sticks to join the happy throng which has chased gloom to its lair." Revelers took over the city. Carnival frivolity and festivities flourished in residential districts, downtown streets, public parks, hotels, and restaurants. The city, declared the reporter, was filled with "a constant ebb and flow of surging humanity, looking for something with which to amuse themselves."[15] The toboggan slides, as expected, drew massive crowds from the moment they opened. Throughout the carnival hundreds of eager children and adults waited with their toboggans for a turn.[16] Photographs in the city's papers underscored the slides' popularity and the involvement of innumerable citizens in this and other festival activities. Day after day front pages depicted a variety of events and individuals: carnival queen candidates, teenaged ice hockey players, toddlers on toboggans, men and women in carnival costumes, bundled-up men racing horses on the frozen Mississippi.[17] The headlines of the city's three white dailies, too, were continually focused on this mass participation.[18]

The carnival parades also highlighted this sense of place-based solidarity. Both years featured a series of parades, with tens of thousands of costumed revelers marching in each one. In 1916 organizers planned three grand parades, and the morning after the first one, which opened the carnival, the city papers crowed, "Great Throng Lines Streets as 20,000 March Past," and "11,000 People and 180 Marching Clubs to Be in Line."[19] The marching clubs represented groups of workers, residents of select neighborhoods, and unaffiliated citizens who had joined the "Carnival Marching Club" organized by officials.

The focus of the largest of all the carnival parades most clearly articulated the carnivals organizers' desire to foster a sense of civic unity. The municipal parade on February 1 explicitly celebrated the workers of the city, with 200 decorated floats and approximately 20,000 marchers representing 163 different marching clubs. Heralded as "the crowning achievement of the St. Paul Outdoor Sports Carnival," the parade drew 150,000 spectators who lined the streets to watch the two-hour procession.[20] Parading through the streets, a diverse group of St. Paulites represented the leaders and the laborers of various employers in the city. Union affiliation, which had become a source of civic strife in the 1910s, was invisible in these parades. Rather, as the souvenir view book indicates, participants marched as representatives of their employers. These marching clubs were composed of men (and some women) who worked in a range of professions and industries, from the newspapers to the railroads, and they wore costumes in the carnival's official colors, demonstrating their connection to all of the other marching workers and residents.[21]

The parades in 1917 were no different. And even though there was no repeat of a "municipal parade" per se, they drew even more participants. The official tabulation for the opening-day parade lists a total of 30,000 marchers with 250,000 spectators cheering them on. To boost turnout, Mayor V. R. Irvin declared three days beforehand that an official business holiday would begin at noon. In his official proclamation he impressed upon the citizens of his city that his declaration of "St. Paul Carnival Day" was linked to a belief that "the success of our carnival depends upon the extent to which our entire citizenship participates in it."[22] He encouraged those who were not actively marching to celebrate nonetheless. On January 30 and February 2, more parades wound through the streets, stirring emotions and, according to the official chroniclers, "evoking great applause from the thousands of admiring spectators."[23] Like the parades of 1916, they brought together an assortment of residents. According to one newspaper account, the 1917 opening-day parade was full of people from "all walks of life, . . . young and old of both sexes. Millionaire factory owners and office boys, women of the exclusive clubs and shop girls, messenger boys and magnates, all walked side by side—at times arm in arm."[24] This interclass solidarity on display was a source of pride for the organizers, who had claimed all along that this was their central goal.

Although the carnivals created such moments of apparent civic unity, the organizers were unwilling to leave them up to chance. Before each year's festivity, the association released sheet music of songs written expressly for the event, songs whose lyrics were clearly intended to underscore the carnival's purpose. "When the summer's over and the snow is on the ground," the 1916 version ran, "Then the natives of St. Paul all gather 'round for a great big jubilee. . . . Every body's dressed right up in carnival array. . . . Hail! Hail! the gang's all here. The people one and all." In 1917 the chorus of a new song, "Back to Old Saint Paul," revived those sentiments. Once again, residents were encouraged to sing, "Hail! Hail! the gang's all here! Shouting for the Carnival."[25]

Creating the image of a unifying event was so important to the carnival organizers that they repeated the theme in the official histories released after the events were over. In addition to recounting the details of the festival days, the souvenir view books highlighted the solidarity displayed. In 1916 they likened the unifying power of the carnival to a living thing with the power to make intimates out of strangers: "The carnival idea . . . at first had a slow growth, but suddenly seemed to dig its roots through the very rock foundations of the city itself and soon blossomed into the most brilliant array of colors the capital city has ever known. Children, young men and women, even the staid old plutocrats of the hill caught the fever and, almost before anyone could explain, the whole population was cavorting around in carnival costume."[26] In 1917 the carnival was touted as an even more powerful equalizer, having enticed both "captains of industry and lowly clerks . . . to rub shoulders together, marching in close ranks to the stirring rat-tat-tat of the drums or blare of the martial music." "Verily," the authors of the *De Luxe Souvenir Book* declared, "the Carnival is a great leveler."[27] Even the national press took up this rhetoric. *Outing Magazine*, a national sporting publication, reported in 1917 that, by providing a "common meeting ground," the carnival had broken through the class stratification that had come to mark life in the city.[28]

Nonetheless, a closer look at the shape of the carnivals' days and the organizers' limited efforts to involve the entire citizenry demonstrates that the celebrations failed to truly unite all the city's residents. While the activities were theoretically available to all citizens, certain segments of the population were both explicitly and implicitly excluded from full participation. Clearly, even in the liminal place and time of a carnival, let alone in everyday life, an experience of place-based solidarity could not be sustained. Yet a widespread insistence that it did exist suggests that an imagined community of St. Paul existed in the minds of some residents, despite alternative understandings and evidence to the contrary.

Carnival revelers may have spread out across the city, but the official carnival events remained tightly concentrated. In 1916 the city of St. Paul covered approximately fifty-five square miles and was growing.[29] Yet all of the high-visibility, communal events of both carnivals were located primarily in the central business district and near the surrounding well-to-do residential areas. Organizers claimed that these locations were the only "natural" ones for the events, but the very act of choosing these spots rather than others, especially for the ostensibly democratic carnival parades, is telling.[30] Beyond serving as a ploy to drum up business, the emphasis on the city's commercial district underscored the degree to which *communal* and *public* were increasingly relative terms that were being defined by the experience and communal vision of the group in power in a given place and with a particular relationship to the economic drivers of the city.

Scholars have persuasively argued that parades communicate messages about solidarity and community in a given locale and reveal established social and ideological hierarchies.[31] Such hierarchies were on grand display in the early years of the twentieth century. During the nineteenth century, the streets had been fairly democratic arenas for civic instruction and demonstration, but by 1900 the multivocal nature of the street had all but disappeared. All across the nation "the street had become the domain of political, industrial, and mercantile elites, as well as a growing class of upper-middle-class professionals."[32] In St. Paul, as in cities across the United States, parade organizers were usually men of business and professional acclaim. They created "public" events that promoted and celebrated the sites of their personal and professional lives. Thus, by positioning the carnivals' so-called public events in spaces marked as belonging to the people who controlled capital, power, and success, the organizers equated the St. Paul community with their own affinity-based network of merchants, professionals, and civic leaders.

In 1916 the two most prominent parades—the opening-day parade and the municipal parade—focused on the downtown commercial area. The marchers did venture outside this realm, but only as far as the fringes of the Summit neighborhood and to Harriet Island, the location of that year's ice fort and many carnival activities.[33] In 1917 the opening-day parade followed nearly the same route as the 1916 municipal parade had. Marchers trooped downtown from the residential neighborhood just north of Summit Avenue and wound through the commercial district before disbanding close to historic and wealthy Ramsey Hill.[34]

By designing the parade routes in the way they did, the carnival organizers imbued the spaces of the wealthy and the professionally successful with exaggerated meaning in the civic community.[35] Emphasizing the epicenter of the city's commercial world implicitly indicated that the market had become a central symbol of St. Paul. Membership in the civic community, the parade layout indicated, was at least peripherally linked to one's familiarity and interaction with these sites of commerce and the social networks that supported and emerged from them. Organizers for the 1917 parades appear to have given little thought to expanding or shifting the 1916 routes to traverse a wider swath of the city—say, into poorer, ethnic, immigrant neighborhoods such as the Lower West Side, the Upper Levee, and Swede Hollow.[36] To be sure, not all activities took place in the downtown area, but parts of the city were consistently overlooked. To this end, the placement of the official carnival slides, too, is telling.[37] For instance, although the committee seemed to be committed to scattering toboggan slides throughout the city, they did not place them in the poorest or most identifiably immigrant neighborhoods. Thus, while many neighborhoods could claim to have a slide in their vicinity, the most marginalized neighborhoods could not.[38]

Carnival activities were made most accessible to members of the classes who were sponsoring the carnivals.[39] In addition, this arrangement ensured that visitors and supporters would see only the most desirable parts of St. Paul, those areas that looked like their own neighborhoods or were most often frequented by their own associates. They would not be subjected to the sights and sounds of the city's most impoverished or marginalized areas, places that the city leaders were becoming increasingly concerned about by the late 1910s. To the outside world, St. Paul's poverty would be invisible and the city's inherent inequality and internal divisions erased. The capital city would sparkle as a symbol of culture, commerce, and successful living—the very traits that would encourage business growth. In this way, the specific sites of the carnival's most public events underscore the degree to which, in the minds of the organizers, neither unity nor community required full access or participation.

Indeed, this self-conscious erasing of certain sections of the city seems to have reinforced the organizers' already limited image of the St. Paul community. Certainly they understood that they were linked to all residents in an instrumental way; after all, the upper classes depended on the labor and business of the lower classes to stay in their privileged positions. But the less well-off were not members of their communities. Such membership was reserved for those with whom the elite shared something closer to reciprocal relationships. The inhabitants of the overlooked neighborhoods were nonessential members of the organizers' imagined St. Paul community. There were ways in which the carnivals celebrated a significant segment of the working class—for instance, through the municipal parade.[40] Yet it is clear that most events were geared toward those with some disposable income. Even if residents of St. Paul's most marginalized neighborhoods had taken the initiative to reach the carnival sites, they would not necessarily have been able to participate in the activities there. In spite of the carnival association's claim that the carnival was "free," there were costs involved—some more explicit than others.[41]

On the most basic level, active participation in the sporting events that formed the core of the programs required special equipment and skills. If a resident did not own skis or skates or any of a number of other specialized items, he or she would have to be content to observe. There seems to have been no provision made for providing such items to interested carnivalgoers.[42] Beyond these invisible costs was the monetary expense of participating in many of the most highly publicized events, including the ubiquitous toboggan slides. Although they were touted as one of the most accessible and popular of the activities, the slides were open only to people who were either wearing a carnival costume or had purchased and were wearing a carnival button. These buttons cost one dollar each in 1917, the costumes considerably more. Thus, the city's poorest citizens were relegated to the "crowds" that supposedly "thronged" the slides throughout the carnivals. The carnival committee claimed in its official recounting that all of the events of 1916 had been free, apparently overlooking necessity of carnival buttons for access. The buttons were not free for everyone in 1916, although exactly who needed to pay is unclear.[43] The children of poverty-stricken residents may have been able to use the slides on the special public school day arranged by the city, but their parents seem to have been left on the sidelines.[44]

At least one St. Paul resident wrote to the carnival committee after the 1916 event and chastised them for being "cheap" and not allowing people on the toboggan slides without a button.[45] But this lone charge had little effect on the organizers, who, in 1917, merely reinforced their policy of charging carnivalgoers for slide privileges. Although they agreed to let children slide for free during the day, all sliders were required to show a button after six o'clock in the evening, and adults were required to do so at all times.[46] Writing to each slide operator before the carnival opened, the organizers said sternly, "We would like the party in charge of your slide to see that no one is allowed to use the toboggan slide except persons wearing the membership buttons [which] are now on sale in two hundred different places at $1.00 each."[47] According to Louis Hill, "limiting the coasting to persons wearing buttons [was] purely a safety first device." He may have been correct, but the result was the same. The limits were not random; they were placed on those who lacked enough disposable income to purchase a button. Being "indiscriminate" about coasters (to use Hill's own wording) apparently meant allowing the city's poorest citizens on the slide.[48] The fee excluded not only those who might not have had a chance to purchase a button but also those who were unable to do so, regardless of desire.

Some of the most celebrated carnival events held at the City Auditorium were likewise limited to a restricted number of paying spectators. In 1917 there was free dancing each night in that space, but the cost of attending most of the other events staged there limited the number and type of people who could use the carnival activities as a way to position themselves within the community of St. Paul.[49] In 1917 the carnival association took out a large newspaper ad to announce its rationale for charging admission to the main carnival pageant. The year before there had been far more interested spectators than seats available in the auditorium, the ad said. Thus, for the 1917 pageant, admission would cost between 50¢ and $1.50. It is hard to tell if the organizers were aware of the message they were sending, but the wording of the ad makes one thing is clear: their imagined carnival community was limited those who could afford costumes and admission and were in a position, as the ad said, to help "defray the cost for *your* Great Outdoor Sports Carnival."[50]

Not even the many carnival parades, as democratic as they seemed, were truly open to the public at large. Anyone could view the parades, but marching required membership in a social club, a steady job at a company that had decided to sponsor a marching unit, or the money to purchase a carnival costume. In many cases social clubs or companies subsidized part of the cost of the carnival outfits, but most marchers had to make some financial investment. On average the outfits were $10 apiece in 1916 and $13 apiece in 1917, another financial barrier to civic participation.[51]

The public face of the carnival leadership contributed to this image of an abbreviated St. Paul community. In addition to their behind-the-scenes influence, wealthy male St. Paulites held key positions in the major events, which helped control the public image of the community of St. Paul. Louis Hill, a fixture in the city's social and business world, made appearance after appearance at both carnivals. In 1916, for instance, he rode in a convertible at the opening parade, christened the carnival slides by sliding down first, and was generally everywhere, front and center. Even the carnival song for that year was dedicated to him.[52] His business associates, who were also members of his intimate community, served as the figureheads of the festivities. In 1916 two of them portrayed rival kings in the battle between winter and spring, the theme around which many of that year's activities were organized. J. P. Elmer, a prominent businessman, occupied the throne of King Boreas, ruler of the north wind, while Ronald Stewart, Hill's vice president, was his nemesis, the Fire King, Ignis Rex. Although they were in costume during all of their public carnival appearances, their identities were not a secret. The local newspapers printed numerous photographs of both men, clearly identifying them and noting their positions in the city's social and business hierarchy. Anyone who read the newspapers would have recognized their kingly status.[53]

In 1917, Hill remained at the helm of the carnival association and was central to many of the festivity's most publicized events. The huge opening parade featured him astride a horse with a star on its flank, leading tens of thousands of marchers along the route.[54] In keeping with the precedent set in 1916, James Ridler, a prominent businessman, played King Boreas, and other business and social elites organized various events and competitions.[55] Thus, the core of the St. Paul community on display was constructed from the ranks of a select set of residents whose loyalties and notions of community were clearly divided between the city in which they lived and the people with whom they shared demographic identifiers and personal and professional intimacies. The carnivals were an attempt to reconcile the two ideas. By promoting themselves as central to the notion of community in St. Paul, the carnival organizers promulgated a limited image of what and who constituted the St. Paul community they were trying to shore up. Class status was obviously part of the equation. The elevation of the wealthy over the poor meant that, even as the planners strove to create an atmosphere that was inclusive, class-based divisions were highlighted and reinforced.

The carnival organizers wanted to unite the citizens of their hometown, but they also wanted to align their own personal St. Paul with a larger national community of revelers, boosters, and businessmen. They understood that they were linked to others who shared their lifestyle and worldview, and they pushed hard to make sure that their ostensibly local carnival would celebrate this particular experience of community. "The spirit of community which prevails here," proclaimed the official souvenir program from 1916, "radiates beyond the confines of the city boundaries."[56] The local papers reflected this belief in their coverage of the event; one headline from 1916 read, "Most Successful Trade Stimulator: Best of All, Though, Is the Awakening of Civic Spirit in City."[57] An ability to greet visitors was seen as part of the march toward creating a "spirit of good fellowship" in the city. Even before the 1916 carnival began, planners were predicting that a "spirit of good fellowship and friendly relations" would arise when "merchants and bankers brought in closer touch with their customers in the Northwest." They even offered a familial frame: "It is a sort of municipal party, in which St. Paul is to have as guests her sister cities."[58] The very unity of the carnival was expected to draw outside interest. According to a published statement from the mayor, by "welding all . . . citizens together in a common spirit of civic pride and affection," the carnival would present the city "advantageously all over the world."[59]

In prospective, real-time, and retrospective accounts of the events, civic leaders and carnival organizers alike seamlessly linked boosterism and civic unity. They truly believed that the two goals were organically linked (and for them this may have been true), but their attempts to introduce externally focused business goals into a civic event was a move away from using geography as the sole acceptable meaning of community in modernizing America. Place-based notions of community remained appealing, at least in theory, but for modern businessmen thinking in terms of national markets, single municipalities were neither the totality nor even the most desirable of all conceivable experiences of community. Place remained important in an imagined sense, but literally sharing space was unnecessary.[60]

Consequently, organizers' sense of obligation to their community of business and social contacts outside of St. Paul was at play in their design of the carnivals. During their early planning for the 1916 event, they advertised it far and wide, as newspaper accounts, carnival histories, and association records all make clear. The business-savvy committee saw the carnival as a means to highlight St. Paul's suitability as a meeting ground for likeminded businessmen, social elites, and savvy politicians from across the nation. They promoted the city as both a destination and a desirable place to live. At least one chronicler remarked that the advertising value of the carnival could not be overstated, and the organizers were quick to thank the local press for recognizing the "immense value to St. Paul of the carnival as an advertisement" and for giving "the carnival a degree of publicity which no other in this or any other country has ever enjoyed."[61] Because the event organizers had already developed contacts and relationships with people around the nation, they believed that bringing these outsiders into the city for a civic event made perfect sense.

Carnival posters appeared as far away as the Pacific Coast, and advertising postcards went to South America and Europe courtesy of a steamship company.[62] The association sent official letters to the mayors and commercial clubs of other cities. Louis Hill sent a letter of invitation to a colleague in Oregon, and other members of the business community also worked to publicize the event outside of St. Paul.[63] Notably, the heads of thirty of the largest wholesale houses in the city joined forces to extend an invitation to merchants across the Northwest, the core of their customer base. The invitation promised that these visitors would be able to enjoy not only the general festival activities but also the opportunity to network at the three grand dinners that St. Paul businessmen would be hosting.[64]

The efforts of these local boosters were successful; visitors to the 1916 carnival numbered in the thousands. With that success as encouragement, the organizers made drawing outsiders to the festivities a driving goal for the 1917 carnival. Determined to fulfill a prophecy made following the previous year's event that "the carnival of the coming year . . . will put the name of the city before [even] more people," delegations traveled to neighboring Wisconsin and as far as Spokane, Washington, to "carry the spirit of the carnival" to potential supporters and entice visitors from "the whole country" to experience the festivities for themselves.[65] The association even went so far as to sponsor a competition, awarding prizes to those St. Paulites who had traveled the farthest and visited the most cities to advertise the event.[66]

In both years, the city's leading white newspapers trumpeted the success of these promoters and promotions, making daily references to visiting groups in the city and publishing photographs of them, often emphasizing the distance they had traveled to participate in the carnival.[67] In 1916, hoping to attract more people from the nation's merchant, business, and social elite, the association even invited President Woodrow Wilson to attend. Although Wilson respectfully declined, many other invitees flocked to the city, arriving in such numbers that its hotels were filled to capacity.[68] The flood of visitors forced some hotelkeepers to set up cots in their hallways.[69]

Not even St. Paul's long intercity rivalry with Minneapolis stood in the way.[70] All animosity was set aside as carnival leaders encouraged that city's businessmen and citizens to participate. In both years St. Paulites took part in advance parades in downtown Minneapolis and invited the residents of their sister city to join the upcoming festivities. At the first parade, skepticism turned quickly into support as Minneapolis citizens warmed to the idea: St. Paul marchers were welcomed, applauded, and cheered as they tramped through hotels and clubs in the Mill City.[71] In 1916, the mayor of Minneapolis encouraged his citizens to take part in the St. Paul festivities, and the next year he was on hand to welcome the advance marchers, even asking his downtown merchants to close their businesses so that their employees could watch the parade.[72] This direct advertising was enhanced after a St. Paul leadership group declared that January 31, 1917, would be Minneapolis Day at the carnival. The enticements worked, and many residents of Minneapolis took part in the activities of both carnivals, tobogganing, skiing, skating, and filling the city's streets. One parade drew 15,000 spectators from Minneapolis; their numbers nearly overwhelmed the intercity streetcar lines.[73]

Carnival organizers were proud of their efforts to attract outside support and participants.[74] To make sure that visitors would be well received, they added events such as an opening-day reception and luncheon for "Visiting Kings and Dignitaries." And in 1916 members of the St. Paul business community took out a full-page ad in the Pioneer Press that opened with "Greetings: we hereby invite you to come to St. Paul to enjoy in fullest measure the pleasure of our Winter Sports Carnival—We want to greet you. We open our homes and hearts to you. We promise you good entertainment, good weather and good cheer. Come to revel in our brisk glowing days. Come to enjoy interesting contests. Come to see our grand and growing city. We beckon you—come on."[75]

Louis Hill made a point to personally welcome visitors who were arriving at Union Depot, the city's magnificent train station. In one highly publicized act, a banquet hosted by and for a delegation from Montana, he offered an official greeting.[76] In 1917, the organizers established an official accommodations bureau whose primary purpose was to provide statistics about the myriad places from which the visitors had come.[77] At least some visitors were grateful for these gestures. For instance, after returning to her home in outstate Minnesota, one visitor announced to her local paper that she had had "one of the best times of her life. The Carnival authorities showed [me] every courtesy, contributing to [my] comfort in every way."[78]

Many average St. Paulites seemed to embrace the outsiders' presence, going so far as to open their homes in order to ease overcrowding in the hotels.[79] In fact, some seem to have seen these visitors as an integral part of the carnivals. The Dispatch urged, "Look citizens! With throngs of visitors . . . to our city [for] the Carnival, it's up to you to mingle and play with them."[80] As the Pioneer Press pointed out vis-à-vis one of the grand parades, visiting clubs, had not only "figured conspicuously" in the event but were "applauded continuously."[81] For some residents, the carnival was an opportunity to broaden their horizons and celebrate their city with all who wished to join them. The welcome they gave reflected an understanding of community that was far from being limited to or defined by place of residence. The fact that this welcome occurred in the midst of an event touted as St. Paul-centered strengthens this argument. For a significant segment of the general citizenry as well as for the organizers, the visiting revelers could be integrated into a notion of community that was based on shared experiences (carnival attendance) and shared loyalties (to the promotion of St. Paul), whether or not they had addresses in the city.

These tens of thousands of visitors were ubiquitous in the city, visibly participating in key carnival events and accounting for much of their perceived success. St. Paul's reputation was boosted by their presence, and, to outsiders, the carnival's power lay in its ability to provide entertainment for people across the nation. After seeing the huge crowds gathered in the city from all over the United States, an eastern journalist who occupied the reviewing stand at the 1917 opening-day parade gushed, "Hereafter, America should claim this carnival and look at it as a thing of which the whole nation should be proud [and] St. Paul must be satisfied to be the mecca to which thousands will travel to participate."[82] According to another journalist, by 1917 the St. Paul carnival had become a "national institution, not a mere civic celebration."[83] This statement indicated that all Americans, not just St. Paulites, were interested in creating links with people around the country.

Even as St. Paul welcomed outsiders, both actually and imaginatively, into the realm of the carnival community, another group of residents remained on the margins. Organizers' effort to attract middle- and upper-class nonresidents was balanced by their almost total lack of interest in attracting the city's African American citizens.[84] Although many working-class, middle-class, and professional black residents lived within walking distance of the carnival core, they were almost completely absent from the activities and rarely appear in recorded images or accounts of either carnival. In the one dramatic instance when they did appear, their marginality was clear.

There is no evidence of African American participation in the 1916 carnival. Not one image of or reference to a black St. Paul resident appeared in the three major white-owned dailies at any point during the weeks leading up to the carnival or during the festival itself. Neither do the association records indicate any interest in addressing or reaching out to the African American population. The souvenir book, which claimed over and over again that the carnival had united a diverse citizenry, does not mention or show an identifiably nonwhite face anywhere in its pages.[85]

The black residents appear to have been equally uninterested in participating in this white-led carnival. At no point leading up to, during, or following the ten days of the 1916 carnival did the *Appeal* mention the event. This exclusion continued in 1917.[86] However, in that year the absence was particularly notable: not only were a few black men featured in some of the high-profile pre-carnival events, but the association also sanctioned a parade that had strong racist overtones. Such blatant exclusion and racism seem to have alienated the city's African Americans from the carnival activities, but they also seem to have spurred an effort to stage an alternative event that made it clear that race-based divisions were central to navigating the experience of St. Paul community, even as shared racial identification could imaginatively link people across locales.

No images of African Americans were printed in the mainstream, white St. Paul newspapers during the 1917 carnival's run, nor did the 1917 *Official Souvenir View Book* include any images of black participants. However, a group of unnamed black men appears in two carnival-related photographs that the *Pioneer Press* published before the carnival, and the same men appear in nearly 20 percent of the ninety-two official photographs taken during the pre-carnival publicity pageants and published in a private album produced by the Camera Art Company, the official carnival studio. Thus, it is clear that African Americans had a role in the carnival activities that was prominent, publicized, and troubling.[87]

Both carnivals were all about pageantry and performance; and in 1917 the trappings of royalty that were part of the image of King Boreas included not only a crown and a royal robe but also four men who, according the *Pioneer Press*, played the role of his personal "attendants" and followed him on all of his official carnival duties. Photographs of these men show that they appear to be black, and their faces stand out in a sea of white as they flank the white king, holding his robe off the ground and shielding his face from the sun and wind with giant fans. In the two images that circulated widely in the white press and in the more than a dozen others included in the Camera Art Company album, the men do not smile; and in keeping with their roles in the pageant, they are always either serving the king from the side or, most commonly, positioned a step or two behind.[88]

While neither the faces nor the bodies of these African American men appeared in any official post-carnival summation or in any press coverage during the days of the fête itself, their existence was not hidden from St. Paul residents. As the Camera Art Company's album photos (such as fig. 31) and the newspaper coverage make clear, they were photographed (and presumably filmed) during the staged pre-carnival festivities at the Town and Country Club on December 31, 1916, and again on January 1 and January 20, 1917.[89] Thousands of local residents attended these promotional events, and many more would have noted the men's presence in the newspaper photographs reproduced in the *Pioneer Press*. Even if they missed the front-page photo on January 2 (fig. 32), they would have seen the multipage carnival supplement published on January 21 and would have read the caption: "Boreas Rex, ruler of the carnival (James Ridler) and his attendants, who will accompany him throughout the week's festivities" (fig. 33).[90]

Who were these men, why they were included in the carnival production, and were they compensated for their efforts? Those details seem lost to official history. There is no mention of their names anywhere in the records, no indication that they even existed.[91] One must assume that they chose to participate of their own free will. Yet the images and the lack of accompanying documentation remain troubling. If the records included other images of African Americans as participants in the carnival, one might assume that they had played this role in addition to others. But this was not the case. Carnival leadership, supporters, newspaper readers, and the people who attended the promotional events were exposed to only one image of black people in St. Paul: the black man as servant.[92] The marginality of this role needs no explication.

The mysteries of the photographs do not offer the only evidence of the way in which race functioned within citywide discourses and experiences of community in 1917. The other involves the grand auto parade that closed out the carnival. As part of a plan to draw Minneapolis residents into the festivities and to underscore the market-driven basis for extra-local community building in the modernizing urban economy, the organizers orchestrated the inclusion of a group of Minneapolis auto dealers into an auto parade scheduled for February 2, the second-to-last day of the carnival. Hundreds of dealers would drive their cars from the Mill City business district to St. Paul before meeting up with the scheduled decorated automobile parade that was to begin at three o'clock in the afternoon. After the Minneapolis vehicles (which would be "fantastically" decorated) had reached the parade route, they would fall into line with the rest of the parade. At the end of the event drivers would park their cars on Eighth Street in downtown St. Paul. City policemen had been instructed to watch the vehicles while their occupants mingled with the crowds during the late afternoon hours before celebrating as a group at the first rendition of the final grand pageant to be held at the City Auditorium that evening.[93] The linked business goals of this collaboration were widely reported: Minneapolis businessmen would help ensure the success of the carnival while promoting their auto-show opening in Minneapolis the next day. Economic boosterism and business alliances were winning the day on both sides of the Mississippi.

The event publicly emphasized the intersecting ideas and practices of economic agendas and community formation, and it was a symbolic extension, on a grander scale, of other carnival events that had included visitors. However, public reaction and press coverage focused largely on the fact that the auto dealers rode into town and toured the city while wearing the white robes of the Ku Klux Klan. This spectacle was no surprise. In fact, it had been planned. Almost a week before the carnival began, and in the same issue as the pictorial supplement depicting King Boreas and his black "attendants," the *Pioneer Press* published a long celebratory article detailing the impetus for and plan of the upcoming auto parade.[94] The piece reported that the manager of the auto dealer association "Walter R. Wilmont has taken the direction of the organization of the parade and invites anybody and everybody to participate, having arranged to supply 1,000 night riders' costumes. 'We intend to show St. Paul that we want to help make the carnival a success.'"[95] The article was accompanied by a photograph of three men, faces exposed, all of them wearing Klan attire (fig. 34). The article refers to the outfits as "white-hooded robes such as were worn by the Ku Klux Klan," apparently to detach these "playful" costumes from their more sinister connotations. Yet the headline above the photograph proclaims, "Minneapolis Ku Klux Clansmen Coming in Force," and a subheadline states, "'Night Riders' Will Attack Carnival." A briefer article run in the previous day's *Pioneer Press* had stated matter-of-factly that "nearly 5,000 persons from Minneapolis in Ku Klux Klan costumes will take part in the Outdoor Sports Carnival parade in St. Paul February 2."[96] The intent was clear.

Such publicity was likely to have created concern among the city's black residents, for even in the urban North the Klan's image and activities were well known by 1917. The revived KKK had made significant inroads into the Middle West, including Minnesota, in the years following its 1915 resurgence, and by the 1920s one-third of its membership in the United States was in the Midwest. It is reasonable to assume that the anti-immigrant, pro-Protestant, white-supremacist, "patriotic" gospel of the revived Klan was present in Minnesota by early 1917; and while there were certainly many groups who faced the intimidation, boycotts, and political actions of the KKK in the state, the specter of race-based physical violence could not have been far from the minds of many local African Americans. Any "new" incarnation of the KKK in Minnesota circa the 1910s emerged both in the shadow of the 1896 attempted lynchings of two black men in St. Paul by a white mob and in a state that would pass an anti-lynching law in 1921 in response to the actual 1920 lynchings of three black men in Duluth attended by some 10,000 spectators. In the 1920s the Klan would dig in its heels in St. Paul, which between 1923 and 1925 became the place of publication for a Klan newspaper, the *Call of the North*.[97]

It was into this context of a history of racial violence, ongoing race-based discrimination and intimidation, and a renewed Klan gaining ground throughout the Midwest that hundreds of men (and some women) wearing "Night Rider costumes" drove into St. Paul during the carnival days, welcomed, encouraged, and expected. So clearly unproblematic was this display that the major newspapers hyped the success of the auto parade and expressed gratitude for the group's presence. Even the record cold on February 2 could not dampen the festivities. The newspapers reported that more than 1,000 cars filled the St. Paul streets as 75,000 spectators cheered them on. A reported 500 cars were from Minneapolis alone. A *Dispatch* head-line declared, "Ku Klux Klan Fantastic," and its article referred to the hooded revelers as "the Minneapolis funmakers" and proclaimed that "the Ku Klux men in their white gowns, added a tone of the fantastic to the parade."[98] On the day after the event the *Pioneer Press* ran two articles side by side. The first had a large-print sub-headline proclaiming "Ku Klux Invade City" followed by a statement linking the success of the parade to the contributions of the Minneapolis contingent who were identified as "scores of Ku Klux Klan in white suits."[99] The second article was organized by a series of subheadings including "Ku Klux Klan Booms Mill City Motor Show," "Parade Boosts Show," and "Women in the Ku Klux Klan." The text that followed pointed out not only that some of the riders were "of the fairer sex" but made clear, once again, the linked economic interests of the two sets of boosters and tied the Klan clothing to the perceived success of the event:

> The procession was a foretaste of the attractions offered by dealers in the annual auto show in Minneapolis today and tomorrow. With that event in view Minneapolis enthusiasts were present in force to help warm up the parade. In addition to a demonstration by truck and sundries manufacturers . . . the Mill City auto fraternity made a con-spicuous showing with their ghostly-costumed Ku Klux Klan. Almost every other machine seemed filled with "night riders."[100]

St. Paul was brimming with visitors, black men were taking on the role of servant to a white king, and carnival organizers had encouraged (and the local newspapers touted) a group of revelers dressed in Klan attire. Yet to read the black press during the carnival days of 1917 was to believe that events in St. Paul were business-as-usual. And perhaps they were for the black residents of the city. Their absence in the white papers and in the widely publicized carnival images elicited no letters to the editor of the *Appeal* nor do any articles in the issues published before, during, or after the carnival hint at either familiarity with such exclusions or overt racism. These absences speak volumes about the role of race in defin-ing or negotiating various experiences and expressions of community in Minnesota's capital city. Only if marginality and experiences of commu-nity limited by racial identity were the norm does the absence of outcry or even commentary make sense. And apparently it was the norm, so much so that not only did the African American residents refuse to acknowledge the presence of the carnival in their city but they quietly made clear their preference for affinity-based community by staging a thinly veiled alternative.

Immediately after the end of the 1916 and 1917 winter carnivals, the black population of St. Paul staged a multiday festival that replicated some of the events of the winter carnivals, added unique experiences, and provided a time and a place for black residents and nonresidents to reinforce their understanding of affinity-based community based on race. In 1916 the event was called the Three Days Carnival, and it was held at Union Hall.[101] Advertisements indicate that it was, at least in part, a vehicle for raising funds to wipe out the remaining debt on the hall. But the admission price of ten cents indicates that it had meaning and purpose outside of a financial one. After all, the outstanding debt was $1,500, which would have been difficult to recoup by collecting dimes at the door.

The timing and structure of the event is more telling. Even though the Three Days Carnival ran from February 14 to 16, the *Appeal* began advertising it on February 5, the day when the city's large carnival came to a close, thereby taking advantage of the energy (and perhaps frustration) built up in the African American community by its relative exclusion. Yet the two-week gap between the carnivals allowed participants to see themselves and their actions as independent of those promoted and hosted by their white counterparts. In their choice of activities, too, the African American organizers simultaneously played off the publicity of the Outdoor Sports Carnival and established a separate event. Participants were encouraged to come in costume to the opening night, when prizes would be awarded for the "best and most comical." The second day's activities highlighted the various African American fraternal organizations; members would come in their full dress regalia. The third night was marked by the crowning of senior and junior carnival queens, voted on by carnivalgoers and chosen from candidates representing various clubs and organizations.[102]

In these activities, participants and organizers articulated their knowledge of the events that were taking place in white St. Paul while asserting their power to shape their own experience of the carnival and its meaning as a community unifier—at least among those with the leisure and the finances to participate. An announcement in the *Appeal* just days before the event began dispelled any doubts. Appropriating the other carnival's slogan, the announcement read: "'Make it a Hot One: The Three Day Carnival at Union Hall."[103] The following year, promoters advertised their carnival under the slogan "Say, make it a Hotter One!" They asked attendees to come in carnival costume and even went so far as to refer to the festivity as an "Indoor Sports Carnival," though it did not involve any true sporting events.[104] Adopting the terminology of the official St. Paul carnival positioned the black residents of the city, at least rhetorically, in the discourse of place-based community, while the act of hosting a separate "carnival" exposed the weakness of this definition of community. What the Union Hall carnival provided was an experience of affinity-based community that could also accommodate a rhetorical nod to a wider community of St. Paul residents—much like that provided by the other event.

Like Hill and his colleagues, the organizers of the Union Hall carnivals emphasized the way in which the events promoted a "true spirit of brotherhood" among participants. While acknowledging some implicit stratification among members of the city's black population, a 1916 article in the *Appeal* noted that in the carnival space and time no "petty jealousies" were exhibited and that "religious, fraternal and social lines were completely ignored." According to the *Appeal*, by achieving this desired unity, the event became "one of the most pre-eminently successful undertakings ever inaugurated in St. Paul," and it gave black St. Paulites a tangible indicator of the power of race to draw them together.

Importantly, like the extralocal notion of community that spurred inclusion of "outsiders" in the Outdoor Sports Carnival, the Union Hall events encouraged participants from Minneapolis as well as St. Paul and, according to the published record, embraced them fully. Likewise, the Minneapolis participants fully supported the goals of their St. Paul counterparts. For instance, a carnival queen candidate from the Mill City went so far as to donate the total of her fundraising efforts to the Union Hall cause, even after withdrawing from the contest. As members of the same racial minority, black residents of the Twin Cities saw themselves as part of a shared community of identity and experience, an affinity-based notion of community that was in many ways stronger than the draw of shared place of residence.[105]

African Americans were not the only St. Paulites who challenged the winter carnival's vision of city-as-community. Members of the city's working classes also saw shared residence as only one aspect of what was increasingly a broader experience of communal ties. For these residents the 1916 carnival gave them a degree of reassurance that they were integral to the experience and success of the city, a reaction that shored up an abstract concept of city-as-community even if daily life supported more class-bound understandings of the term.[106] The carnival's structure and organization had encouraged such imaginings. Actively recruited by carnival planners, working-class citizens constituted the bulk of the carnivalgoers who made events such as the municipal parade grand successes. Many were employed by bosses who had subsidized carnival costumes or closed workplaces so that workers could participate in parades. On the surface, then, it appears that these citizens believed that they were in a reciprocal and therefore potentially communal relationship with the more prosperous or elite members of the association. Yet events in the weeks after the carnival revealed that such a notion of imagined community tied to place of residence was hard to hold on to when economic forces delineated and illuminated alternative communal allegiances based on class status, one's place in the commercial world of the city, and the power that went along with the same.

After the 1916 carnival ended, the carnival association received numerous medical claims on behalf of working-class citizens who said that they had been injured during the carnival by faulty equipment or neglect. Most of these residents never saw a doctor to verify their injuries but apparently made these claims because they knew that the association had liability insurance.[107] In taking action against the association and, by proxy, against the city elite, they were inserting themselves more fully into the community that the carnival leadership represented. If residence in St. Paul had, in fact, offered an assurance of membership in this community, the plaintiffs would have been compensated, for communal relations imply responsibility for those in one's community. Yet the response of the carnival leaders challenged this notion, revealing how economic concerns and a relationship to the structures of power could override shared location. Even when claims were paid, motives were complicated. When he was notified about the cases, Louis Hill made it clear that he wanted them to quickly disappear. For instance, after receiving a phone call from an allegedly injured young woman, he remarked to his attorney that "she seemed to think she was entitled to some damages" and that he wanted to offer some "reasonable settlement" to avoid "having her talking about the matter" with anyone else.[108]

Even more telling was the tone that carnival organizers took with local businessmen following the 1917 carnival. After tallying up the event's expenses, the association set out to recoup some of its losses and targeted the small businesses in the vicinity of the carnival activities. In their solicitation letters, the organizers explained that they had provided a service to the businesses and thus deserved the owners' financial support.[109] But business owners were indignant at the thought that they owed anything to the association. "We have already made a donation to the Association and have also purchased a number of buttons," wrote the owner of the United States Bedding Company. "Therefore we do not see our way clear to make this additional donation. . . . We felt that we have already done our share towards this carnival fund."[110] There is no evidence of how the association followed up on this particular refusal, but at least one member of the association, Mr. W. H. Burns, was sent door to door to solicit funds from unresponsive business owners in the area just west of downtown. Planners hoped that these proprietors would be shamed into making further donations, and records of these solicitation attempts indicate the animosity felt on both sides.

When approached, some of the targeted businessmen pleaded lack of funds; others claimed they lacked the authority to make financial decisions for the company; still others simply stalled, asking the solicitor to return later. The majority of business owners simply refused to give any money. Many explicitly expressed their lack of support for the entire carnival idea and argued that they had made nothing from the event. Statements such as "Says he made nothing and will give nothing," "Had [already] donated enough to the Carnival," and "Positively refused, and seemed sore that he should be called on" fill the pages of W. H. Burns's journals as well as the report he submitted to the carnival committee. It seems that there were few post-carnival supporters and that most of this small number were the city's largest merchants and those who had close personal ties to the organizers.

The business owners saw themselves at odds with the carnival committee; one man actually accused Burns of "doubling up" on him. But Burns's records indicate his own sense of distance from the needs of the men he was approaching. He found their stance offensive and felt no compunction about revealing his annoyance, even at the risk of offending a potential donor. After one businessman claimed to have mailed a check, Burns, "doubting his statement," decided to call on him the following day, when he told the potential donor that he was questioning his veracity. In his written reports Burns peppered his remarks about refusals with commentary about the owners' ethnicity. Writing about someone named T. H. Courney, he noted that the man was "a cranky Irishman," a status that apparently helped explain the refusal. In Burns's estimation, being Jewish also made a businessman a potential problem. He linked one man's refusal to his status as a "cranky Jew" and wrote that the owners of Ted's Family Liquor Store wouldn't donate funds because they were "two Jews [who] use the other for an excuse."[111]

The spirit of divisiveness implicit in these interactions challenges any assertion that the carnivals had successfully reinscribed a nineteenth-century ideal of a city or town as communal unit marked by deep reciprocity. Rather, the animosity and individualistic sentiment that rings throughout these records indicates the inability of such a cultural event to dramatically alter perceived differences between, say, small-business owners and the civic leadership. A person's specific place in the commercial fabric of the city (and the nation) was more significant than even his or her general place in the world of commerce writ large. Outside the liminoid spaces of the carnival, the two groups saw themselves not as members of one community—which would have required and implied common concern and led them to work for a mutually desirable outcome—but rather as competitors battling over their rights to and ownership of limited resources.

Equally instructive is a letter to the carnival organizers from a member of the middle class, a letter that challenged the notion that St. Paulites had believed in place-based unity even *during* the carnival's run. The author was an employee of the city's prestigious West Publishing house who had written to complain about the fee for the carnival slides. But in the course of laying out those concerns, he also indicted the carnival's relationship to civic unity. His concern about the slide fee was only partially linked to the money involved. Chiding the organizers, he wrote that, "aside from this feature of its absurdity, your rule is apt to reflect discredit upon the Carnival." He believed that by enforcing such exclusionary rules the carnival committee would expose its ulterior motives. "One likes to feel," he explained, "that the Carnival is more or less for the entertainment of St. Paul and its visitors, although, of course, we all know that it is a business proposition, and that you are in it for what you can get out of it."[112]

No matter how much the carnival organizers touted their sense of responsibility to all of the city's residents, those residents remained aware of the hollowness of that claim. The organizers' actions make it clear that they were focusing on their peers and working to reinforce their own position within the economic structure of the city, the region, and the nation. They also suggested that St. Paul was a community only in an abstract sense, identifiable only from a safe distance and usually understood, constructed, and mediated through the market and its mechanisms. One final act post-1917 carnival served as an apt announcement of this position, linking as it did questions of class, race, and place.

Despite the rhetorical success of the 1917 carnival and its organizers' apparent unassailable commitment to a 1918 version, the financial success of the event was never certain. Thus, in an effort to "help defray the deficit of the St. Paul Outdoor Sports Carnival," planners staged a follow-up event for Saturday, February 10, just a week after the carnival had ended. For 50¢ (adults), 25¢ (children), or $1 (for a box seat), spectators could watch a two-mile dog-team race at the state fairgrounds featuring the top four finishers from the carnival's signature event: the Red River to St. Paul race, won by Fred Hartman. Attendees could also participate in skijoring, snowshoeing, and push-ball contests; and members of marching clubs were encouraged to come in costume.

With this plan for revenue generation in place, organizers just needed the general public to buy tickets, so they advertised in local newspapers, including the *Appeal*. On the morning of February 10, just a week following the close of the St. Paul carnival and two days after the close of the Union Hall event, African American residents opened their weekly copy of that paper and found a large ad for the fairgrounds fundraiser. It began with "Everybody's Going to the Dogs" and ended with the ubiquitous "Make it a Hotter One."[113] The message of this ad was that as long as the city's black residents were willing to spend money to help city leaders and event organizers recoup their financial investments, they were welcome to imagine themselves to be part of "everybody." The irate (white) author of the letter complaining about slide costs may not have know that his suggestion about community-as-commodity had other evidentiary support. In the minds of the white event organizers, there were enough members of the African American community willing to consider attending the fundraiser to warrant an advertisement, and in this one action they laid bare the complexity of community in modernizing America. On display was a concept of community that could hold in balance structural racism and class division within a place of residence *and* ideas of a communal identity shaped by access to shared economic status or aspiration.

Although the carnival organizers had hoped that their events would reunite the factions that were increasingly threatening the economic success of the city, they had not bargained that the carnivals might actually reveal the deep roots of those divisions or the difficulty of redefining community in a landscape of economic, social, political and demographic change. The carnival band might have played "Hail! Hail! The gang's all here, The people one and all," but the reality was quite different. For African Americans and the very poor, membership in a community defined by place appears to have been tenuous at best. Both were largely invisible at the carnival proper—from the planning stages to the final frame of the carnival documentary. Nowhere were their voices heard. Nowhere were their faces seen as co-participants. Nowhere was there any substantial evidence that they were part of the community that carnival promoters were selling. For them, place-based community and intimate or emotional community were separate entities, even city leaders tried to pretend that these residents' financial participation would be a tool for entrance into an imagined city-as-community. To a lesser degree, the same held true for working- and middle-class white St. Paulites.

By the late 1910s, the pull of affinity-based notions of community driven by shared race, class, ethnicity, religion, or experience had complicated, displaced, and paralleled notions of community based on place. The carnival organizers' decisions and the citizens' responses illustrate this trajectory: locale was merely one way of thinking about community, and for many it was not a very powerful one. Affinity and geography were in dynamic tension. In many cases the social networks created and nurtured by the forces of the growing market economy and the linked world of commerce were at the center of these affinities.

The carnival days revealed three experiences, expressions, and ideas of community in St. Paul: affinity-based (by choice or structural limitations) among city residents, affinity-based and broader than the city limits, and an imagined community in which all residents coexisted by virtue of their connection to the city itself. It was clear that one's relationship to economic, political, and social power influenced which and how many of these communities an individual could embrace simultaneously. This pattern was not created in the space and time of the carnival but was a manifestation and reassertion of patterns that had become well established in St. Paul and other cities by the late 1910s. These patterns would continue to shape life in modernizing America and beyond.

More than anything, the Outdoor Sports Carnivals of 1916 and 1917 underscored an already-present reality: that for St. Paulites demographic variables, which were often tied to one's relationship to the market, were more powerful factors in determining a person's understanding of his or her membership in a given community than was any claim of residency within the city limits. When the pull of affinity-based community came up against notions of place-based community, the former won out. Community was increasingly linked to and experienced as a set of relationships both wider and narrower than any one city, yet community could still be discussed and understood as tied to place. No matter how much the carnival organizers touted their sense of responsibility to the entirety of the city's residents, those residents were aware of the limits of this claim. Yet, ironically, while the organizers' actions make it clear that their primary experiences of community involved those St. Paulites (and non-residents) who were most like them in status, class, and lifestyle, their privileged position made it possible for them, more than for others, to hold on to and promote a multifaceted, renegotiated understanding of community in which place and affinity could coexist and all of the city's residents could be imagined as such. This image of community strikingly anticipates the image of Carol Kennicott's beloved St. Paul in *Main Street* and her understanding of community in that city. Diversity, autonomy, and segmentation did not translate into the death of communal relationships; rather, they redefined and reinforced the concept. In the opening two decades of the twentieth century, demographic and affinity-based communal bonds—which had always marked the lives of Americans in some way—had gained both currency and prominence. In addition, the market, especially in cities, had eroded the possibility of uncomplicated place-based notions of community. From this had emerged a complicated, nuanced, and widely accepted understanding of community that allowed for divisions and hierarchies of many sorts while still embracing a rhetoric of location. It was in cities that this conception of community flourished. The scale, scope, and dynamism of urban America made this possible. Notably, Sinclair Lewis portrayed St. Paul not as an oasis from the many long-standing divisions of small towns such as Gopher Prairie but as a place where diversity and division were embraced and fully compatible with community as it had come to be understood by 1920. Only in this way could citizens like Carol have positive experiences of affinity-based community that they understood as being tied to a place of residence. For Louis Hill and the other members of the city's business and cultural elite, as for Carol Kennicott, the relationships created and shaped by a market economy (and one's position within it) over two transformative decades proved to be the key to successfully embracing geography and affinity as equally valid and rewarding experiences and definitions of community in modernizing America. Or of being unable to do the same. The carnivals, then, tell us not so much about a brand-new experience of community emerging for the first time in 1916 and 1917 but about its permanence and pervasiveness on the eve of the modern era.

CONCLUSION

THE COMPLEXITIES OF COMMUNITY

Lessons for Our Time

In 1918 a Philadelphia publishing house brought out a new civics textbook for use in public high schools across the nation. Intended to introduce young Americans to the structure of civil society, *Our Community: Good Citizenship in Towns and Cities* included an entire chapter devoted to "The Community." Community, the authors affirmed, remained a central concept in modern America. But despite the confident definite article in the chapter's title, the authors struggled to integrate the singular definition they offered with the contemporary examples that filled the chapter's pages. They recognized that neither the meaning nor the experience of community could be simply or monolithically limned.

In response to their own question, "What is a community?" the authors concluded that both shared location and shared interests formed essential aspects of it. "A community," they wrote, "consists of a group of people, living in a single locality, having common interests, and subject to common laws."[1] Yet this concise definition did not encompass all the versions of community they described. Beginning with the home and expanding outward to schools, athletic teams, the town, the state, and the nation, the chapter identified a wide variety of forms that community could take. In each case, the authors instructed, the establishment of community required some sense of shared place, some sense of "common interests," and an element of reciprocity.[2] Even so, the specific examples they offered illustrated that the importance of each component was debatable. In some cases one or more of these three foundational elements was present in only a minute amount.

In certain instances community implied shared residence in specific physical locations easily identified, bounded, and traversed. In other cases the geographic referent was much broader: state or nation. Sometimes common interests were easily identified and numerous; at other times they marked out common denominators that allowed for smooth governmental and social functioning. Reciprocity might require a community member to make substantial physical and psychological exertions on behalf of another member of the community, or it might merely require paying taxes. By 1918, as the authors' examples made clear, the term *community* identified a wide range of relationships, ideas, and experiences simultaneously. Modernizing Americans could call relationships communal that were linked only peripherally to a specific place or to the shared intimacy and reciprocity that had marked community in generations past. In the end, *Our Community* suggested that the meaning of the term had been transformed. No longer did community demarcate simply the close, emotional relationships common in nineteenth-century usages of the word. Rather, the concept and the experience encompassed a broad sweep of emotional and utilitarian interactions at local, national, and global levels. This understanding of community could hold up in an industrial, increasingly diverse, quickly changing nation whose present looked very different from its past and whose future was largely unknown.

Our Community was published in response to and in alignment with a 1915 U.S. Bureau of Education report titled "The Teaching of Community Civics," and it was adopted by school districts nationwide in the waning days of the 1910s.[3] The textbook offered a city's youngest residents a simplified version of the discourse on community that was shaping contemporary sociological thought. In particular, it paralleled the thesis in Robert MacIver's 1917 *Community: A Sociological Study,* which defined communities in relation to associations. Associations, he explained, were limited, exclusive groups of people with common goals; his examples included families, church congregations, and labor unions. Communities, however, were much like commonweals. They needed to have borders (although these could be broader than a nation), and the people who claimed membership in them needed to share some element of common life such as manners, traditions, or modes of speech. Such a definition left a great deal of latitude for those imagining or crafting experiences of community that were compatible with the modern age. Communities, in MacIver's formulation, were political mergers of disparate peoples united by some broad similarity. He seemed little concerned about the depth of these similarities or whether, as communities, they elicited deep reciprocal bonds among members. In his formulation communities might involve such connections, but they did not have to. They could vary in size, and any one community could also be a component of a larger community. They were neither bound by municipal lines nor always separate from them. And any man, woman, or child could be a member of many communities simultaneously.[4]

Yet as both MacIver and the textbook authors indicated, a shift in the usage of *community* had not eliminated the desire or the experience of mutuality-based, emotional relationships. By 1918 Americans had proven turn-of-the-century scholars such as Edward Ross wrong. Society had not killed community. The emotional bonds that had once been thought to exist only in small towns could also exist in American cities. Even the textbook authors described emotional relationships in the form of family and neighborhood connections. Like MacIver, they underscored the ways in which such intimate relationships could be seen as the building blocks of larger civil society.

What had changed were the locations and singularity of these relationships. No longer did Americans understand such intimate relationships to bind all members of a particular municipality. No longer did Americans assume that the borders of their hometowns or current cities marked the borders of their communities. Instead, as the textbook authors implicitly asserted and MacIver conceded, they found communal relationships with narrower subsets of residents in their places of residence, even as they nurtured ones that stretched far beyond the limits of those places.

As the textbook emphasized, this new notion of community engaged in a complicated dance with older notions that were linked to place and reciprocity. Americans who could claim membership in the middle or upper classes, the business world, or the political realm saw municipalities as communities. This belief, this dream, this imagined community of deep horizontal comradeship held sway with city leaders in St. Paul. Like the textbook authors, these men were able to conflate the disparate experiences of intimate community and utilitarian community present in their own lives—at least rhetorically. Most local elites operated on the assumption that this combination was available to all. After all, their own intimate communities were tied to the presence of at least a surface image of civic solidarity. Their relationship to the political and economic structures that organized cities and towns (the basis of much community discourse even in the 1918 textbook rendering) allowed them the privilege of holding three experiences and definitions of community in balance simultaneously: imagined place-based unity, narrow relationships within the city boundaries tied to shared demographic and social identities, and reciprocal community connections reaching across the nation and the world.

But the majority of St. Paulites who, intentionally or not, participated in the renegotiation and redefinition of community in the opening years of the twentieth century remained skeptical. Although many would have acknowledged that they shared some loose affinity with other residents of the city—a common "civic identity," to use Mary Wingerd's useful phrase—the cultural products they created and left behind suggest that there were other types of communal relationships that shaped their everyday lives in more immediately recognizable ways and that were narrower and broader than geography, even as imagined community played a role.[5] Sinclair Lewis highlighted this phenomenon in *Main Street,* published just two years after *Our Community.* Carol Kennicott's imagined unity with the city of St. Paul and its inhabitants occupied a category in her mind that was different from her connections with the guests at the Marburys' dinner party, with whom she shared more demographic attributes and closer intimacies. In modernizing St. Paul, cultural products helped produce and reaffirm this type of limited emotional community, even as culture became increasingly important as the basis for civic identity.

City leaders backed projects that proclaimed inclusiveness while they attempted to reinforce the possibility of a unified St. Paul, even if only in abstract form. To this end, Como and Phalen parks were painstakingly developed to include recreational spaces for all kinds of popular activities, and the City Auditorium stood, in classical glory, in the city center. Yet these efforts could not persuade all residents that the city was an intimate community in the ways in which narrower affinity-based groups were. As *Main Street* would illustrate, modern American cities were too large and too heterogeneous; it was the city's "generous indifference" that Carol longed for from the confines of Gopher Prairie. Even though she could imagine the city as a community, her own intimate communal experiences were with much smaller groups, and she was grateful for this fact. She could hide from and block out those residents whose gazes felt intrusive and whose lives did not align with her vision of self and city. Carol stands in for many St. Paul residents whose daily activities, choices, and decisions renegotiated and redefined what community would mean and look like in the modern era. Instead of working to reverse the trend, they embraced these more complex and less universal experiences of community to further their own public or private agendas.

A wide range of everyday activities in the cultural realm as well as the cultural production promoted by social, political, and economic leaders shaped and reflected these newer communal experiences. The creation of Union Hall and the popularity of neighborhood parks announced that St. Paulites were regularly interacting with people whose daily lives most closely matched their own, whether by force or by choice. Because of restrictive covenants, zoning decisions, and discrimination as well the growth of architecturally distinctive neighborhoods divided by economic status and ethnic identity, residents had become increasingly connected to those who lived closest to them. However, the use of buildings to mark these communal distinctions went beyond home construction, for during these years St. Paulites continued to frequent and even erect new ethnic parishes, despite the completion of a cathedral that Archbishop Ireland promoted as universal.

More explicit were the ways in which St. Paulites used photographs to reflect their ideas about community in their hometown. The choices of newspaper editors, especially those in charge of the city's white dailies, clarified the way in which their mental image of St. Paul resembled their own intimate communities (in this case, of other white, male, middle-, and upper-class residents) even as they purported to stand in for the city as a whole. Family photographs provided a counterpoint but often suggested the same disconnect between the diversity of the city and the uniformity of daily life. The Gardner and Dunn collections proclaim the narrow limits of each family's intimate communities, which were tied at least in part to racial prejudice and economic opportunities that were available only to whites. Race divided St. Paulites, but class and a relationship to the market were equally important, a message underscored by Aronovici's 1917 housing report. By highlighting the presence of the poor in St. Paul and presenting them as objects on display, it implicitly removed them from any possible inclusion in the real or imagined communities of the report's viewers. In and through each of these images, produced and reproduced, emerged a more complex narrative of who and what *community* meant.

The winter carnivals of 1916 and 1917 brought into focus the fundamental transformation of community that, by the end of the decade, had come to embrace and balance a definition that was tied to legal or civic responsibilities and an experience that was connected to narrower, limited, relations—sometimes intimate, sometimes reciprocal—that might reach far beyond the city's borders. Even as they noted the affinity-based connections that marked their own experiences of community, the carnival leadership believed mightily in their ability to convince St. Paulites that mere residence in the city meant they were members of the carnival community and, by extension, St. Paul. The complexity and limits of this new public understanding of the term was nowhere more explicit than in the *Pioneer Press*'s final editorial about the 1917 carnival, published the day after the event ended. The article referred to the carnival as a "great community affair" and spoke highly of a specific set of St. Paulites: those who had administered and funded the event, those who had let their employees participate, and all of the marchers and boosters, apparently regardless of place of origin.[6] By excluding certain segments of the St. Paul population while embracing residents of far distant municipalities, the organizers revealed their own adherence to an increasingly malleable understanding of community. One's place in the world of commerce, for instance, could help erase potential bifurcation of roles. Furthermore, the organizers highlighted the growing insignificance of locality in the formation of intimate communities even as they held on to a belief in cities as imagined communities that were worth defending.

By the end of the 1910s, the nation was undergoing dramatic shifts in immigration, migration, and the scale of industrial capitalism along with the attendant political, intellectual, and cultural responses. Communities had solidified across municipal boundaries while narrower ones had coalesced within city borders. As the carnivals demonstrated, city leaders welcomed their counterparts from across the nation because those men had become a community that shared interests, status, proximity to economic drivers, the rewards of industrial capitalism, and the worlds of business and leisure. In contrast, racial and ethnic minorities had never had the luxury of equating place and community in an uncomplicated way; for them, city limits had long been less important.

By 1918 many St. Paulites seemed familiar with this social order even if they were at times troubled by it. For marginalized groups, clear divisions could be preferable to the rhetoric of place-based unity. In the wake of the winter carnivals, for instance, the small business owners were angry not so much about being excluded from the community of the carnival as by the leadership's false statements regarding their inclusion in the first place. Like many other residents, they were well aware by 1917 that any claim to a singular, intimate, reciprocal, citywide community was imagined. These small business owners certainly identified as St. Paulites. They embraced their civic identity. But they and many people around the nation associated themselves with a locality on the basis of a more or less shared set of cultural norms that helped distinguish their hometown from all other places. This imagined community could coexist with other understandings of the term. As MacIver argued in 1917 and as the federal government suggested in its 1915 report on teaching civics, a sense that a given place was distinct from all others was central to any identification with that place.

Civic identity was pervasive in St. Paul and in many cities across the country in the opening years of the twentieth century.[7] But identifying with a city was not the same as experiencing or imagining that city as a community. Moreover, civic identity was not universal. For some segments of the St. Paul population, the city was a secondary affiliation and not one that was ever imagined as a community. When African Americans decided to throw their own winter fêtes, they implicitly asserted their understanding that the imagined city-as-community did not include them. By appropriating the slogans and the structure of the winter carnivals, they sent a message that they were aware of their alienation; and by involving African Americans from Minneapolis in their activities, they confirmed their own experiences of an affinity-based community that transcended place.

By 1920, then, St. Paulites had multiple, overlapping, and sometimes competing ideas about community. Intimate community was found most often and most powerfully in relationships with those who shared specific experiences and interests, even if imagined communities tied to more general commonalities also took up room in some people's minds or lives. These experiences of community did not ignore place, but the experience of mutuality and reciprocal relationships was both narrower and broader than the city limits and could require or produce more or less intense experiences of mutuality or reciprocity. St. Paulites identified with their city but only fostered place-based communal bonds with residents with whom they shared similar life experiences. They were willing, and increasingly able, to search for people who shared their views and life experiences but did not live within the boundaries of their hometown. The places that people identified with were no longer clearly demarcated geographic spaces. Increasingly they were defined by experience and relationships and free from municipal boundaries. Place and affinity were more closely related than place and municipality were.[8] And, critically, residents had a newer idea of community that did not require actual reciprocity but only imagined it.

The heterogeneity and size of cities made this understanding and pattern of communal relationships ubiquitous in urban America by 1920. Residents could segment themselves along racial, ethnic, and socioeconomic lines within a city's borders. Structural inequality, residential segregation, and the forces of industrial capitalism and its attendant hierarchies of power in modern American life meant that there were fewer compelling reasons for residents to try to bridge the gaps. As Ross had claimed, relationships in cities were driven by affinity; thus, in one respect, it is fair to say that he was right: urban life did reshape the meaning of community. But in a twist that Ross never imagined, community—especially a renegotiation of it for a modern age—also shaped urban life. Americans did not lose interest in intimate, communal relationships. Rather, they sought them out in their neighborhoods, at their churches, with business associates, and in conversations with fellow immigrants. They didn't lose interest in finding or creating community. They simply renegotiated what could be included in that community. They expanded the meaning of the term. For those who wished to or were able, it became possible to envision an imagined unity that, thanks to the "generous indifference" of city life, allowed for the possibility that everyone in the city was part of one's own world. This search for community, this renegotiation and reconceptualization of the concept and of the places and ways in which it formed and was defined, shaped life in America's cities as much as cities shaped what community would come to mean in the modern era.

Exploring how modernizing Americans produced, negotiated, redefined, and experienced community a century ago leads us to reevaluate the same quest in the period since. It also encourages reflection on the opportunities and challenges that the redefinition presents to Americans today. What becomes clear is that throughout the twentieth-century Americans lived in a world in which community, both the definition and the experience, was aligned simultaneously and complexly with both geography and affinity. In 1963 the sociologist Roland Warren reaffirmed that "mere similarity of interest does not in itself make a sociological community, nor does mere geographic proximity of residence." Rather, he explained, "the term community implies something both psychological and geographical."[9] This definition mirrored those of his early twentieth-century predecessors, and it has proven resilient to the present day. It is at the core of such astute insights as Pico Iyer's claim that the entire concept of belonging in a postindustrial, global, transnational world exists on a fine edge between the twin pulls of location and affinity.[10]

The complexity faced by modernizing Americans and the tensions it created in the early twentieth century remain surprisingly salient in the twenty-first. Conversely, what many twenty-first-century Americans think of as relatively new concerns turn out to have a long history. What is and should be meant by community, who is and is not embraced by the term, how to shore up the notion in an era of unprecedented technological and demographic change: these are both new and old concerns. A full century after the winter-carnival squabbles, Americans are still caught up in a quest to foster community in cities and towns across the nation. The rise of planned communities, the new urbanism of the late twentieth century, and even recent efforts to shop and eat locally remind us of the persistent desire to equate place with reciprocal relationships and intimate connections, even if those outcomes require excessive regulation and effort and raise additional questions along the way.[11]

The story told in *Modern Bonds* should also remind us of the persistent belief that products and activities in the broad cultural sphere (for instance, architecture, public art, city-based community reading programs, and city planning) are important tools for shaping an ideal of place-based community experiences. Yet most contemporary Americans, like their early twentieth-century counterparts, find themselves drawn into close communal relationships with those who share some particular interest, ideology, lifestyle, or demographic variable, whether or not they share a place of residence. Shared residence remains a significant marker of communal bonds, but economic, demographic, and social drivers have continued to organize cities in ways that collapse place with shared gender, class, racial, or ethnic identities. Thus, place-based communal bonds more often than not coexist alongside of or woven through a number of other networks and relationships that are also labeled *community*.

Moreover, the term itself remains ambiguous—and intentionally so. Today there are as many, if not more, types of relationships that are called communities as there were listed in the pages of *Our Community* a century ago. So many twenty-first-century Americans find themselves in the same quandary as the St. Paulites booking the early 1900s. In the end, it is this tension—the persistence of a desire to conflate community and place combined with a reality that community is often defined as a set of relationships disconnected from locale—that often creates the fear that community has been lost. Reclaiming the history of redefining community may help assuage these concerns even as it helps us view skeptically those situations in which community is invoked to obscure class, racial, gender, or other divisions.

What *Modern Bonds* establishes is that contemporary analyses and anxieties are both not new to our own era and emerged from the struggles of the early twentieth century. At that time, when an older understanding of community was seen to be under attack—in the midst of unprecedented change not unlike what contemporary observers claim for our own time—diverse Americans contested and renegotiated its meaning.

On the one hand, Americans maintained a spoken and unspoken desire to hold on to a sense of locality-based community. On the other hand, most Americans daily experienced community in less place-based forms. And the era saw a growing acceptance of both understandings to coexist, to fit into, and to continue to exist alongside one another.

Recognizing that locality, affinity, and community often seem to be at odds with one another in the twenty-first century does not mean that Americans should abandon efforts to shore up locality-based community. But before we claim that community itself no longer exists or that the only good community is local community, we might do well to look back at the lives of the subjects of this book. If we recognize that Americans' understanding of community in the industrial era was significantly transformed without becoming completely detached from place, we might be able to make sense of the current anxious response to even more complex and disentangled ideas of community in our postindustrial, global world.[12]

In turn-of-the-century St. Paul there was concern about the separation of locality from community, yet residents managed to find places and people with whom they could form intimate bonds. Sometimes those bonds were local, sometimes they were not, but, regardless, they were important to the people who shared them. What urban Americans did during the opening decades of the twentieth century was to find a way forward by reconceptualizing community for all who have come along since. By complicating what had seemed fixed, by embracing intersectionality, and by creating—intentionally or unintentionally through everyday activities in the cultural sphere—new experiences and definitions of the concept, they opened the possibility for something called community to persist in a modern (and even postmodern) era, even if that something was significantly different from earlier incarnations.

This is not to say that striving for a return to locality-based community is futile or that it has no merits. On the contrary, it might go far to help solve some of the nation's most pressing local problems, from funding civic projects, to improving education, to reducing crime, to creating opportunities for all to thrive. But the rhetoric of community has also proven to be compatible with policies and practices that are far from universally inclusive, so we must engage in honest, complex conversations about what it is we are talking about when we talk about community.

Such an approach is necessary (as this book's subjects were well aware) if we are to lessen the divisions among people of various economic classes, races, religions, and ethnic groups in both cities and the nation at large; for these divisions, as this book has shown, often emerge from structural inequalities. In the meantime, we need to note, reaffirm, and build upon the positive aspects and articulations of communal relationships wherever and among whomever they exist. This must be the basis for our own era's engagement with the concept.

Finally, like St. Paulites in the early 1900s, Americans in the twenty-first century use images, buildings, green spaces, and public festivals to mark the boundaries of and possibilities for our communities. This book, then, is more than a window to the past; it is a call for Americans to be aware of the influence that cultural products, in all their forms, can have on creating, destroying, transforming, or renegotiating definitions or experiences of community. Any serious commitment to reviving place-based community today will require municipal governments, city planners, neighborhood associations, and citizen activist groups to study how the things they build and destroy, capture on film or social media, and ignore in public and private add to or detract from a sense of belonging and connection among those who work, play, and live in a single geographic location. Furthermore, if cultural products are shaped exclusively by one or another group in a given locality, the result will be not a shoring up of place-based unity but the reinforcement of smaller, more limited, affinity-based communities within or extending beyond the municipality. Such communities certainly have merit; but if cultural production is to serve a unifying end, all groups must be part of the effort in a meaningful way. They must be involved from the beginning as co-creators. Otherwise, even if an imagined city-as-community is possible for some, it will cease to be possible for all. The St. Paulites at the center of this book knew this only too well.

The story this book tells—and its reminder both of how an earlier broadening of the concept of community was carried out and the implications of that broadening—is important in our own time. It has the power to both assuage current concerns about communal life and offer some insight to those of us invested in the task of crafting meaningful and just lives for all on scales both large and small.

ABBREVIATIONS

AA Archives of the Archdiocese of St. Paul and Minneapolis

DPR Archives of the Department of Parks and Recreation, St. Paul

JTD James Taylor Dunn and Family Papers, Minnesota Historical Society, St. Paul

JWGD J. W. G. Dunn Photograph Album Collection, Minnesota Historical Society, St. Paul

MNHS Minnesota Historical Society, St. Paul

RCHS Ramsey County Historical Society, St. Paul

SHPO State Historic Preservation Office, St. Paul

SPOSCA St. Paul Outdoor Sports Carnival Association Records, Minnesota Historical Society, St. Paul

SPC St. Peter Claver Parish Archives, St. Paul

NOTES

INTRODUCTION

1. "Minneapolis Ku Klux Clansmen Coming in Force," *Pioneer Press,* January 21, 1917, sec. 4.

2. Thomas Bender, *Community and Social Change in America,* (New Brunswick, NJ: Rutgers University Press, 1978).

3. Robert D. Putnam, *Bowling Alone: The Collapse and Revival of American Community* (New York: Simon and Schuster, 2000); Robert N. Bellah, Richard Madsen, William M. Sullivan, Ann Swidler, and Steven M. Tipton, *Habits of the Heart: Individualism and Commitment in American Life* (Berkeley: University of California Press, 1985). Key communitarian texts include the following works by Amatai Etzioni: *The Spirit of Community: Rights, Responsibilities, and the Communitarian Agenda* (New York: Crown, 1993); *Rights and the Common Good: The Communitarian Perspective* (New York: St. Martin's, 1995); and *The New Golden Rule: Community and Morality in a Democratic Society* (New York: Basic Books, 1996). Also see Amatai Etzioni, ed., *New Communitarian Thinking: Persons, Virtues, Institutions, and Communities* (Charlottesville: University Press of Virginia, 1995). Theda Skopcol is the most important exception to these general trends in the 1990s and early 2000s. In 1997 she responded to Putnam's assertion with a detailed look at alternative forms of relationship building and interdependence in the American past. Her findings led her to question his declension theory as well as his methodology. See "The Tocqueville Problem: Civic Engagement in American Democracy," *Social Science History* 21 (Winter 1997): 455–79.

4. See Bender, *Community and Social Change;* John C. Walsh and Steven High, "Rethinking the Concept of Community," *Social History* [Canada] 32, no. 64 (1999): 255–73; and Craig Calhoun, "Community: Toward a Variable Conceptualization for Comparative Research," *Social History* 5 (January 1980): 105–29, especially Calhoun's statement: "The relationship between community as a complex of social relationships and community as a complex of ideas and sentiments has been little explored" (107).

5. The fact that sociologists were preoccupied with identifying and recording change (not continuity) helped to fuel this perception.

6. Edward Alsworth Ross, *Social Control: A Survey of the Foundations of Order* (1901; reprint, Cleveland: Case Western Reserve University, 1969), 432.

7. Thinkers who offered variations on the complete declension theme included Robert Park, Jane Addams, Mary Parker Follett, and John Dewey.

8. Louis Wirth, "Urbanism as a Way of Life," in *On Cities and Social Life: Selected Papers,* ed. Albert J. Reiss, Jr. (Chicago: University of Chicago Press, 1964), 80. This image of the city drove urban sociology for years.

9. Much information in this paragraph has been culled from Bender's work. The moment of declension in American communities has been set at various points by various scholars. Some claim the breakdown began shortly after the founding of the original colonial settlements, while others implicate the late nineteenth century, the 1920s, or even the years after World War II. See Bernard Baylin, *The New England Merchants in the 18th Century* (Cambridge: Harvard University Press, 1959); Stephen Therstrom, *Poverty and Progress: Social Mobility in a Nineteenth Century City* (Cambridge: Harvard University Press, 1980); Robert Wiebe, *The Search for Order, 1877–1920* (New York: Hill and Wang, 1967); Roland Warren, *The Community in America* (Chicago: Rand McNally, 1963); Maurice Stein, *The Eclipse of Community* (New York: Harper, 1964); and Alan Ehrenhaldt, *The Lost City: Discovering the Forgotten Virtues of Community in the Chicago of the 1950s* (New York: Basic Books, 1995).

10. Bender, *Community and Social Change,* 5–11. While nodding to the process of problematizing community as a historical concept, Bender did not erase the community-society polarity. In his account, community persisted in modernizing America but was largely independent of other, often more expansive, networks or relationships.

11. Craig Calhoun, "History, Anthropology, and the Study of Communities: Some Problems in Macfarlane's Proposal," *Social History* 3, no. 3 (1978): 368; Calhoun, "Community: Toward a Variable Conceptualization," 108–9. For the line of thought to which Calhoun is responding, see Max Weber, *The Theory of Social and Economic Organization,* trans. A. M. Henderson and Talcott Parsons, ed. Talcott Parsons (New York: Oxford University Press, 1947).

12. Carroll Smith-Rosenberg, "The Female World of Love and Ritual: Relations between Women in Nineteenth-Century America," *Signs* 1 (August 1975):1–29; Herbert Gutman, *Work, Culture, and Society in Industrializing America* (New York: Knopf, 1976).

13. For a concise overview and critique of this rhetoric, see Miranda Joseph, *Against the Romance of Community* (Minneapolis: University of Minnesota Press, 2002). She reminds us that feminist and poststructuralist scholars have made clear that there is "racism, sexism, and violence entailed in explicit or implicit attempts to constitute nations and liberal states as communities" (viii).

14. Benedict Anderson, *Imagined Communities: Reflections on the Origins and Spread of Nationalism,* rev. ed. (London: Verso, 1991). While Anderson discussed the nation, I contend that his discussion of a perceived, deep, horizontal comradeship

among those not personally known to one another is a useful framework for understanding the renegotiation of relationships among people in smaller geopolitical entities and among affinity group members far removed from one another during the expanding, industrial, modernizing era. His claim that cultural production (for him, the circulation of print) is an essential ingredient in producing and representing such imagined communities is instructive for understanding the mechanisms through which the notion of geo-referenced community could be maintained and challenged in modernizing St. Paul.

15. See Bender, *Community and Social Change;* Calhoun, "Community: Toward a Variable Conceptualization"; and Richard R. Beeman, "The New Social History and the Search for 'Community' in Colonial America," *American Quarterly* 29 (Autumn 1977): 19–38. Network theory, drawn from anthropology and made popular in the 1930s by Robert Redfield, "deliberately seeks to examine the way in which people may relate to one another in terms of several different normative frameworks at one and the same time and how a person's behaviors might in part be understood in light of the pattern of coincidence of these frameworks" (J. Clyde Mitchell, "The Concept and Use of Social Networks," in *Social Networks in Urban Situations: Analyses of Personal Relationships in Central African Towns*, ed. J. Clyde Mitchell [Manchester, UK: Manchester University Press, 1969], 49). According to Barry Wellman and Barry Leighton, network theory lets a scholar approach data without prejudice and allows for the possibility that any social aggregate is a community, or not ("Networks, Neighborhoods, and Communities: Approaches to the Study of the Community Question," *Urban Affairs Quarterly* 14 [March 1979]: 363–90). In short, as Walsh and High write in "Rethinking the Concept of Community," by challenging historians to see community "as a social process predicated on relationships," network theory "place[s] community in the social spaces of everyday interactions and exchanges [and] communal boundaries [are] defined by the extent of these social networks" (260–61).

16. Walsh and High, "Rethinking the Concept of Community," 262.

17. The idea of imagined communities is relevant here but is not the sum of my discussion or the experience of St. Paul.

18. See Ross, *Social Control,* 432, 434.

19. Ross's formulation of the problem of community in cities was the model for other scholarly work in sociology, including Wirth's "Urbanism as a Way of Life," which remains important and recapitulates many of Ross's assertions. On the general impact of Ross, see Julius Weinberg, *Edward Alsworth Ross and the Sociology of Progressivism* (Madison: University of Wisconsin Press, 1972), 89.

20. See Jean Quandt, *From the Small Town to the Great Community: The Social Thought of Progressive Intellectuals* (New Brunswick, NJ: Rutgers University Press, 1970), 10. Addams's work at Hull House exemplified this trend. See Jane Addams, *Twenty Years at Hull House* (New York: Macmillan, 1910), for a sense of her belief in the power of neighborhood-based reciprocity and capacity building.

21. See Jane Addams, *Newer Ideals of Peace* (New York: Macmillan, 1907). For a brief explanation of how Addams connected local ethnic neighboring and global humanitarianism in that book, see Marilyn Fischer, "Cosmic Patriotism and Spiritual Internationalism: Jane Addams's Newer Ideals of Peace," *Newsletter of the Society for Historians of the Gilded Age and Progressive Era* 26, no. 1 (2006): 1. Also see Mary Parker Follett, "Community Is a Process," *Philosophical Review* 28, no. 6 (1919): 576–88.

22. See James Shortridge, *The Middle West: Its Meaning in American Culture* (Lawrence: University of Kansas Press, 1989), 34.

23. Ibid., 33–35.

24. Ibid., 8.

25. Quoted in Jon K. Lauck, *The Lost Region: Toward a Revival of Midwestern History* (Iowa City: University of Iowa Press, 2013), 82.

26. Ibid., 28, 87. Lauck's work follows that of Cayton and his collaborators, particularly Andrew R. L. Cayton and Peter S. Onuf, *The Midwest and the Nation: Rethinking the History of an American Region* (Bloomington: Indiana University Press, 1990); and Richard Sisson, Christian Zacher. and Andrew R. L. Cayton, eds., *The American Midwest: An Interpretive Encyclopedia* (Bloomington: Indiana University Press, 2006). I agree with Lauck's entreaties to revisit midwestern history and culture but reject his critiques of recent historiography and his emphasis on regional identity as such.

27. In this book, I build on the foundation set by a number of Midwest-focused works: Lizabeth Cohen, *Making a New Deal: Industrial Workers in Chicago, 1991–1939* (New York: Cambridge University Press, 1990); William Cronon, *Nature's Metropolis: Chicago and the Great West* (New York: Norton, 1991); Jon Gjerde, *The Minds of the West: The Ethnocultural Revolution of the Middle West, 1830–1917* (Chapel Hill: University of North Carolina Press, 1997); Thomas J. Sugrue, *Origins of the Urban Crisis: Race and Inequality in Post-War Detroit* (Princeton: Princeton University Press, 1996); Catherine McNichol Stock, *Main Streets in Crisis: The Great Depression and the Old Middle Class on the Northern Plains* (Chapel Hill: University of North Carolina Press, 1992); and Richard White, *The Middle Ground: Indians, Empires, and Republics in the Great Lakes Region, 1650–1815* (New York: Cambridge University Press, 1991). Since 2000, key works include Adam Arenson, *The Great Heart of the Republic: St. Louis and the Cultural Civil War* (Cambridge: Harvard University Press, 2011); David Blanke, *Sowing the American Dream: How Consumer Culture Took Root in the American Midwest* (Athens: Ohio University Press, 2000); Patrick J. Carr and Maria J. Kefalas, *Hollowing Out the Middle: The Rural Brain Drain and What It Means for America* (Boston: Beacon, 2009); Kathleen Mapes, *Sweet Tyranny: Migrant Labor, Industrial Agriculture, and Imperial Politics* (Urbana: University of Illinois Press, 2009); Jim Norris, *North for the Harvest: Mexican Workers, Growers, and the Sugar Beet Industry* (St. Paul: Minnesota Historical Society Press, 2009); Daniel K. Richter, *Facing East from Indian Country: A Native History of Early America* (Cambridge: Harvard

University Press, 2001); Timothy B. Spears, *Chicago Dreaming: Midwesterners and the City, 1871–1919* (Chicago: University of Chicago Press, 2005); and Wayne A. Weigand, *Main Street Public Library: Community Places and Reading Spaces in the Rural Heartland, 1876–1956* (Iowa City: University of Iowa Press, 2011).

28. Rich Arpi, personal correspondence with the author, January 9, 2017.

29. Katherine Spear, *St. Paul Foreign Born Population Studies* (St. Paul: St. Paul Planning Board, 1934), MNHS.

30. In the urban North, the black population rarely exceeded 5 percent of the total population. A comparison of the twelve largest midwestern cities in 1910 shows that the percentages ranged from a high of 9.3 percent in Indianapolis down to 0.3 percent in Milwaukee. Only four were higher than 5 percent. Even in Chicago the percentage of blacks among the city's residents was 1.9 in 1900, 2.0 in 1910, and 4.1 in 1920. See Jon C. Teaford, *Cities of the Heartland: The Rise and Fall of the Industrial Midwest* (Bloomington: Indiana University Press, 1993), 189; Joe William Trotter, Jr., *Black Milwaukee: The Making of an Industrial Proletariat, 1915–1945* (Urbana: University of Illinois Press, 1985), tabs. 1.1 and 2.1; and Alan H. Spear, *Black Chicago: The Making of an Urban Ghetto, 1890–1920* (Chicago: University of Chicago Press, 1967), 12. On St. Paul, see David Taylor, "Pilgrim's Progress: Black St. Paul and the Making of an Urban Ghetto, 1870–1930" (Ph.D. diss., University of Minnesota, 1977), tab. 1.

31. For an overview of this era, see William D. Green, *Degrees of Freedom: The Origins of Civil Rights in Minnesota, 1865–1912* (Minneapolis: University of Minnesota Press, 2015), Kindle edition. On discrimination (including a 1909 attempt by white parents to segregate an elementary school) ibid., loc. 5681. On tensions between the city's black leaders and others (particularly recently arrived southern blacks), see ibid., loc. 5153. Also see David Vassar Taylor, *African Americans in Minnesota* (St. Paul: Minnesota Historical Society Press, 2002); David V. Taylor and Paul Clifford Larson, *Cap Wigington: An Architectural Legacy in Ice and Stone* (St. Paul: Minnesota Historical Society Press, 2002); and "William 'Billy' Williams Served 14 Minnesota Governors," *African American Registry*, http://www.aaregistry.org.

32. See Jackson Lears, *The Rebirth of the Nation: The Making of Modern America, 1877–1920* (New York: HarperCollins, 2009); Leon Fink, *The Long Gilded Age: American Capitalism and the Lessons of a New World Order* (Philadelphia: University of Pennsylvania Press, 2014); and Nell Irwin Painter, *Standing at Armageddon: A Grassroots History of the Progressive Era* (New York: Norton, 2008).

33. Mary Lethert Wingerd, *Claiming the City: Politics, Faith, and the Power of Place in St. Paul* (Ithaca: Cornell University Press, 2001).

34. Walsh and High, "Rethinking the Concept of Community," 269. Note that Bender, in *Community and Social Change*), signaled this problem as early as 1978, when he made clear that more scholarship on the history of community would only be possible if and when historians began to look at sources and patterns beyond the census tract., 124.

35. For preliminary work in this area, see Francis Rothenhoeffer, "'The Clustered

Spires of Frederick': The Cultural Creation of Local Community Identity, 1745–1995" (Ph.D., diss., George Washington University, 1996;) and Sally Griffith, *Home Town News: William Allen White and the "Emporia Gazette"* (New York: Oxford University Press, 1989).

36. Other transformational, interdisciplinary works that use this approach and are models for my work include Rhys Isaac, *The Transformation of Virginia 1740–1790* (Chapel Hill: University of North Carolina Press, 1999); John Kasson, *Amusing the Million: Coney Island at the Turn of the Century* (New York: Hill and Wang, 1978); Karal Ann Marling, *Wall-to-Wall America: Post Office Murals in the Great Depression* (Minneapolis: University of Minnesota Press, 2000); and Courtney Baker, *Humane Insight: Looking at Images of African American Suffering and Death* (Urbana: University of Illinois Press, 2015).

37. As Joseph has argued in *Against the Romance of Community*, community's expansive definition and consistently positive meaning means it can support any number of competing political, ideological and economic agendas. Her critique of the relationship between capitalism and community is a call, once again, for a critical rethinking of any simplistic approach to divorcing community from capitalism or modernity or identity or place as well as an opportunity to consider what links exist between modernizing urban America and the newer, more expansive, yet limited (and limiting) understanding of community common among everyday Americans and leading scholars, public intellectuals, politicians, and the middle class as a whole.

38. Marc J. Dunkelman, *The Vanishing Neighbor: The Transformation of American Community* (New York: Norton, 2014).

39. J. D. Vance, *Hillbilly Elegy: A Memoir of a Family and Culture in Crisis* (New York: HarperCollins, 2016); Arlie Russell Hochschild, *Strangers in Their Own Land: Anger and Mourning on the American Right* (New York: New Press, 2016).

40. Elena Pulcini, "Rethinking Community in a Global Age," *IRIS*, April 3, 2010, 87–117. Also important is Pico Iyer, *The Global Soul: Jet Lag, Shopping Malls, and the Search for Home* (New York: Knopf, 2000).

41. Michael McGerr, *A Fierce Discontent: The Rise and Fall of the Progressive Movement in America, 1870–1920* (New York: Free Press, 2009).

42. Sinclair Lewis, *Main Street* (1920; reprint, New York: Bantam, 1996), 20, 503.

43. See Joseph, *Against the Romance of Community;* and Miranda Joseph, "Community," in *Keywords for American Cultural Studies*, 2nd ed., ed. Bruce Burgett and Glen Handler (New York: New York University Press, 2014).

CHAPTER 1: "GENEROUS INDIFFERENCE"

1. Sinclair Lewis, *Main Street*, ed. Morris Dickstein (1920; reprint, New York: Bantam, 1996), 121.

2. Ibid., 114.

3. Hamlin Garland's *Main Travelled Roads* (1891), Theodore Dreiser's *Sister Carrie* (1900), Edgar Lee Masters's *Spoon River Anthology* (1915), Willa Cather's *The Song of*

the Lark (1915), and Sherwood Anderson's *Winesburg, Ohio* (1919) also anticipated or were part of the revolt from the village school.

4. See Thomas Bender, *Community and Social Change in America* (New Brunswick, NJ: Rutgers University Press, 1978); and Herbert Gutman, *Work, Culture, and Society in Industrializing America* (New York: Knopf, 1976).

5. Booth Tarkington addressed the topic in *The Gentleman from Indiana* (1899) and *The Magnificent Ambersons* (1918). See also Dwight W. Hoover, "Social Science Looks at the American Small Town," in *The Small Town in America: A Multidisciplinary Revisit,* ed. Hans Bartens and Theo D'haen (Amsterdam: VU University Press, 1995), 19.

6. See Page Smith, *As a City upon a Hill: The Town in American Literature* (New York: Knopf, 1966), particularly 258–83. American literature of the nineteenth century was full of celebratory images of small-town life, which many new urbanites held on to as they encountered the vastly different life in American cities. However, just as "urban businessmen began to applaud the town as the embodiment of American virtues, of the Protestant ethic of thrift, industry, piety, hard work, and rugged individualism, the writers began to take this same complacency and use it to expose the crassness, greed, complacency and self-righteousness of American middle-class culture." The idealization of the small town was in full force by the end of the nineteenth century, and it "did not truly become the object of the novelist's attack until it had been largely integrated into the dominant urban culture" (266).

7. Quoted in James M. Hutchisson, *The Rise of Sinclair Lewis, 1920–1930* (University Park, PA: Pennsylvania State University Press, 1996), 12.

8. Meredith Nicholson, *The Valley of Democracy* (New York: Scribner's, 1918), 8, 15.

9. Edward Alsworth Ross, *Social Control: A Survey of the Foundations of Order* (1901; reprint, Cleveland: Case Western Reserve University, 1969), 432. Although Ross was the first major American scholar to take up this issue, the German scholar Ferdinand Tönnies was the first scholarly figure to raise questions about the viability of community in the urban centers of the industrialized world. He coined the now-common terms *gemeinschaft* (community) and *gesellschaft* (society). Tönnies's formulation of this division turned on the idea that, in large urban centers, the intimate, face-to-face relationships that had defined and organized rural societies for centuries would be broken down. However, he acknowledged that new forms of community could and would come to replace them. While Tönnies wrote specifically about Germany, his concerns were felt in the United States. On Tönnies, see Bender, *Community and Social Change,* 32–34.

10. Ross, *Social Control,* 432.

11. Ibid., 434.

12. Ibid.

13. Bender, *Community and Social Change,* 38.

14. On communitarians, see Jean Quandt, *From the Small Town to the Great*

Community: The Social Thought of Progressive Intellectuals (New Brunswick, NJ: Rutgers University Press, 1970). Also see Marilyn Fischer, "Cosmic Patriotism and Spiritual Internationalism: Jane Addams's *Newer Ideals of Peace*," *Newsletter of the Society for Historians of the Gilded Age and Progressive Era* 16, no. 1 (2006): 1; and Mary Parker Follett, "Community Is a Process," *Philosophical Review* 28, no.6 (1919): 576–88.

15. Robert MacIver, *Community: A Sociological Study*, 4th ed. (1917; reprint, London: Cass, 1970).

16. On the relationship between associations and community, MacIver acknowledges that "no student of the actual social life of the present can help being struck by the enormous number of associations of every kind . . . which today more than ever before enrich communal life" (ibid., 23).

17. MacIver articulates the nuanced difference between community and association in ibid., chap. 2. Here, I argue that by 1920 abstraction, instrumentality, and affinity all constituted critical (and often overlapping) elements of intimate community.

18. M. P. Follett, "Community Is a Process," *Philosophical Review* 28, no. 6 (1919): 583.

19. Lewis, *Main Street*, 521.

20. See Martin Bucco, *Main Street: The Revolt of Carol Kennicott* (New York: Twayne, 1993), chap. 1.

21. Mark Schorer (among others) also makes this assertion in *Sinclair Lewis: An American Life* (New York: McGraw-Hill, 1961).

22. Grace Hegger Lewis, *With Love from Gracie: Sinclair Lewis, 1912–1925* (New York: Harcourt, Brace, 1951), 333.

23. Schorer's massive biography has been the basis for much of the scholarship that has followed. Yet the book is often criticized for its negative and sometimes even damaging presentation of Lewis. For a more recent biography, see Richard R. Lingeman, *Sinclair Lewis: Rebel from Main Street* (New York: Random House, 2002). Also see George Killough, introduction, in Sinclair Lewis, *Main Street* (New York: Penguin, 2008), 5–13.

24. Schorer, *Sinclair Lewis*, 3, 5–6.

25. Lewis, *With Love from Gracie*, 88.

26. August Darleth, *Three Literary Men: A Memoir of Sinclair Lewis, Sherwood Anderson, Edgar Lee Masters* (New York: Candlelight, 1963), 11–12.

27. Schorer, *Sinclair Lewis*, 108.

28. Schorer gives a brief account of Helcion Hall in *Sinclair Lewis*, 112–14. For a first-person account of life there, see Edith Summers Kelley's retrospective in Mary Byrd Davis, "Helcion Hall: An Experiment in Living," *Kentucky Review* 1, no. 3 (1980): 29–51. Kelley spent six months at Helcion Hall and was briefly engaged to Lewis.

29. Schorer, *Sinclair Lewis*, 112–13. The residents included Columbia University

professors as well as suffragettes, editors, and freelance writers. They were joined periodically by William James, Emma Goldman, and John Dewey, among other well-known guests.

30. Quoted in ibid., 115. Schorer does not offer citations for his quotations.

31. Ibid., 234.

32. Lewis, *With Love from Gracie*, 96. Although *Main Street* was published in 1920, Lewis seems to have been conceptualizing for about fifteen years, ever since his return to Sauk Centre from Yale. After reading Garland's *Main Traveled Roads,* he realized that he too, had a novel in him—a novel about "the 'village virus'—. . . how it getteth into the veins of a good man & true," as he recorded in a diary entry dated September 13, 1905. On this process and for the citation, see Bucco, *Main Street*, vii; Lingeman, *Sinclair Lewis*, 24; and Schorer, *Sinclair Lewis*, 93–98, 100–102. The 1916 visit seems to have solidified the project.

33. Quoted in Schorer, *Sinclair Lewis*, 238.

34. An announcement about a public reading of his play even appeared in the society pages of St. Paul's largest daily paper, the *Pioneer Press,* January 18, 1918.

35. Schorer, *Sinclair Lewis,* 249.

36. On Lewis's moves and travel itinerary during this period, see Bucco, *Main Street*, xi–xiii.

37. Schorer details the many views on this argument in *Sinclair Lewis,* 251–53.

38. See Smith, *As a City upon a Hill.*

39. Sinclair Lewis, "Self Portrait, Berlin, August 1927," in *The Man From Main Street: Selected Essays and Other Writings, 1904–1950,* ed. Harry E. Maule and Melville H. Crane (New York: Random House, 1953), 49.

40. Darleth, *Three Literary Men,* 22.

41. Dickstein's introduction to Lewis, *Main Street* (xvii) and Bucco's *Main Street* (3–5) make this point. The latter points out that the years of Lewis's coming of age exactly mirror Carol Kennicott's (3).

42. In 1920 Sinclair Lewis was an average talent who had produced works of limited literary note, although reviewers applauded his fresh new voice. This changed with the 1920 publication of *Main Street,* which catapulted him into the spotlight and marked the beginning of his uneasy relationship with the critical literary world. On this relationship, Bucco, *Main Street,* chap. 3; Martin Bucco, ed., *Critical Essays on Sinclair Lewis* (Boston: Hall, 1986); intro; and Hutchisson, *Rise of Sinclair Lewis,* intro.

43. For two approaches to the issue of dividing realism from naturalism, see Donald Pizer, ed., *The Cambridge Companion to American Realism and Naturalism: Howells to London* (Cambridge: Cambridge University Press, 1985), intro; and Eric J. Sundquist, ed., *American Realism: New Essays* (Baltimore: Johns Hopkins University Press, 1982), intro.

44. Quoted in Sundquist, *American Realism,* 13. Also see Pizer, *Cambridge Companion,* 8.

45. The term *realism* often refers to literature produced between the end of the Civil War and up to World War I. Some argue, however, that American realism began with Dreiser's *Sister Carrie* in 1900 and ended with either John Dos Passos or Ernest Hemingway three decades later. Still others see it as an influence throughout the twentieth century. See Sundquist, *American Realism*, 4.

46. H. L. Mencken, "Portrait of an American Citizen," *Smart Set* 64 (January 1921): 138–44.

47. Pizer, *Cambridge Companion*, 9.

48. This is Bucco's wording in *Critical Essays*, 4.

49. T. K. Whipple, review of *Main Street*, *New Republic*, April 15, 1925, 3–5.

50. Carl Van Doren, *Sinclair Lewis: A Biographical Sketch with a Bibliography by Harvey Taylor* (1933; reprint, Port Washington, NY: Kennikat, 1969), 22.

51. Pizer, *Cambridge Companion*, 10.

52. In the mid-1940s, John T. Flanagan asserted that, while there were some "solid merits of the novel, . . . the enormous and sudden success of *Main Street* was partly circumstantial" ("A Long Way to Gopher Prairie: Sinclair Lewis' Apprenticeship," *Southwest Review* 32 [Autumn 1947]: 403–13).

53. Alfred Kazin celebrates the work of Lewis (*Main Street*) and Sherwood Anderson (*Winesburg, Ohio*), identifying them as part of a group he calls the "'new realists' who brought new life into the American novel by dramatizing [contemporary changes] in terms of common experience" (*On Native Grounds: An Interpretation of American Prose Literature* [1942; reprint, Garden City, NY: Doubleday 1956], 162, 164). Continuing in this vein, George J. Becker that the multitude of themes in *Main Street* was one of its chief problems, yet, "whatever the deficiencies of *Main Street* as a novel . . . it is important as the original trumpeting of Lewis' discontent, as his first gesture of flinging open every window and door and letting the fresh air of the prairie turn smugness and conventionality head over heels" ("Sinclair Lewis: Apostle to the Philistines," *American Scholar* 21 [Autumn 1952]: 423–32).

54. In the age of the New Criticism, interest in and scholarship about both Lewis and the novel tapered off, and the latter's reputation suffered. As late as 1986, Joel Fisher was able to begin an article with the words "Sinclair Lewis' critical reputation could not easily be lower than it is at present" ("Sinclair Lewis and the Diagnostic Novel: *Main Street* and *Babbit*," *Journal of American Studies* 20, no. 3 [1986]: 421–33).

55. Not all scholars agree that there has been such a dramatic shift in the scholarship on realism. For instance, Amy Kaplan's *The Social Construction of American Realism* (Chicago: University of Chicago Press, 1988) helped bring new attention to realist works, even in an era that she believed was still dismissive of realism. Both Lewis and *Main Street* have benefited from a renewed interest in the genre in the 1980s and 1990s, evidenced in an annotated bibliography in Hutchisson's *Rise of Sinclair Lewis*, 202–40. Other important essay collections are Michael Connoughton, ed., *Sinclair Lewis at 100: Papers Presented at a Centennial Conference* (St. Cloud, MN: St. Cloud State University, 1985); Bucco, *Critical Essays on Sinclair Lewis*; and James

Hutchisson, *Sinclair Lewis: New Essays in Criticism* (Troy, NY: Whitston, 1997). All explore *Main Street* through a variety of lenses, including feminist theory, modernism, transnationalism, gender, cross-regional identities, and connections to the visual arts. Also see Bucco, *Main Street: The Revolt.*

56. Lewis, *Main Street*, 12.

57. In *Main Street Blues: The Decline of Small Town America* (Columbus: Ohio State University Press, 1998), Richard O. Davies makes clear that, in the half-century following the Civil War, leading citizens and merchants in small towns enthusiastically embraced the new capitalist ethos driving the larger American economy and shaping its culture. As he writes, small towns had begun to embrace "the crass, bottom-line aggressiveness of the Gilded Age" (56).

58. Lewis, *Main Street*, 12.

59. Ibid., 13.

60. Ibid., 12.

61. "In the community," Ross argued, "the secret of order is not so much control as concord" (*Social Control*, 432). As he sees it, community is maintained by virtue of the fact that there is agreement among and between those individuals who make up the community. Thus, if a geographic location were made up of people with diverse worldviews, community would be hard to come by.

62. Lewis, *Main Street*, 19.

63. Ibid., 70.

64. Ibid., 48.

65. Ibid.

66. Ibid., 60.

67. Ibid., 103.

68. Ibid.

69. Ibid., 109–10.

70. Ibid., 309.

71. Ibid., 115, 117

72. Ibid., 117.

73. Ibid., 124.

74. Ibid., 286.

75. Ibid., 285.

76. Ibid., 373.

77. Ibid., 98

78. Ibid., 130. Caren J. Town writes about this scene in "'A Scarlet Tanager on an Ice Floe': Women, Men, and History on *Main Street*," in *Sinclair Lewis: New Essays in Criticism*, ed. James Hutchisson (Troy NY: Whitson, 1997), 80–93.

79. Lewis, *Main Street*, 130.

80. Ibid.

81. Ibid., 17. Mendota is the name of the original Native American settlement in the area that would become St. Paul. To the Mdewakanton people, Mendota was the center of the world. American explorers and military personnel began settling

the area in the 1830s, and it became the general site of the first permanent Euro-American settlement in Minnesota. By the early twentieth century, Mendota was the name of a separate municipality across the Mississippi River from St. Paul.

82. Ibid., 18.

83. Ibid.

84. I categorize Carol's St. Paul as an "imagined community" because it is similar in form to the imagined communities of nations that Benedict Anderson describes in *Imagined Communities: Reflections on the Origins and Spread of Nationalism,* rev. ed. (London: Verso, 1991), 6–7.

85. Lewis, *Main Street,* 130. As I will discuss later in the book, one of the most impoverished immigrant areas of St. Paul in 1900–20 was known as Swede Hollow.

86. Ibid., 131.

87. Ibid.

88. Ibid., 132.

89. Ibid., 12.

90. Here, Lewis alludes to the research approach to cities that marked the work of turn-of-the-century sociologists at the University of Chicago and elsewhere. As chapter 2 will discuss, there was a major effort to observe, catalog, and eradicate poverty and poor housing in St. Paul in 1917.

91. Lewis, *Main Street,* 18.

CHAPTER 2: IMAGES AND IMAGINING

1. Eastman Kodak led the trend in providing inexpensive camera technology, introducing the Brownie camera in 1900. Incorporated in 1899, by the early 1900s the St. Paul Camera Club occupied the top floor of a downtown building, and its membership records list a hundred individuals in good standing. The club provided space and supplies for developing images, offered opportunities for exhibiting work, and arranged outings to scenic spots in the area. See the pamphlet "The First Hundred Years of the St. Paul Camera Club," pamphlet collection, MNHS.

2. So central were photographs to the construction of communal identities in this era that they even factor into *Main Street*—for instance, in helping to persuade Carol that a desirable life awaits her in Gopher Prairie. When Will is wooing her, he shows her pastoral images of the Minnesota countryside and a photograph of a "sagging woman" and a "bedraggled" baby. He points out that Carol can help them if she marries him. Toward the end of the novel, as he tries to convince her to return to Gopher Prairie after her year in Washington, he "tosse[s] over to her thirty prints of Gopher Prairie and the country about." The tactic works. As Lewis tells us, "Without defense, she was thrown into it." The emotional power of the images even allows her to overcome her critique of Will's predictable methods. See Sinclair Lewis, *Main Street* (1920; reprint, New York: Bantam, 1996), 20, 503.

3. John Berger, "Understanding a Photograph," in *Classic Essays in Photography,* ed. Alan Trachtenberg (New Haven, CT: Leete's Island, 1980), 292. In Berger's

estimation photographs celebrate "neither [an] event itself nor the faculty of sight in itself." Rather, "a photograph is already a message about the events it records" (ibid.).

4. Laura Wexler asserts that "photography was part of the master narrative that created and cemented cultural and political inequalities of race and class" ("Seeing Sentiment: Photography, Race, and the Innocent Eye," in *The Familial Gaze*, ed. Marianne Hirsch [Hanover, NH: University Press of New England, 1999], 252).

5. American scholars, drawing from the semiotic theory of Barthes, have written extensively about the cultural work that photographs do, arguing persuasively that the cultural context in which a photograph is produced and received shapes its message and meaning. See Roland Barthes, "The Photographic Message," in *Photography in Print: Writings from 1816 to the Present*, ed. Vicki Goldberg (New York: Simon and Schuster, 1981) 521–33; Alan Trachtenberg, *Reading American Photographs: Images as History, Matthew Brady to Walker Evans* (New York: Hill and Wang, 1989), xiii–xviii; Alan Sekula, "On the Invention of Photographic Meaning," in Goldberg, *Photography in Print*, 452–573; and Marianne Hirsch, *Family Frames: Photography, Narrative, and Post Memory* (Cambridge, MA: Harvard University Press, 1997). From the decision to take a picture of a certain subject, to its composition, to whether to disseminate it or mount it in an album, to whether to add text to an image, to which audience receives the image, each decision places a photo within one or another cultural context. Trying to discern the nature of community from photographs requires sensitivity to all of these decision points and their implications, many of which the photographers most likely never imagined.

6. The series of images I explore in the chapter shed particular light on the myriad experiences of community while leaving open the possibility of more detailed explorations of each as an individual group. I chose to draw most of my evidence from the holdings of the Minnesota Historical Society, in part due to ease of access (their holdings are in the public domain), in part because a statewide agency can offer a more varied and representative collection of images than a smaller, more specialized archive can. The society's holdings include professional studio portraits, family photographs and albums, social reform photography, and a complete collection of St. Paul newspapers from 1900 to 1920.

7. I use *album* here to refer to both albums and collections of photographs belonging to a family but not necessarily preserved in album form. There are eight family albums in the MNHS collections but many more collections of family photographs that are not bound in formal albums.

8. Hirsch asserts that the importance of studying family photographs lies in the fact that "when we photograph ourselves in a familial setting, we do not do so in a vacuum." Rather, "we respond to dominant mythologies of family life, to conceptions we have inherited . . . [because] the familial gaze is always inflected by numerous other institutional gazes." She suggests that this is true because family photographs are uniquely located "precisely in the space of contradiction between the myth of the ideal family and the lived reality of family life" (*Family Frames*, xii,

xvi, 8). In "'Sweet it is to scan . . .': Personal Photographs and Popular Photography" (in *Photography: A Critical Introduction*, ed. Liz Wells [London: Routledge, 1997]), Patricia Holland writes that "personal photographs . . . are made specifically to portray the individual or the group to whom they belong *as they would wish to be seen* and as they have chosen to show themselves to one another. . . . The photographs that we keep for ourselves . . . are treasured . . . for their *context* and for the part they play in confirming and challenging the identity . . . of their users" (107). On the insights to be gained from analyzing what and who is not pictured in family photographs, see Ellie Reichlin, "'Reading' Family Photographs: A Contextual Analysis of the Codman Photographic Collection," *Old-Time New England* 71, no. 258 (1981): 115–49; and John Kouwenhoven, *Half a Truth Is Better Than None: Some Unsystematic Conjectures about Art, Disorder, and American Experience* (Chicago: University of Chicago Press, 1982).

9. Hirsch takes up this issue as she explores whether or not the mere inclusion of otherness in her own family album indicates an authentic broadening of the boundary of family or truly represents a total embracing of the other or the outsider (*Family Frames*, 47–53).

10. I found seven other collections of family photographs that would have been options for analysis, including two that belonged to St. Paul women. However, as an African American family, the Gardners provide a dramatic contrast to the Dunns, who exemplify the dominant demographic group in St. Paul. Subsequently, the similarities between the two collections come into sharper relief. Hirsch's approach to exploring the anomalous images in family albums shaped my approach to these collections, as did her meditation on a white family's album, which includes pictures of an African American boy they hosted for a summer (*Family Frames*, 41–47).

11. I refer to "Rondo neighborhood," "Rondo district," or just "Rondo" because those names have relevance to today's African American community in St. Paul. Scholars have pointed out, however, that the name was applied to the area later in the twentieth century, after the era under study here. It was located on the city's western plateau, centered around lower St. Anthony, Central, and Carroll avenues. It eventually expanded westward along Rondo and St. Anthony avenues toward Lexington Parkway. See David Taylor, foreword, in "Pilgrim's Progress: Black St. Paul and the Making of an Urban Ghetto, 1870–1930" (Ph.D. diss., University of Minnesota, 1977), 48–49; David Taylor, foreword, in *Voices of Rondo: Oral Histories of St. Paul's Black Community*, ed. Kate Cavett (Minneapolis: Syren, 2005), xii–xv; David Taylor, *African Americans in Minnesota* (St. Paul: Minnesota Historical Society Press, 2002).

12. *United States Census, 1910*, William J. Gardner, St. Paul, ward 8, Ramsey County, MN, ED 109, sheet 2B, family 35, NARA microfilm publication T624 (Washington, DC: National Archives and Records Administration, 1982), roll 719, FHL microfilm 1,374,732; *United States Census, 1920*, William J. Gardner, St. Paul, ward 8, Ramsey County, MN, ED 91, sheet 6A, line 11, family 136, NARA microfilm publication T625 (Washington, DC: National Archives and Records Administration, 1992), roll 855, FHL microfilm 1,820,855.

13. Like most other family photograph collections, the Gardner collection is composed mainly of snapshot images of the family home and members of the immediate family, with a few images of non-family members sprinkled among the more than 150 photographs dated between 1900 and 1920. Although the MNHS has prints of some of the family's photos, it does not hold the actual albums or the complete collection of loose photographs. There is a paucity of African American family albums in public collections generally. Thanks to the generosity of the Gardner family, I was able to gain some access to two of the original albums (from which some of the MNHS images had been drawn) and could compare the holdings to the more complete collection. There is no clear documentation regarding the full extent of the collection or who took, developed, and arranged the images I have analyzed. Regardless, it is clear that the focus of both the Gardner and Dunn family collections is primarily on the immediate family members and their respective residential districts within the city. Regardless of the limitations posed by the Gardner collection, the number and condition of its existing images allow us to see an African American family in a variety of times and places through the eyes of its own members

14. bell hooks, "In Our Glory: Photography and Black Life," in *Picturing Us: African-American Identity in Photography*, ed. Deborah Willis (New York: New Press, 1994), 48.

15. Ibid, 49. The importance of having access to such a collection of self-representative images cannot be overstated.

16. On the links between race and class status as well as on the structural limitations to black economic life in Minnesota during this era, see William D. Green, *Degrees of Freedom: The Origins of Civil Rights in Minnesota, 1865–1912* (Minneapolis: University of Minnesota Press, 2015), part 3. See also Taylor, "Communities in the Twin Cities," in *African Americans in Minnesota*, n.p.; foreword, *Voices of Rondo*, xv; and *Remember Rondo: A Tradition of Excellence* (St. Paul: Remember Rondo Committee, 1995), 6. Most of the African Americans living in Minnesota at this time held unskilled, low-wage jobs as recounted in Taylor, "Communities in the Twin Cities" and "The Twin Cities from 1910 to 1980," both in *African Americans in Minnesota*, n.p. For information on aggregate data regarding the jobs they held, see Taylor, "Pilgrim's Progress," apps. C and D. For comparison, the statistics for Cleveland at the turn of the twentieth century show that 57.4 percent of the black males worked in jobs categorized as "unskilled" or "domestic." Similar statistics hold true for other northern cities. On Cleveland, see Kenneth Kussmer, *A Ghetto Takes Shape: Black Cleveland, 1870–1930* (Urbana: University of Illinois Press, 1976). On Milwaukee, see Joe William Trotter, Jr., *Black Milwaukee: The Making of an Industrial Proletariat, 1915–45* (Urbana: University of Illinois Press, 1985). Service work was respectable, and a worker could generally earn a living wage (*Remember Rondo*, 9).

17. "Christmas at 369 Jay St. (now Galtier), St. Paul, 1912, Ralph, Dorothy and William Gardner," I.108.31, William J. Gardner Photograph Collection, MNHS.

18. "With the Youngsters," privately held by Evelyn Hill and Rosella Limon.

19. "Ida, Mildred, Marie, 1920," privately held by Evelyn Hill and Rosella Limon.

20. "William J Gardner Family, St. Paul, 1912 (L-R: Marie, Ethel, Ida, Mildred, Agnes, Gladys, Bill, Ralph and Baby Dorothy in front of Ethel)," I.108.40, William J. Gardner Photograph Collection, MNHS; "Carrie Gardner Williams and Ethel Gardner Sheets, 369 Jay St. & St. Anthony, St. Paul, c. 1910," I.108.13, William J. Gardner Photograph Collection, MNHS; "Gladys, Ralph, Uncle Bill, Dorothy," circa 1920, I.108.10, William J. Gardner Photograph Collection, MNHS.

21. "While on a Family Outing at Como in 1912," privately held by Evelyn Hill and Rosella Limon.

22. Post-1920 images in the collection show older Gardner children, family, and friends at Como Park and Como Lake. There are also two images that are circa 1920 and might have been taken at Lake Phalen, but this can't be confirmed.

23. "William and Ralph Gardner, 260 W. 3rd St. (Below tunnel), St. Paul, 1916," I.108.2, William J. Gardner Photograph Collection, MNHS.

24. The exact location is noted on the back of the photograph in the MNHS collection. The boys' outfits bear a nominal resemblance to some worn by other carnival attendees of 1916, yet there are few public photographs of any children in costume. These costumes may have been for the Union Hall winter celebration (see chapter 5), but that is just a speculation.

25. "Boys shoveling snow at 369 and 375 Jay St. (now Galtier), St. Paul, 1912 (Bill and Ralph Gardner)," I.108.1, William J. Gardner Photograph Collection, MNHS.

26. On the 1889 law, see *Remember Rondo, 9*; and Arthur McWatt, "Small and Cohesive: St. Paul's Resourceful African-American Community," *Ramsey County History* 26 (Spring 1991): 4–15. This law had grown from two earlier laws (1885 and 1887), which had purported to outlaw discrimination in public accommodations, places of entertainment, and eating establishments but contained loopholes and absences that allowed much discrimination to continue unpunished. On the long and complex efforts to strengthen this law, see Green, *Degrees of Freedom*, chaps. 7 and 10. Although the law did not keep illegal discrimination from occurring, it did offer a semblance of equality. Note that, in Cleveland, a city with a black population very similar in size to St. Paul's, there was explicit discrimination at city parks into the 1910s. See Kussmer, *Ghetto Takes Shape*, 58.

27. Green, *Degrees of Freedom*, chap. 15.

28. On this phenomenon in St. Paul, see ibid.; Taylor, "Pilgrim's Progress," 48–51, 220; Taylor, "The Twin Cities 1910–1980"; and Calvin Schmid, *Social Saga of Two Cities: An Ecological and Statistical Study of Social Trends in Minneapolis and St. Paul* (Minneapolis: Minneapolis Council of Social Agencies, 1937), 182–83 and chart 96. The increased racism in northern cities in the 1910s is discussed in Eric Monkhonnen, *America Becomes Urban: The Development of US Cities and Towns, 1780–1980* (Berkeley: University of California Press, 1988), 202. On racism in other midwestern cities, see Jon C. Teaford, *Cities of the Heartland: The Rise and Fall of the Industrial Midwest*

(Bloomington: Indiana University Press, 1993), 192; On Detroit, see Oliver Zunz, *The Changing Face of Inequality: Urbanization, Industrial Development, and Immigrants in Detroit, 1880–1920* (Chicago: University of Chicago Press, 1982). St. Paul generally followed this trend toward dramatically segregated neighborhoods, although at a slower pace. It did not have an identifiable, nearly exclusively black area of the city until the 1930s (Taylor, "Pilgrim's Progress," 258). The slow pace of this residential concentration in the Gardners' immediate neighborhood (supported by data in the 1910 and 1920 censuses) makes the selectivity of their photographs even more instructive.

29. The Rondo neighborhood was located in ward 8, where 1,592 blacks lived in 1920. In the same year 1,784 black St. Paulites lived in all the other wards combined (Taylor, "Pilgrim's Progress," tab. 2). By 1930, the percentage of black residents in the Rondo district was even greater (Schmid, *Social Saga of Two Cities,* chart 95).

30. In 1920, 66 percent of Rondo residents were black (Taylor, "Pilgrim's Progress," 49). For data on the Gardners' neighborhood, which had a significant white population, see *United States Census, 1920,* St. Paul, ward 8, Ramsey County, MN, United States, ED 91).

31. Roy Wilkins, *Standing Fast: The Autobiography of Roy Wilkins* (New York: Viking, 1982), 29.

32. William F. Williams (Billy) and Ella Williams, sister and brother, lived in the same home on West Central Street during both the 1910 and the 1920 censuses. See *United States Census, 1910,* William F. Williams, St. Paul, ward 8, Ramsey County, MN, United States, ED 109, sheet 2A, family 32, NARA microfilm publication T624 (Washington, DC: National Archives and Records Administration, 1982), roll 719, FHL microfilm 1,374,732; and *United States Census, 1920,* William F. Williams in household of Ella Williams, St. Paul, ward 8, Ramsey County, MN, United States, ED 91, sheet 21B, line 71, family 569, NARA microfilm publication T625 (Washington, DC: National Archives and Records Administration, 1992), roll 855, FHL microfilm 1,820,855. See also the excellent map *St. Paul's Rondo Neighborhood: 1920–1960,* by James Peter Gerlich (2008).

33. Dorothy O.'s last name is spelled both "Ochme" and "Ohme" in the Gardner records. Despite extensive research in city directories and census records, I have not determined who she is, where she lived, or what her relationship was to the Gardners. There are no listings of any families with the last name Ohme residing near the Gardners' or the Williams' homes. Conversations with Gardner family members Evelyn Hill (in August 2006) and Rosella Limon (in August 2017) could not confirm her identity. Limon's recollections of the neighborhood in the 1940s indicate that there were white children living in rented apartments near the home and that children would play together. Limon's hypothesis is that Dorothy O. was a neighborhood child (perhaps of a renting family) and friend. In two additional images a relatively fair-skinned child appears in a more posed group photo with child members of the Gardners' extended family. According to Limon (in August

2017), three of the children are certainly members of the extended family, but the identities of the others (including the fair-skinned girl) are unrecorded; they might be neighborhood children.

34. "Dorothy G. Dorothy Ohme," circa 1915, privately held by Evelyn Hill and Rosella Limon.

35. "Dorothy Gardner, Dorothy Ohme, 1918," privately held by Evelyn Hill and Rosella Limon.

36. "Confirmation at St. Peter Claver, c. 1910," I.108.32, William J. Gardner Photograph Collection, MNHS. The ages of the Gardner children in 1910 are based on information in *United States Census, 1910*. I have determined this photograph to be from about 1905, although a note on the back claims it is from about 1910. Carrie Gardner is listed as being 20 years old in 1910. The girl in this photo appears to be a teenager. The same is true of a number of the images in the collection at the MNHS, which are dated circa 1920 but are likely older, given the ages of the subjects.

37. My knowledge about the Gardners' active participation in parish life is based on conversations with Hill and Limon and is supported by pictorial evidence (including studio portraits of the children on sacramental days and photos of the boys as altar servers and choir members). See also Bill Gardner, transcript of interview (c. 1992), SPC, which details his family's long-standing relationship with the parish. It is among a set of typewritten transcripts of interviews conducted at the time of the St. Peter Claver centennial celebration in 1992.

38. Arthur McWatt, "Frederick McGhee," unpublished manuscript written on the occasion of the St. Peter Claver centennial celebration (c. 1992), SPC. McGhee was not only active in the life of the parish but has been credited with involving the Catholic church in St. Paul in racial justice matters. For more on McGhee, see Green, *Degrees of Freedom*.

39. The 1911 *St. Paul City Directory* lists McGhee's residence as 665 University Avenue. He died in 1912, which may also account for this absence.

40. This stratification was becoming marked in places such as Cleveland by the end of the nineteenth century and was apparent in both church affiliation and residential differentiation (Kussmer, *Ghetto Takes Shape*, 91–92, 97–98). In Milwaukee, too, by the mid-1910s there was a growing black middle class dominated by a very small business and professional elite (Trotter, *Black Milwaukee*, chap. 3). On St. Paul, see Peter J. DeCarlo, "Loyalty within Racism: The Segregated Sixteenth Battalion of the Minnesota Homeguard," *Minnesota History* 65/66 (Summer 2017): 208–19; and Taylor, "The Twin Cities from 1910 to 1980."

41. Dunn had been interested in and proficient at photography since his teenage years in Philadelphia in the 1880s. For more about his early life and the cameras he used, see the small privately printed book by his son James Taylor Dunn, *John W. G. Dunn: Fisherman, Photographer and Nature Lover* (Marine of the St. Croix, Minn.: J. W. G. Dunn Libraries of the St. Croix Watershed Research Station, 1996), MNHS.

42. In *Half a Truth*, Kouwenhoven provides a useful definition of snapshots:

"predominately photographs taken quickly, with a minimum of deliberate posing on the part of the people represented and with a minimum of deliberate selectivity on the part of the photographer so far as vantage point and the 'framing' of the image [is] concerned" (149).

43. Joseph Pennell, "Is Photography Among the Fine Arts?" *Contemporary Review* (December 1897), cited in Naomi Rosenblum, *A World History of Photography* (New York: Abbeville, 1984), 298.

44. Formally, one of the most interesting elements of Dunn's images and the one that stands in sharp contrast to the Gardner snapshots is his use of averted gazes, a common stylistic practice of well-known pictorialists.

45. By 1916 Dunn was a partner in the real estate and insurance firm of Cushing, Dunn, and Driscoll (James Taylor Dunn, memo to Gareth Heibert, December 13, 1956, "History of Oxford Skating Club" file, JTD).

46. I selected the Dunn collection from among a set of photograph collections in the MNHS archive that could be identified as belonging to white residents of St. Paul, were focused on the years 1900–20, and included a significant percentage of photographs of the city itself. The extensive focus on family members matched the Gardner collection, while the pictorialist aesthetic created a formal contrast. In addition, as members of the growing upper middle class of white professionals, the Dunns represent a segment of the population that had set the tone for social and cultural life in St. Paul for decades and that would continue to do so in the decades that followed. Furthermore, they lived on the western edge of St. Paul, a fast-growing area marketed to members of the professional class who were looking to escape from the urban core and that was predominately (if not exclusively) white. Thus, because the Dunns represented a segment of the St. Paul population that was in some ways as self-consciously defined and unified as the working-class black population to which the Gardners belonged, their albums offered a useful basis for comparison. The nine St. Paul-focused albums in the Dunn collection each hold between sixty and a hundred photoprints covering the years between 1897 and 1919. In total, there are forty-nine albums in the collection. Those that do not focus on St. Paul show images of Dunn's home state of Pennsylvania, the woods and lakes where he hunted and fished, and various random locations. The images are predominately 3-inch-by-3-inch prints attached deliberately and symmetrically to the pages of the albums. Although compiling photo albums in the early twentieth century was fairly common, Dunn's care, concern, and professionalism were unusual, judging by the other albums in the MNHS.

47. See JWGD, box 2.

48. "1033 Lincoln Ave, St. Paul," photo by J. W. G. Dunn, collection III.9.4, box 2, album "Minnesota 1897–8, 1902–4," JWGD.

49. Photo by J. W. G. Dunn, in ibid.

50. "Jack, March 1904," photo by J. W. G. Dunn, in ibid.

51. Photo by J. W. G. Dunn, in ibid.

52. Notably, the occupants of these houses (or those in figures 13 and 14) are nowhere to be seen. Similarly, the photographs do not include images of the family's maid, a young woman who lived in their home during part of the era under investigation.

53. Photo by J. W. G. Dunn, collection III.9.8, box 4, album "A Nice Boy and his Home 1903–1904," JWDG.

54. "The Garden, St. Paul, 1918," photo by J. W. G. Dunn, collection III.9.7, box 3, album "Minnesota 1913–1919," JWDG.

55. The albums from 1913 include some additional photographs of a camping trip.

56. In this album, there are a few images of the Dunn children in front of their local elementary school (the Lincoln School) as well as a few that include glimpses of the neighbors' houses, but the Oxford Club photos are more numerous and relate directly to the world the photographer inhabited.

57. Photo by J. W. G Dunn, collection III.9.7, box 3, album "Minnesota 1913–1919," JWDG.

58. See Dunn, memo to Heibert; and membership records, 1921–22, "History of Oxford Skating Club" file, in JTD.

59. The roster included between four hundred and six hundred members a year and drew families from the emerging white middle-class neighborhoods from Dayton, Marshall, and Inglehardt avenues to St. Clair Avenue and from Pleasant Avenue out into and beyond Lexington Avenue (Dunn, memo to Heibert).

60. In *Changing Face of Inequality*, Zunz asserts that race and class began to define city neighborhoods after 1920.

61. Dunn, memo to Heibert.

62. This reading of Dunn's photographs is supported by the recollections of his eldest son, who recounted his father's constant involvement with the club from the moment of its founding (Dunn, memo to Heibert).

63. The literature on reform photography and especially on Riis and Hine is significant. Scholars from a variety of disciplines have written provocatively on their techniques and the implications thereof. See, for instance, Trachtenberg, *Reading American Photographs;* Peter Hales, *Silver Cities: The Photography of American Urbanization, 1839–1915* (Philadelphia: Temple University Press, 1984); Maren Stange, *Symbols of an Ideal Life: Social Documentary Photography in America, 1890–1950* (New York: Cambridge University Press, 1989); Sally Stein, "Making Connections with the Camera: Photography and Social Mobility in the Career of Jacob Riis," *Afterimage* 10 (May 1983): 9–16; and Walter Rosenblum and Naomi Rosenblum, *America and Louis Hine: Photographs, 1904–1940* (New York: Aperture, 1977). Riis's most famous photographs were eventually reproduced in *How the Other Half Lives: Studies among the Tenements of New York* (New York: Scribner's, 1890),and Hine's most important work was for his *Pittsburgh Survey* (1909–14) and for the National Child Labor Committee (1908–18).

64. The sixteen photographs that do include human subjects suggest the outlines of Riis's and Hine's influence. Riis's is more pronounced because these images

tend to be group photographs and are accompanied by generalizing captions that fail to identify the individuals or tell their stories. The one exception is an image of a small boy, which, by virtue of its gentle nature, hints at Hine's work. However, the subject of this latter picture is not identified, nor is his story told. In the end he becomes merely a prop.

65. Carol Aronovici, *Housing Conditions in the City of Saint Paul* (St. Paul: Wilder Charity, 1917), 9, MNHS.

66. Ibid.

67. The report was not an unqualified success; and although there was much support for the changes suggested, some people resented Aronovici's intrusion into city business. His plan to create a new subdivision to ease housing problems never came to fruition. The city did pass its first housing ordinance in 1918 "regulating the Construction, Enlargement, Alteration, Repair, Inspection, and Safeguarding of buildings, and the Safe-guarding of the Health of occupants by the regulation of Sanitary Provisions and the Protection of Real Property Used for Dwelling Purposes in the City of St. Paul" (Gary Phelps, "Aronovici's Campaign to Clean up St. Paul," *Ramsey County History* 15, no. 2 [1980]: 13).

68. John Tagg, *The Burden of Representation: Essays on Photographies and Histories* (Amherst: University of Massachusetts Press, 1988), 131.

69. Ibid., 131–32.

70. Aronovici, *Housing Conditions in the City of Saint Paul*, 56.

71. For this reading of "Hebrew Master," see Hales, *Silver Cities*, 194; Aronovici, *Housing Conditions in the City of Saint Paul*, 64.

72. Aronovici, *Housing Conditions in the City of Saint Paul*, 8.

73. Ibid., 35.

74. Ibid., 36.

75. Most of those listed as members of the housing commission of the St. Paul Association also appear in the *Dual City Blue Book* for 1917, which lists the names and addresses of the most elite families and individuals in the Twin Cities. The photographer's identity is unrecorded, but probably he or she shared at least some of the social and economic identities of the group supporting the survey.

76. Stange, *Symbols of an Ideal Life*, 86–87.

77. On the power of newspapers to shape or reflect norms of society, especially in the early years of the twentieth century, see Sally Griffith, *Home Town News: William Allen White and the "Emporia Gazette"* (New York: Oxford University Press, 1989). She highlights the "mutual interaction between newspaper and audience" and discusses the influence of a "newspaperman's power to describe events [for] through his choice of language, [he can affect readers'] means of thinking about them" (180–81). Such an observation is useful when discussing photographs; even more than words, the images a newspaper employs can affect not only how readers think about events but also the events (and people) they think about.

78. While there were numerous labor and ethnic papers in St. Paul in this era (including the well-known *St. Paul Union Advocate*), I have limited my focus for

comparative purposes and because of the relative paucity of images in these other newspapers at the time.

79. In November 2000, an employee at the *Pioneer Press* confirmed that there are no circulation records for the years under investigation. The other two papers are defunct. The *Daily News* had a circulation of 36, 950 in 1905, and while that continued to grow during the next fifteen years, sources indicate that it was the smallest of the three throughout its entire existence (Herbert Y. Weber, "The St. Paul *Daily News*—Toward a Monopoly Press in St. Paul, Minnesota" (master's thesis, University of Minnesota, 1965), 5–6.

80. Founded in 1885 and headquartered in St. Paul, the *Appeal* was one of the nation's leading and longest-running African American newspapers during the late nineteenth and early twentieth centuries. At its height, it offered six separate editions in six cities and advertised itself as "An American Paper." By the end of the 1910s, it was publishing only in St. Paul and Minneapolis. It ceased publication in 1923.

81. *Pioneer Press,* December 4, 1904 Sec. 2; *Pioneer Press*, December 8, 1904; *Pioneer Press*, January 5, 1905.

82. The photos that grace the pages of two randomly chosen issues (the *Dispatch* from April 1910 and the *Pioneer Press* from September 1914) exemplify this stasis. Given the emphasis on world events in September 1914 and the fact that photographic images of World War I proliferated in the papers, the choice of local photographs and the image they presented might have been more conscious and telling then than at any other time.

83. More outside images appeared as Word War I approached and European concerns began to dominate.

84. *Dispatch*, April 16, 1910; *Dispatch* April 19,1910; *Dispatch*, April 21, 1910.

85. *Dispatch*, September 6, 1914.

86. See, for example, *Dispatch*, September 6, 1914, sec. 3.

87. It was rare for a St. Paul woman's photograph to appear in the news pages. For example, in a survey of every edition of the *Dispatch* printed in April 1910, I found only one woman's picture in a section of the paper generally devoted to regular news. She is not pictured alone but as the "Mother" in a family portrait of recent Dutch immigrants to St. Paul (*Dispatch*, April 2, 1910, 4).

88. "Miss Alice Michaud has gone to Seabreeze, Fla. She was accompanied by her mother Mrs. A. E. Michaud 797 Linwood place," *Pioneer Press*, January 21, 1917, MNHS.

89. See, for example, *Dispatch*, April 21, 1910.

90. There is no substantial scholarship on photographs of women in newspapers in this era. However, Julia Golia includes some brief discussions of photographs and other visual images in "Courting Women, Courting Advertisers: The Women's Page and the Transformation of the America Newspaper, 1895–1935," *Journal of American History* 103, no. 3 (2016): 606–28.

91. Take, for example, the coverage of the storm-caused destruction of the High Bridge in early August 1904. The two photographs in the *Pioneer Press* (August 22,

1904) do not focus on the houses or people (mostly poor and immigrant) who lived in the area underneath it.

92. Donald J. O'Grady, *The Pioneer Press and Dispatch: History at Your Door, 1849–1983* (St. Paul: Northwest Publications, 1983), 64–67,. Also see Weber, "St. Paul *Daily News*," 2.

93. For example, there is no obvious difference in the scope or selectivity of the *Daily News*'s coverage of the winter carnival.

94. See Golia, "Courting Women."

95. For bibliographic information on Adams, see Taylor, "Pilgrim's Progress," 90–100; and Green, *Degrees of Freedom*. Green argues that the rise of the *Appeal* was a significant event in the history of race relations and the African American experience in Minnesota.

96. For an in-depth discussion, see Taylor, "Pilgrim's Progress," chap. 3; Taylor, "Leadership and Organizations," in *African Americans in Minnesota,* n.p.; and Green, *Degrees of Freedom.*

97. "Residence of J. Q. Adams, 527 St. Anthony Avenue, St. Paul," *Appeal,* September 24, 1910, and October 28, 1911, MNHS; "Residence of F. L. McGhee 665 W. University Avenue, St. Paul," *Appeal,* September 24, 1910, and October 28, 1911, MNHS. While it is hard to establish the exact position and social standing of the residents of each house pictured, their addresses and their general appearance indicate that their owners were fairly well off. In addition, there are virtually no pictures of extremely small or plain houses (of the four-room type that Roy Wilkins describes his aunt and uncle living in) or of apartment buildings or rooming houses where the poorer members of St. Paul's black population would have resided.

98. Evidence suggests that the specific photographs printed—especially of the homes and businesses—were linked to sponsorship. That is, subscribers had to pay to have their home included (Adina Gibbs, interview by David Taylor, December 18, 1970, Minnesota Black History Project, 1970–73, Oral History Collection, MNHS).

CHAPTER 3: DESIGNING FOR COMMUNITY

1. Samuel G. Smith, "Social Forces in the Life of St. Paul," (Minnesota, s.n. between 1890–1899), MNHS. For essays exploring the historical links between architecture and community identity and experience in the United States, see Carter L. Hudgins and Elizabeth Collins Cromley, eds., *Shaping Communities: Perspectives in Vernacular Architecture,* vol. 6 (Knoxville: University of Tennessee Press, 1997).

2. William H. Wilson, *The City Beautiful Movement* (Baltimore: Johns Hopkins University Press, 1989), 27.

3. On the general growth patterns of American cities and their expansion in the late nineteenth and early twentieth centuries, see Eric H. Monkhonnen, *America Becomes Urban: The Development of U.S. Cities and Towns, 1780–1980* (Berkeley: University of California Press, 1988).

4. Paul Boyer, *Urban Masses and Moral Order in America, 1820–1920* (Cambridge, MA.: Harvard University Press, 1978), 149, 175.

5. In the world of architecture and art (as opposed to purely American literature), the period between 1870 and 1917 is referred to as the American Renaissance
because of the renewed sense of nationalism and self-confidence and a coming-
of-age that many in the United States felt was the modern equivalent of ancient
Rome's empire and the European Renaissance. The 1979 exhibit "The American
Renaissance" at the Brooklyn Museum encouraged a reengagement with this
era and its flourishing in technological and architectural areas. See Richard Guy
Wilson, "The Great Civilization," in *The American Renaissance, 1876–1917* (New
York: Pantheon, 1979), 11–74.

6. Wilson (in *The City Beautiful Movement*, chap. 3) takes issue with the idea that
the exposition marked the beginning of the era of comprehensive planning in the
United States. Yet there appears to be evidence from other sources that indicates
a relationship between the creation of the White City and a large-scale interest in
organizing and planning cities across the nation.

7. Julius Gy Fabos, Gordon T. Milde, and V. Michael Weinmayr, *Frederick Law
Olmstead, Sr., Founder of Landscape Architecture in America* (Amherst: University of
Massachusetts Press, 1968), 91.

8. Jon C. Teaford, *Cities of the Heartland: The Rise and Fall of the Industrial Midwest*
(Bloomington: Indiana University Press, 1993), 138–39.

9. For a full discussion of the model homes described by housing advocates in
the 1910s, see Gwendolyn Wright, *Moralism and the Model Home: Domestic Architecture
and Cultural Conflict in Chicago, 1873–1913* (Chicago: University of Chicago Press, 1980),
chap. 8. This type of housing was not intended only for the nation's poor but was
also described as very desirable for modern families. In St. Paul, housing reformers advocated for it in the 1910s, but it was not adopted by the middle class until the
1920s, when cottages and bungalow began appearing in their neighborhoods.

10. The most ambitious housing reform plan in St. Paul—to build a subdivision of small middle-class homes for members of the working class—was never
fully developed, but it is detailed in Carol Aronovici, *Housing Conditions in the City
of Saint Paul* (St. Paul: Wilder Charity, 1917). For a general discussion of the construction of many municipal buildings and downtown business structures during
this era, see Jeffrey A. Hess and Paul Clifford Larson, *St. Paul's Architectural History*
(Minneapolis: University of Minnesota Press, 2006), chap. 2. As per the chapter
title, they refer to the years between 1875 and 1920 as the era in which "St. Paul
Comes of Age" (37–100).

11. For a general history of the settlement and growth patterns of St. Paul,
its neighborhoods, and overall trends in architecture, see Patricia A. Murphy,
"Introduction: Historic Sites Survey of Saint Paul and Ramsey County" (March
1981), MNHS; and Patricia A. Murphy and Susan W. Granger, "Historic Sites Survey
of Saint Paul and Ramsey County, 1980–1983, Final Report" (May 1983), MNHS.

12. Leslie Weisman, *Discrimination by Design: A Feminist Critique of the Man-
Made Environment* (Urbana: University of Illinois Press, 1992), 2, 9.

13. Constructed from logs, the chapel measured a mere eighteen by twenty feet. In 1847 an additional eighteen feet was added, but later that year the structure was abandoned due to its poor condition. Also in 1847 the area received its first bishop, Joseph Cretin, who was responsible for building the city's first cathedral, a stone building in the Lowertown district, not far from the Mississippi. When this building became too small for the city's growing Catholic population, a second cathedral—at Sixth and St. Peter streets—replaced it. It became the mother church of the archdiocese in 1888. See Franklin T. Ferguson, "The Cathedral of St. Paul," *Minnesota History* 39 (Winter 1964): 153–162.

14. *St. Paul City Directory, 1903,* and *St. Paul City Directory, 1920,* MNHS. I cite these figures as approximate because they do not include churches that met in spaces other than their own specific buildings or those listed as "Missions" or "Salvation Army."

15. This number comes from evidence in a database of building dates for St. Paul area structures, compiled as part of a history-architecture inventory, SHPO.

16. On another city's relationship with its ecclesiastical architecture, see Diane Shaw, "Building an Urban Identity: The Clustered Spires of Frederick, Maryland," *Perspectives in Vernacular Architecture* 5 (1995): 55–69. For recollections of St. Ambrose in the poor neighborhood of Swede Hollow, see Gentille Yarusso, "An American Newcomer—The Italians" (1973), MNHS. On the new, non-denominational and architecturally unique People's Church, built in 1889 and rebuilt post-fire in 1912 along Pleasant Avenue, a lovely street running beneath Summit's mansions, see Alison McKibbin Bigelow, correspondence, Charles H. Bigelow Family Papers, box 2, MNHS. On Pilgrim Baptist Church, one of three black churches in St. Paul, see its Ladies' Aid Society minutes, attendance, and dues records, 1910–21, MNHS. On the way in which Mary Hill's close relationships were shaped by her Catholic identity, see Craig Johnson, *James J. Hill House* (St. Paul: Minnesota Historical Society Press, 1993); and Mary T. Hill, "Diaries and Transcripts," Mary T. Hill Papers, MNHS.

17. Using the case of St. Paul Lutherans as an example, note that with forty-four Lutheran churches scattered throughout the city in 1920, it seems likely that Lutheran residents sometimes opted for a place of worship close to home. More generally, while it is hard to ascertain the specific membership statistics and demographic makeup of each parish, I assume that the presence of an available church in any given location meant increased homogeneity within that congregation. The result was to reinforce existing class-based divisions that were linked to residential areas of the city.

18. Mary Lethert Wingerd notes that there was a pattern of church hopping among St. Paul Catholics: regardless of the parish to which they officially belonged, they would frequently visit other churches on specific feast days or simply for a change of pace (*Claiming the City: Politics, Faith, and the Power of Place in St. Paul* [Ithaca: Cornell University Press, 2001], 64). Also see Hill, "Diaries and Transcripts."

19. Daniel Patrick O'Neill, "St. Paul Priests, 1851–1930: Recruitment, Formation and Mobility" (Ph.D. diss., University of Minnesota, 1979), 15–16.

20. Masses were said in the mother tongues of the various congregations, although eventually Archbishop Ireland's Americanization focus (connected to fears of ethnic Catholics during World War I) led him to ban the practice (Wingerd, *Claiming the City*, 234–35).

21. Geoffrey Gyrisco, "East Slav Identity and Church Architecture in Minneapolis, Minnesota," in *Exploring Everyday Landscapes: Perspectives in Vernacular Architecture*, ed. Annemarie Adams and Sally McMurray (Knoxville: University of Tennessee Press, 1997), 7:200. The same trend can be seen in St. Paul. In *Claiming the City*, Wingerd illustrates the importance of ethnicity there well into the twentieth century.

22. At least twelve of the forty-nine church buildings erected in this period can be identified as belonging to ethnic subsets of a number of faith traditions. I determined this figure by cross-referencing a list of churches that historical preservationists have identified as being built between 1900 and 1920 with other known sources that indicate ethnic affiliation of parishes. Data on build dates is from the history-architecture inventory, SHPO.

23. Guild of Catholic Women, annual report (May 1912), 17, AA.

24. Hess and Larson, *St. Paul's Architectural History*, 86–87.

25. Ibid., 88.

26. Pilgrim Baptist may be an exception, but broader patterns of racial segregation in the city complicate the evidence. A study of the addresses of the women involved in the church's Ladies Aid Society indicates that membership was drawn primarily from the upper Rondo area; virtually no members lived in the area below Dale.

27. According the *St. Paul City Directory, 1903*, Pilgrim Baptist was on Cedar at the southwest corner of Summit; St. Peter Claver was on Aurora, near Farrington; and St. James AME was on Fuller, at the northwest corner of Jay. For maps of the relationship between these churches and the black population of St. Paul, see David Taylor, "Pilgrim's Progress: Black St. Paul and the Making of an Urban Ghetto, 1870–1930" (Ph.D. diss., University of Minnesota, 1977), 47; *St. Paul's Rondo Neighborhood: 1920–1960*, by James Peter Gerlich (2008).

28. "Pilgrim Baptist Church: A Brief Resume of History," Records of Pilgrim Baptist Church, MNHS.

29. Ministers' Union, minutes, MNHS. The black churches may have been involved in the union, but that there is no convincing evidence that they were.

30. Wingerd discusses this political capital in *Claiming the City*.

31. "Race Prejudice is held a Blot against Americans," *Twin City Star*, December 14, 1912.

32. M. Geraldine Williams, "St. Paul Items," *Minneapolis Messenger*, September 17, 1921.

33. Father Stephen Theobald, the first black man to be ordained at St. Paul Seminary, was named pastor of St. Peter Claver in 1910. See Kathryn Goetz, "St.

Peter Claver Church, St. Paul," http://www.mnopedia.org; Arthur McWatt, "Frederick McGhee," unpublished manuscript (c. 1992), SPC; and Williams, "St. Paul Items."

34. Goetz, "St. Peter Claver Church, St. Paul."

35. Arthur McWatt, "One Hundred Years Ago: St. Peter Claver's History," *Ramsey County History* 27 (Fall 1992): 25

36. Taylor, "Pilgrim's Progress," 172.

37. Guild of Catholic Women, annual reports (1911–18), AA.

38. Society of St. Vincent de Paul of St. Paul, annual reports (1915, 1920), AA.

39. Taylor, "Pilgrim's Progress," 172. There is little evidence indicating that this tension separated black Catholics from their Protestant counterparts in St. Paul in any meaningful way, yet religious differences cannot be ignored in an attempt to understand the complicated intersection of religion and race in the city.

40. St. Bernard's design was so unusual that it instantly became a local icon in this German, working-class, north-side neighborhood when it was completed in 1905 (Hess and Larson, *St. Paul's Architectural History,* 87).

41. A survey of the city's churches as depicted in photographs (in the collection of MNHS) provided the evidence for this argument.

42. John Ireland, "The New Cathedral of St. Paul: Letter of the Most Reverend Archbishop John Ireland" (1905), MNHS.

43. Masqueray had received numerous awards in his native country and had also been named the chief designer and consulate for the 1904 Louisiana Purchase Expedition in St. Louis. On the selection of Masqueray, see Ferguson, "The Cathedral of St. Paul."

44. "Cathedral of St. Paul, Summit and Dayton, St. Paul, c. 1905," circa 1915, MR2.9 SP5.1, 165, MNHS. Note that there are two dates on this image. The correct one is 1915. The building did not exist in 1905.

45. For details about the capitol, see "State Capitol, Learn," http://www .mnhs.org.

46. E. L. Masqueray, "Religious Architecture and the Cathedral of St. Paul and Pro-Cathedral of the Immaculate Conception," *Western Architect* (October 1908): 43–48. See also Ferguson, "The Cathedral of St. Paul," 161; and Eric Hansen, *The Cathedral of Saint Paul: An Architectural Biography* (St. Paul: Cathedral of St. Paul, 1990), 23.

47. Hansen, *Cathedral of Saint Paul,* 23.

48. While supporting the creation of small ethnic parishes, Ireland was concerned as early as 1888 about the degree to which anti-Catholic sentiment was fueled by the growing numbers of immigrant Catholics from non-English-speaking countries and the inability of non-English-speaking Catholics to defend the faith to their Anglo neighbors. In a speech that year, he exhorted German Catholics in Minnesota to make sure their children were educated in English and that their religious education was carried out in English as well as in their mother tongue because English was the language of daily life. See James Michael Reardon, *The*

Catholic Church in the Diocese of St. Paul: From Earliest Origin to Centennial Achievement (St. Paul: Northcentral, 1952), 265.

49. Ireland, "The New Cathedral of St. Paul."

50. *Acta et Dicta* 1, no.1 (St. Paul: St. Paul Catholic Historical Society, 1907), 101.

51. Some of the vibrancy of the smaller churches can be attributed to the exclusive nature of the cathedral as parish. The cost of a pew there was expensive.

52. In *Moralism and the Model Home,* Wright points out that domestic architecture illuminates norms concerning not only "family life, sex roles . . . [and] social equality" but also "community relations" (1).

53. Discussing neighborhoods in St. Paul is a difficult because the names that modern historians and scholars use were not necessarily used by the residents themselves. According to Susan Roth of the Minnesota State Historic Preservation Office, most neighborhood contours were fluid, and there is little evidence on how self-conscious residents were about the specific neighborhoods in which their homes existed (personal communication, January 4, 2002). In my discussion here, I draw largely on the neighborhood classifications and boundaries established by the 1981–83 Historic Sites Survey conducted by the Saint Paul Heritage Preservation Committee and the Ramsey County Historical Society (Murphy and Granger, "Historic Sites Survey, Final Report").

54. See Wingerd, *Claiming the City,* intro. Also see the images of standard middle-class homes in pattern books as such as Montgomery Ward's *Building Plans of Modern Homes,* (1914), MNHS. Most of the styles advertised there could be found in St. Paul between 1900 and 1920.

55. *Saint Paul Architecture* (St. Paul: Minnesota City Planning Department, 1975), 4–5.

56. *Building the Future from Our Past: A Report on the Saint Paul Historic Hill District Planning Program* (St. Paul: Old Town Restorations, 1975), 42.

57. See introduction of any edition of the *Dual City Blue Book* from the years 1900–1920 for this reminder of its purpose. My assertion that so many of the names corresponded to the Hill district is based on surveying the Blue Books published between 1900 and 1924.

58. *Building the Future,* 54.

59. On the industrial and commercial growth of St. Paul from its founding through the 1930s, see Calvin Schmid, *Social Saga of Two Cities: An Ecological and Statistical Study of Social Trends in Minneapolis and St. Paul* (Minneapolis: Minneapolis Council of Social Agencies, 1937), 19–36.

60. *Building the Future,* 38.

61. My discussion of Victorian ideals is drawn from Clifford Clark, Jr., *The American Family Home, 1800–1960* (Chapel Hill: University of North Carolina Press, 1986), chap.

62. Quoted in ibid., 104.

63. Thorstein Veblen, *The Theory of the Leisure Class: An Economic Study of Institutions (New York: Macmillan, 1899).*

64. Architectural historians at least since Dell Upton in the 1970s have discussed

the way in which buildings construct, communicate, reproduce, and normalize social identities and hierarchies. However, Abigail Van Slyck offers a more complex, sophisticated understanding of the cultural and social work of buildings based on integrating the work of Judith Butler. As she writes, "social identity [is] a less stable quality that is always in the process of construction performed every moment by each individual. Thus, social identity does not exist in any fixed way prior to the buildings designed to support and sustain those performances" ("The Spatial Practice of Privilege," *Journal of the Society of Architectural Historians* 70 [June 2011]: 236).

65. Ibid., 213.

66. "James J. Hill residence, 240 Summit Avenue, St. Paul, c. 1905," MR2.9 SP2, 100, negative no. 742, MNHS.

67. See Johnson, *James J. Hill House*.

68. Van Slyck, "Spatial Practice of Privilege," 214.

69. Such eastward-looking designs were the consistent pattern for architect-designed homes in St. Paul in the decades bridging the turn of the twentieth century (Hess and Larson, *St. Paul's Architectural History*, chap. 2). In "Spatial Practices of Privilege" Van Slyck notes that the eastern aristocratic families looked, in turn, to England in the late nineteenth century.

70. I obtained this information by looking up the addresses of the various people mentioned in Hill's diaries between 1912 and 1914 ("Diaries and Transcripts").

71. This small group included Mary's childhood friend Seraphina Ireland, a Catholic nun and the archbishop's sister.

72. Wingerd, *Claiming the City*, 44.

73. Hess and Larson, *St. Paul's Architectural History*, 44–45.

74. For a fuller discussion of the legislation, see Earnest R. Sandeen, *Historic Summit Avenue* (St. Paul: Living Historical Museum, 1978), 29–32. No doubt there was significant self-congratulation two years later when Aronovici's report concluded that apartment houses in St. Paul were widely associated with poverty and slum conditions in multiple areas of the city. The 1915 ordinance provided some measure of security from potential changes in the demographics of the Summit neighborhood.

75. *St. Paul Architecture*, 27–28.

76. Fitzgerald spent his childhood in St. Paul consciously "hovering socially on the edge" of high society as his family moved around the edges of the Summit neighborhood. Their final home, on Summit near the intersection of Dale, served as a perfect metaphor for Fitzgerald's sense of being on the periphery. Dale marked the end of the grandest part of Summit and proceeded downhill flanked by more modest homes. See Arthur Mizener, *The Far Side of Paradise: A Biography of F. Scott Fitzgerald* (Boston: Houghton Mifflin, 1949), 13–14.

77. Samuel H. Morgan, "Flexible Flyers, Trolleys to Wildwood and the Wondrous Tree House on Grand Hill," *Ramsey County History* 30 (Summer 1995): 22–26.

78. The Hills' house was not the only impressive façade in the neighborhood,

and today much of the Summit Hill area is marked as a the National Register historic district (Murphy and Granger, "Historic Sites Survey, Final Report," 161). Another home on Summit Avenue, the Lightners', belonged to a family whose social world was also closely linked to their residential area. See Bonnie MacDonald, "One Splendid Pile of Brown Stone: The Young-Lightner Double House, 322–324 Summit Avenue," (B.A. thesis, University of Minnesota, 1998).

79. *Building the Future,* 50–53, 58.

80. Sandeen applies this classification to most of the west-end Summit Avenue homes he discusses (*Historic Summit Avenue,* 109). One of the most noticeable changes in domestic architecture of the early twentieth century was a dramatic decline in the number of projecting wings, dormers, and porches, elements that had marked many Victorian homes. The resulting shape was often a simplified cube or rectangle.

81. The smaller, simpler homes of the early twentieth century were linked to shifting ideas about the requirements of a moral society. As part of a new social order linked to progressive ideals and visions, their younger residents prized efficiency, dignity, and economy above the individualism of the Victorians. See Wright, *Moralism and the Model Home,* chap. 8, for a full discussion of this topic. While the full-on development of small, ideal, bungalow styles did not become commonplace in St. Paul until the 1920s, the new residential architecture in the western Hill district shows that many homeowners adhered to basic idea about housing reform.

82. On standardized house plans and designs in American history, see Daniel D. Reiff, *Houses from Books: Treaties, Pattern Books, and Catalogues in American Architecture, 1738–1950: A History and Guide* (University Park: Pennsylvania State University Press, 2000), which offers a visual description of the standard design from which the Dunn house appears to have been derived (167, fig. 259).

83. On the general move toward this more conservative style, see *Building the Future,* 50.

84. See the following: *Saint Paul Architecture,* 4–5; Paul Clifford Larson, "Dayton's Bluff Preliminary Report, 1989," 22–32, SHPO; Wright, *Moralism and the Model Home,* chap. 8; and Judith Martin and David Lanegran, *Where We Live: The Residential Districts of Minneapolis and St. Paul* (Minneapolis: University of Minnesota Press, 1983), 87.

85. Membership records, 1921–22, "History of Oxford Skating Club" file, JTD.

86. Lynch's main argument is laid out succinctly in Michael Frisch, *Town into City: Springfield, Massachusetts, and the Meaning of Community, 1840–1880* (Cambridge, MA: Harvard University Press, 1972), 133–34.

87. The area's boosters claimed that more than seven hundred new homes would be built in the area in 1905 alone. In reality, about 150 homes built in the district between 1900 and 1920 (Dayton's Bluff Commercial Club, *Picturesque Dayton's Bluff* [St. Paul: Jackson and Smith, 1909], 1, MNHS).

88. See Larson, "Dayton's Bluff Preliminary Report, 1989," 22–32.

89. For clear drawings of the predominant forms of new home construction, see Carole Zellie, *The Dayton's Bluff Historic District Handbook* (St. Paul: City of St. Paul, 1992), 7–8.

90. Dayton's Bluff Commercial Club, *Picturesque Dayton's Bluff*, n.p.

91. Ibid.

92. Larson, "Dayton's Bluff Preliminary Report, 1989," 22–32.

93. Taylor lays out the details of this mixture of people and residential/commercial spaces in "Pilgrim's Progress."

94. *St. Paul Architecture*, 28; *Building the Future from Our Past*, 58.

95. While African Americans continued to reside in a number of different wards in the city into the twentieth century, by 1900 the majority lived in Rondo. For a visual depiction of the population shift see Schmid, *Social Saga of Two Cities*, chart 98; and David Taylor, "The Twin Cities from 1910 to 1980" and the map "African American Neighborhoods in the Twin Cities, 1860–1990," in *African Americans in Minnesota* (St. Paul: Minnesota Historical Society Press, 2002) , n.p.

96. There is little secondary source material about Rondo's architecture. In the 1960s much of the neighborhood was razed as part of urban renewal. As a result, the fairly detailed historical knowledge that exists about residential architecture in other neighborhoods does not exist for Rondo. My assertions here are based on inferences and trends indicated in writings about the areas directly surrounding what became known as Rondo. See *St. Paul Architecture*.

97. The area was the site of some new construction, as verified by data in the history-architecture inventory, SHPO.

98. Roy Wilkins, *Standing Fast: The Autobiography of Roy Wilkins* (New York: Viking, 1982), 29.

99. Ibid., 30.

100. For black families in Rondo and in St. Paul in general, home ownership was elusive. A majority of those in Rondo were renters, as were their counterparts in poorer sections of the city. On rental trends in Rondo, see Taylor, "Pilgrim's Progress"; and David Taylor, "Communities in the Twin Cities," *African Americans in Minnesota*, n.p. On rental trends among poor African Americans, see Aronovici, *Housing Conditions*, 15.

101. Thanks to Bruce Schulman for coining *embourgeoisement* and pointing out the pervasiveness of the pattern in my study.

102. Adina Gibbs, interview by David Taylor, December 18, 1970, Oral History Collection, MNHS.

103. Ibid.

104. Taylor, "Pilgrim's Progress," 48–49; David Taylor, foreword, in *Voices of Rondo: Oral Histories of St. Paul's Black Community*, ed. Kate Cavett (Minneapolis: Syren, 2005), xv; Taylor, "The Twin Cities from 1910 to 1980."

105. In 1917 these areas correspond to district 16 on the "Key to Survey" map, a district marked, according to the surveyors, by "Poor and Good [homes] Side by Side" and "Once good, but depreciated, See "Density of Population Chart, St. Paul,

MN. Compiled for the Housing Survey, July 1917," in Aronovici, *Housing Survey*, 12–13. In 1937 social scientists wrote, "The large colored section in St. Paul, where approximately 2,600 of the 4,001 Negroes in the entire city live, does not represent a slum area" (Schmid, *Social Saga of Two Cities*, 180).

106. This division is referred to clearly in the recollections of one Rondo resident who lived in the area as a child in the early 1920s. See Eula T. Murphy, "Growing Up in St. Paul: Looking Back at the Black Community," *Ramsey County History* 27 (Winter 1992–93): 12–15. How widespread this was is unclear.

107. Many homeowners in the western section of the Hill district had non-English ethnic surnames, which might indicate that they were descendants of nineteenth-century European immigrants. On the issue of restrictive practices, see Taylor, "Pilgrim's Progress," 43–44; Peter J. DeCarlo, "Loyalty within Racism: The Segregated Sixteenth Battalion of the Minnesota Homeguard," *Minnesota History* 65/66 (Summer 2017): 218.

108. "Saint Paul, a Week's Record in Minnesota's Capital," *Appeal*, June 25, 1910; Taylor, "The Twin Cities from 1910 to 1980."

109. "Minneapolis News," *Twin City Star*, July 17, 1915.

110. The fact that not even the most elite members of the African American community appear in the *Dual City Blue Books* indicates the degree to which their race excluded them from real or imagined membership in the elite community of the city. On the general racial discrimination faced by black Minnesotans, see DeCarlo, "Loyalty within Racism."

111. Aronovici's survey provides a clear geographic breakdown of the types of houses that denoted poverty. See the chart "Key to Survey" in his *Housing Conditions*, 13. The principal retail district (district 6 on the map) offered residents "cheap hotels" for accommodation. Just west of that area was a section of the city (district 5) with many apartment houses. To the east (district 7) was a collection of lodging houses that were flanked on the northeast by another area (district 9) featuring housing structures described as "badly depreciated." The areas of the city nearest the river itself were also marked by identifiably poor housing. The Upper Levee, an area under the high bridge on the flats of the eastern bank of the Mississippi, had "Shacks Close together," while the "Principal Characteristics" of the West Side Lower Levee and the flats directly across the river from downtown were "Congested and Poor," "Squatters and Renters," and "Laborers—Scattered."

112. Sanborn Map Company, *Insurance Maps of St. Paul* (1903), 2:174, MNHS.

113. "Swede Hollow, Phalen Creek, 6th Street Bridge, c. 1900," MR2.9 SP2, 100, negative no. 11417, MNHS.

114. Aronovici, *Housing Conditions*, 20.

115. See Gentille Yarusso, "La Scola Lincoln," unpublished manuscript (1973), MNHS; and Yarusso, "An American Newcomer."

116. Mollie Price, "Swede Hollow: Sheltered Society for Immigrants to St. Paul," *Ramsey County History* 17, no. 2 (1982): 19.

117. Ibid., 18. On the Swedish residents who lived in the hollow until the turn

of the twentieth century, see Nels M. Hokenson, "I Remember St. Paul's Swede Hollow," *Minnesota History* 41 (Winter 1969): 363–71.

118. Polly Nyberg and Jerome Bette, "Swede Hollow: A Community's Love Affair with Its Past," *Common Ground* 3 (Fall 1974): 4–11.

119. Larry Millet, *Lost Twin Cities* (St. Paul: Minnesota Historical Society Press, 1992), 284.

120. Laurence A. Ball, "The St. Paul Auditorium," speech delivered on November 12, 1908, to the Brooklyn Engineer's Club, reprinted in *Brooklyn Engineer's Club*, vol. 85 (New York: Brooklyn Engineer's Club, 1909), 295, MNHS.

121. "Saint Paul Convention Center" (St. Paul: Polk, 1907), 7.

122. Ibid., 5

123. "Chance for Everybody to See the Auditorium," *Pioneer Press*, April 3, 1907. The article indicates that prices for tickets ranged from 25¢ to $3.

124. *Report of the Board of Auditorium Commissioners of the City of Saint Paul for the Year Ending December 31, 1909*, 640, MNHS.

125. The white press did note in passing that there were a "few districts" without representation at the grand opening, which leads me to speculate that the Rondo area may have been one of them.

126. Discerning the ethnic or racial identity of the groups who used the auditorium is challenging because the account of renters generally list only the name of the individual who was responsible for payment, not his or her affiliation. Its use for benevolent societies' event is noted in the caption of a photo of the auditorium in the *Appeal*, July 24, 1909.

127. In 1918, a decade after the opening of the City Auditorium, W. T. Francis, a black attorney and leading St. Paul resident, addressed the leaders of the city's new public library in an impassioned speech detailing the "humiliation" that the city's black residents had already received from representatives of other supposedly public institutions. In particular, he referred to the new YMCA, a building funded in part with the dollars of African American St. Paulites. Yet "when . . . the new building was completed, we were informed that out membership would be discontinued and that our presence at the new quarters was undesirable." He indicated that the same type of segregation had occurred when black residents had tried to use the Wilder Baths, which the philanthropist Amherst H. Wilder had donated for the use of the "worthy poor" of St. Paul. The city's African American residents were concerned that they would receive the same type of treatment at the St. Paul Public Library ("Francis Condemns Wrongs against Negro Americans," *Twin City Star*, April 6, 1918).

CHAPTER 4: COMMUNITY AND OPEN SPACE

1. Olmstead is best known for his design of New York's Central Park in 1858. For more on him, see William H. Wilson, *The City Beautiful Movement* (Baltimore: Johns Hopkins University Press, 1989). Cleveland was the first person to develop an organic approach to landscape design with his 1855 plan for Sleepy Hollow

Cemetery in Concord, Massachusetts. However, both he and his work were most influential in the Middle West. For an exploration of his writings and influence, see Daniel J. Nadenicek and Lance M. Necker, introduction, in H. W. S. Cleveland, *Landscape Architecture, as Applied to the Wants of the West: With an Essay on Forest Planning on the Great Plains* (1873; reprint, Amherst: University of Massachusetts Press and the Library of American Landscape History, 2002), xi–lxxii.

2. Quoted in Paul Boyer, *Urban Masses and the Moral Order in America, 1820–1920* (Cambridge, MA: Harvard University Press, 1978), 237. On Olmstead's belief that parks were useful tools for democratizing city dwellers and reconciling differences, see Wilson, *City Beautiful Movement*, 10.

3. It was clear by the 1910s that, even as responsibility for developing and completing comprehensive schemes was shifting to a new group of professional city planners, the concerns of the City Beautiful movement were still present. Parks, boulevards, and playgrounds remained central to large-scale city planning schemes throughout the Progressive Era.

4. Boyer, *Urban Masses,* 221.

5. The City Practical approach to urban change was led by a new group of citizens—professional planners and city managers—who challenged the aesthetic focus of the City Beautiful as they searched for ways to organize and shape urban areas and populations. It led to such aggressive attacks on the City Beautiful ideology, as in Cass Gilbert's 1909 proclamation that there was a need for "the city useful, the city practical, the city livable, the city sensible, the city anything but the city beautiful. . . . If it is to be a city beautiful it will be done naturally" (Wilson, *City Beautiful Movement,* 287).

6. The park system that Nussbaumer oversaw was hindered by a municipal system that included little permanent funding for parks, leaving it dependent on an annual appropriation granted from the city's common council out of the general fund. See Patrice Bass, "The Early History of the St. Paul Park System, 1872–1907" unpublished manuscript (1997), 24, personal copy shared with the author; and *St. Paul City Directory* (1915), MNHS.

7. "President's Address," in *Annual Report of the Board of Park Commissioners of the City of St. Paul* (1903) , 32, DPR.

8. Wheelock was also the editor–in–chief of the *Pioneer Press.*

9. Galen Crantz defines and distinguishes between the terms *pleasure grounds* and *reform parks* in *The Politics of Park Design: A History of Urban Parks in America* (Cambridge, MA: MIT Press, 1982).

10. "Chamber of Commerce. The Park Question Discussed," *Dispatch,* April 6, 1874.

11. *Annual Report of the Board of Park Commissioners of the City of St. Paul,* (1894–95), 10, 18–19, DPR.

12. During this lecture Cleveland admonished Chicago planners for attempting to create a linked park system on the outskirts of town and warned the St. Paul Chamber of Commerce about its pitfalls—especially the fact that the parks would

end up outside the reach of the city's poor and would therefore be of no benefit to them ("Prof. Cleveland's Lecture," *St. Paul Pioneer,* February 17, 1872).

13. In 1873 the *St. Paul Pioneer* first criticized this situation. See Bass, "Early History," 12–13.

14. From *1893–94 Annual Report,* quoted in Bass, "Early History," 31. See D. L. Curtice, *Map of St. Paul: Prepared Specially for R. L. Polk & Co's City Directory* (1910), Minnesota Historical Society Map Collection, MNHS; and D. L. Curtice, *Curtice's Standard Guide Map of the City of St. Paul* (1915), Minnesota Historical Society Map Collection, MNHS.

15. Bass, "Early History," 32–33. The goal of meeting the needs of all members of the public was extended in 1901 with the installation of an electric boat launch to make boating accessible to those who were weak or invalid.

16. See, for example, *Report of the Department of Parks, Playgrounds and Public Buildings of the City of St. Paul, 1914–1919,* 3, 5, 15, 16, 25, DPR; and *Annual Report of the Board of Park Commissioners of the City of St. Paul* (1909), DPR.

17. *Annual Report of the Board of Park Commissioners* (1902), DPR.

18. *Annual Report of the Board of Park Commissioners* (1899–1900), 23, DPR.

19 Fred Nussbaumer, "Report of the Superintendent of Parks, 1918," in *Report of the Department of Parks, Playgrounds and Public Buildings, 1914–1919* 16.

20. *Annual Report of the Board of Park Commissioners* (1910), 66, DPR; (1911), 32, DPR.

21. Quotation from the *Report of the Board of Park Commissioners of the City of St. Paul for 1912,* 16; "Report of the Superintendent of Parks, 1918," in *Report of the Department of Parks, Playgrounds and Public Buildings, 1914–1919,* 15, DPR.

22. *Annual Report of the Board of Park Commissioners of the City of St. Paul* (1908,), 34, DPR.

23. Nussbaumer, "Annual Report for the Superintendent of Parks for the Year 1917," in *Report of the Department of Parks, Playgrounds and Public Buildings, 1914–1919,* 12, DPR.

24. Nussbaumer, "Report of the Superintendent of Parks, 1918," in *Report of the Department of Parks, Playgrounds and Public Buildings, 1914–1919,* 15, DPR

25. Information on the streetcar extension appears in the *Annual Report of the Board of Park Commissioners of the City of St. Paul,* 1905, 13, DPR. Among low-cost activities, swimming suits could be rented for 15 cents each and were free to children before noon (Fred Nussbaumer, "Report of Superintendent of Parks [1918]," in *Report of the Department of Parks, Playgrounds, and Public Buildings, 1914–1919,* 15, DPR.

26. Nussbaumer made the comment about people paying for the parks in "An Ideal Public Park," in *Trees, Fruits, and Flowers of Minnesota: Embracing the Transactions of the Minnesota Horticultural Society* (Minneapolis: Harrison and Smith, 1902), 112–14. For an overview of the Nussbaumer years, see "The City Itself Work of Art: A Historical Evaluation of Como Park for the City of St. Paul, Minnesota" (November 1996), unpublished document, SHPO.

27. Nussbaumer, "Report of the Superintendent of Parks," in *Report of the Department of Parks, Playgrounds and Public Buildings, 1914–1919,* 7, DPR.

28. Nussbaumer, "An Ideal Public Park," 112–14.

29. "President's Address" (1903), 1156. This assertion is interesting, given that the Minneapolis park system was designed by Cleveland and heralded as an exceptional example of his work.

30. Cleveland and his adherents promoted the idea of grand parkways radiating from the center of the city to outlying parks.

31. Fred Nussbaumer, "Report of Superintendent of Parks (1911) in *Twenty-First Annual Report of the Board of Park Commissioners of the City of St. Paul*, 24; Nussbaumer, "Report of the Superintendent of Parks" [1919], in *Report of the Department of Parks, Playgrounds and Public Buildings, 1914–1919*, 25–27, DPR. There were numerous calls over two decades for the city to complete the proposed parkway system linking residential areas and parks. In the 1919 report Nussbaumer stridently chastised the city for having privileged business needs over a redemptive and unified park system.

32. There is no direct evidence of appeals to residents of particular races or to women. However, the emphasis on meeting the needs of the working class seems to have included all members of that group, regardless of other demographic variables.

33. According to one printed report Como park was regarded in 1903 as "one of the most popular parks in the country," drawing 1.3 million visitors annually.(Such a claim is hard to verify). See "The President's Address," in the *Annual Report of the Board of Park Commissioners* (1903), 16. In 1919 the total number listed in the annual report was 465,200. Of these, the report noted, 75,250 were picnickers, 377,900 attended the band concerts, and 12,050 were tennis and baseball players. In addition there was a large unrecorded number of visitors who "enjoyed the scenic beauty and cool shade of the park" (Nussbaumer, "Report of the Superintendent of Parks" [1919], in *Report of the Department of Parks, Playgrounds and Public Buildings, 1914–1919*, 24.) Note that there was no systematic data gathering. In 1918 the beach area alone at Phalen Park drew 90,000 people, while the sixty-six open air concerts given that year drew an additional 250,000 (Nussbaumer, "Report of the Superintendent of Parks, 1918," in *Report of the Department of Parks, Playgrounds and Public Buildings, 1914–1919*, 15, DPR; and "Report of the Superintendent of Parks" [1919], in *Report of the Department of Parks, Playgrounds and Public Buildings, 1914–1919*, 23, DPR). These numbers suggest that the two major parks attracted large, diverse crowds—even as they also drew visitors from cities other than St. Paul.

34. Henry Castle, *History of St. Paul and Vicinity: A Chronicle of Progress and a Narrative Account of the Industries and People of the City and Its Tributary Territory* (Chicago: Lewis, 1912), 1:612.

35. See Delia Cheney's photographs, 1889–1909, MNHS; and *Annual Report of the Board of Park Commissioners of the City of St. Paul* (1909).

36. Crantz, *Politics of Park Design*, 196.

37. The Gardner photographs (from 1900–20) do not depict the family members participating in any of the park's activities or recreational opportunities.

38. See, for example, the photograph of the St. Anthony Park Congregational Church Ladies' Aid picnic at Phalen Park in 1905, RCHS. The Pilgrim Baptist

Church Ladies' Aid Society held a special meeting at Phalen in June 1911 (minutes, Ladies' Aid Society Records, vol. 1, MNHS).

39. Castle, *History of St. Paul and Vicinity*, 377.

40. *Annual Report of the Board of Park Commissioners of the City of St. Paul, 1894–95*, 19.

41. Stephen Carr, Mark Francis, Leanne G. Rivlin, and Andrew M. Stone, *Public Space* (New York: Cambridge University Press, 1992), 31.

42. In ibid., Carr et al. argue that public spaces can connect bind together a community by bringing together heterogeneous groups who would otherwise retreat into the private sphere, but I see faint evidence of this in St. Paul in the modernizing era.

43. The literature on the U.S. park movement makes some distinctions between parks and playgrounds, but my focus here is on the presence of smaller spaces for gathering and recreation, regardless of the form they took. For a brief discussion of the terms, see Crantz, *Politics of Park Design*, 65.

44. Because of the limited funding available to the park board, land purchased or donated by private interests could not realistically be turned down. See *Annual Report of the Board of Park Commissioners* (1909), 3.

45. This number includes small squares and triangles, as well as the land for one playground.

46. These numbers are based on data from the "Park Statistics" chart in *Annual Report of the Board of Park Commissioners* (1909), 53.

47. The two neighborhood parks considered to be "most important" were Merriam Terrace and Langford Park located in neighborhoods expressly developed as insular suburbs in the garden city model of the late nineteenth century. On the insularity of suburban neighborhoods in the nineteenth century, see Clifford Clark, *The American Family Home, 1800–1960* (Chapel Hill: University of North Carolina Press, 1986), 98–99

48. *Report of the Board of Park Commissioners of the City of St. Paul for 1901*, 13, DPR.

49. *Annual Report of the Board of Park Commissioners of the City of St. Paul, 1905*, DPR.

50. The minutes of the board meeting on April 3, 1911, indicate that a person named Garry D. W. Sherman had asked it to take some action toward improving the park system in the area between the west end of Isabel Street Boulevard and two or three blocks west of Smith Avenue High Bridge. His request was referred to the park superintendent, who was supposed to confer with him (St. Paul Park Board records, box 3, vol. 2, 1908–14, MNHS). There is no listing for "Garry D. W. Sherman" in either the *Dual City Blue Book* (1911–12) or the *St. Paul City Directory* (1911), both in the MNHS.

51. "Annual Report of the Superintendent of Parks of the City of St. Paul for the Year 1917," in *Report of the Department of Parks, Playgrounds and Public Buildings, 1914–1919*, 10, DPR. In spite of the board's desire to round out the park system's series of neighborhood parks, there was never a push to add to or improve recreational facilities in Rondo.

52. The playground movement at the turn of the century furthered the ideals of previous urban reformers and municipal park advocates. Playgrounds were seen as central educating and socializing agents that might promote civic unity. On the goals and beliefs of national playground advocates, see Boyer, *Urban Masses*, 242–45. In St. Paul the rhetoric surrounding the expansion of the city's playground facilities was in lockstep with this national agenda. As Nussbaumer acknowledged in 1917, "It cannot be questioned that playgrounds for children are a necessity of satisfactory city life." They provided not only opportunities for "healthy exercise" but also were key to proper "character building" among the city's youngest citizens ("Annual Report of the Superintendent of Parks of the City of St. Paul for the Year 1917" in *Report of the Department of Parks, Playgrounds and Public Buildings* [1914–1919], 13, DPR). This comment was similar to one he had made nearly a decade earlier: "The playgrounds of the City do a great deal of good and are of immense benefit of the children" (*Annual Report of the Superintendent of Parks of the City of St. Paul* [1908], 35).

53. Carol Aronovici, *Housing Conditions in the City of Saint Paul* (St. Paul: Wilder Charity, 1917), 66.

54. Ibid.

55. On these competitions, see Castle, *History of St. Paul*, 397–98, and any number of the annual reports in the later part of the 1910s.

56. In 1922 a local Presbyterian minister purchased land in Rondo for the creation of playground for "colored children." The fast and furious negative response of the black community to what looked like a backhanded approach to segregating the city's playgrounds indicated that they were seen as sites of possible interaction or segregation. See *Minnesota Messenger*, April 29, 1922, 4.

57. See Jean Quandt, *From the Small Town to the Big City: The Social Thought of Progressive Intellectuals* (New Brunswick, NJ: Rutgers University Press, 1970), 46.

CHAPTER 5: "MAKING IT A HOT ONE" FOR SOME

1. F. Scott Fitzgerald, *Flappers and Philosophers*, ed. James L. W. West III (Cambridge: Cambridge University Press, 2000), 43. Fitzgerald claims that his description of the ice palace in the story "The Ice Palace" comes from the recollections of older family members who told him about the palaces of the 1880s carnivals. However, scholar James L. W. West thinks Fitzgerald probably saw the 1917 ice fort in St. Paul. On Fitzgerald's claims see West, appendix 2. On West's suggestion, see 355. Other scholars disagree with West's suggestion. See Patricia Hampl and David Page, eds., *The St. Paul Stories of F. Scott Fitzgerald* (St. Paul: Minnesota Historical Society Press, 2004), 77.

2. See Mary Lethert Wingerd, *Claiming the City: Politics, Faith and the Power of Place in St. Paul* (Ithaca: Cornell University Press, 2001), 117–23.

3. *De Luxe Souvenir View Book: A complete pictorial history of Saint Paul's Outdoor Sports Winter Carnival of nineteen hundred and sixteen showing how "we made it a hot one"* (St. Paul: Carnival Publishing Company, 1916), foreword, SPOSCA.

4. See Clifford Geertz, *The Interpretation of Cultures* (New York: Basic Books, 1973), 448; and Allesandro Falassi, ed., *Time out of Time: Essays on the Festival* (Albuquerque: University of New Mexico Press, 1967), intro. Addressing the notion of carnivals as liminal spaces, several scholars demonstrate that that even the topsy-turvy nature of many festivals reinforces this status quo. See Roger Abrahams and Richard Bauman "Ranges of Festival Behavior," in *The Reversible World: Symbolic Inversion in Art and Society*, ed. Barbara A. Babcock (Ithaca: Cornell University Press, 1977), 193–208; and Robert H. Lavenda, "Festivals and the Creation of Public Culture: Whose Voice(s)?," in *Museums and Communities: The Politics of Public Culture,* ed. Ivan Karp, Christine Mullen Kreamer, and Steve D. Lavine (Washington, DC: Smithsonian Institution Press, 1997), 76–104.Exploring the rhetoric of community in small-town festivals in Minnesota in the 1980s and 1990s, Lavenda writes that "the appropriation of 'our community' by . . . organizers . . . is generally accepted by other segments of the population who share their vision of a harmonious community of mutually supportive equals [but, it is] the tension between this ideal and the daily experiences of uninvolved individuals who are linked by fragile, contingent social ties in the town [that] engenders the characteristic earnest and non-ironic official voice of the small-town festival" (77). This was the phenomenon that shaped the 1916 and 1917 St. Paul winter carnivals. See also Robert Lavenda, *Cornfests and Water Carnivals: Celebrating Community in Minnesota* (Washington, DC: Smithsonian Institution Press, 1997). These scholars challenge claims made by Jean Spraker about the breakdown of normal boundaries during winter carnivals in St. Paul in general ("The Rollicking Realm of Boreas: A Century of Carnivals in St. Paul," *Minnesota History* 49 [Winter 1985]: 322–31).

5. The names of all of the carnival organizers appear in the elite records of the *Dual City Blue Book, 1916–1917* (St. Paul.: Polk, 1917).

6. "Most Successful Trade Stimulator," *Pioneer Press,* January 28, 1916.

7. George M. Waters, letter to St. Paul Outdoor Sports Carnival Association, January 23, 1916, box 1, SPOSCA.

8. "St. Paul Wants Men Who Have Time for Play Hill Declares," *Pioneer Press,* January 30, 1916.

9. Thomas Bender, *Community and Social Change in America,* (New Brunswick, NJ: Rutgers University Press, 1978), 114.

10. By mid-January the work had begun. See "Drill and Review Given by Battery A in Honor of Party Boosting Carnival," *Pioneer Press,* January 18, 1916.

11. "Shop Windows are Taking on Carnival Appearance," *Pioneer Press,* January 17, 1916; "Two boys Cheat L. W. Hill of First Ride Down Slide," January 19, 1916;. "Ramsey Street Slide is Christened by Big Crowd," *Pioneer Press,* January 22, 1916; "Merrymakers in Gay Colored Suits Seen Everywhere," *Pioneer Press,* January 23, 1019; Paul Clifford Larson, *Icy Pleasures* (Afton, MN: Afton Historical Society Press, 1997), 104.

12. "3,000 Pose in Costumes for Movies," *Pioneer Press,* January 1, 1917; "Carnival Success Certain, King Says After Maneuvers," *Pioneer Press,* January 2, 1917; "City is Saturated with Enthusiasm for Outdoor Fete," *Pioneer Press,* January 21, 1917; Larson, *Icy Pleasures,* 103.

13. Quotations from *Official Souvenir View Book . . . Jan. 27–Feb. 3, 1917. A Pictorial history of St. Paul's Outdoor Sports Winter Carnival of nineteen hundred and seventeen showing how "we made it a hotter one"* (St. Paul, 1917), foreword, SPOSCA; "18,000 March in Carnival Pageant," *Daily News*, January 23, 1917; "Section of Boreas' Mighty Army on Parade Before Cameras," *Pioneer Press*, January 24, 1917.

14. Larson, *Icy Pleasures*, 101–2.

15. "Winter Outdoor Games Hold City in Firm Grasp, Thousands Being Recruited to Ranks Every Day," *Pioneer Press*, January 30, 1916.

16. *De Luxe Souvenir View Book*, 1916, foreword.

17. See editions of the *Daily News* and the *Pioneer Press* during the run of the carnival.

18. "Winter Outdoor Games," *Pioneer Press*, January 30, 1916. The publicity value of the newspaper coverage was not lost on the organizers, who thanked the *Pioneer Press*, the *Dispatch*, and the *Daily News* in both newspaper accounts and their official post-carnival view books. See *De Luxe Souvenir View Book*, 1916, foreword; and *Official Souvenir View Book*, 1917, foreword.

19. "For Two Hours Great Throng Lines Streets as 20,000 March Past," *Pioneer Press*, February 2, 1916; "Big Parade Opens Carnival Night," *Daily News*, January 27, 1916.

20. "For Two Hours," *Pioneer Press*, February 2, 1916.

21. See Wingerd, *Claiming the City*; and *De Luxe Souvenir View Book*, 1916.

22. "Mayor's Carnival Proclamation Calls for Half Holiday in St. Paul Saturday," *Daily News*, January 24, 1917.

23. *Official Souvenir View Book*, 1917.

24. "Line, Six Miles Long, Two Hours, 20 Minutes Passing Review Stand," *Pioneer Press*, January 28, 1917. The paper notes the significant number of "girls" in every marching club.

25. Norman H. Landman and Harry Wassel, "Come to the Carnival at Old St. Paul" (Saint Paul: Landman and Wassel Music Publishers, 1916); Harley Rosso, "Back to Old Saint Paul" (Sidney, OH: Ohio Publishing, 1917). Jean Spraker argues that these lyrics give "an indication of the part the Carnival has played as a medium for grappling with issues of class and community in a democratic society" ("Come to the Carnival at Old St. Paul: Souvenirs from a Civic Ritual Interpreted," *Prospects* 11 [October 1986]: 235).

26. *De Luxe Souvenir View Book*, 1916.

27. *Official Souvenir View Book*, 1917, foreword.

28. "St. Paul men will tell you quietly that in years past all has not been as it should be. . . . Up on the hill the men who ruled the business of the city; down on the flats the homes of the workers" (Albert Britt, "St. Paul—The City That Discovered Winter," *Outing* 69 [March 1917]: 674–75). Spraker takes Britt at his word in "Rollicking Realm of Boreas," 325.

29. *St. Paul City Directory* (1915), 17, MNHS.

30. "Enthusiasm [was] shown in the down town sections where naturally the carnival must be staged" (*De Luxe Souvenir View Book*, 1916, foreword).

31. See Louis Marin, "Notes on a Semiotic Approach to Parade, Cortege, and Procession," in Falassi, *Time out of Time*, 220–28.

32. Thomas M. Spencer, *The St. Louis Veiled Prophet Celebration: Power on Parade, 1877–1995* (Columbia: University of Missouri Press, 2000), 2.

33. In the early part of the century Harriet Island was a site of a great deal of middle-class activity, especially in the summer.

34. For details of 1916 carnival routes, see *Dispatch*, January 27, 1916; *Daily News*, January 27, 1916; *Daily News*, February, 1, 1916; and *Pioneer Press*, February 2, 1916.

35. In "Notes on a Semiotic Approach," Marin underscores the degree to which choosing certain places for a parade gives those spaces a "meaningful structure" (223).

36. For details of the parade route in 1917, see *Pioneer Press*, January 24, 1917.

37. The official slides were those whose construction and maintenance was funded at least in part by the carnival committee (*Pioneer Press*, January 28, 1917).

38. There were more slides at the 1917 carnival than there had been in the previous year's, but the same general limitations applied. A list of the official locations appears in "Would You Slide or Skate? Here's Your Opportunity," *Pioneer Press*, January 27, 1917; and in the pre-carnival souvenir program, which sold for ten cents, Saint Paul Outdoor Sports Carnival (1917), *Official Souvenir Program (Saint Paul Outdoor Sports Carnival, Jan. 27—Feb 3, 1917: "Make it a Hotter One"* [St. Paul: Webb, 1917], MNHS.

39. Many of the city's wealthiest businessmen resided in the Hill district, Dayton's Bluff, and Ramsey Hill. These neighborhoods were relatively close to the center of carnival activities, which were held in the public areas most closely associated with the organizers' everyday work lives: the business district, Ramsey Hill, and the area around the capitol.

40. On the municipal parade, see "Largest Parade of Kind Tuesday, Aim," *Dispatch*, January 29, 1916; and "Line of March for Municipal Pageant," *Pioneer Press*, February 1, 1916.

41. It is strange that the *De Luxe Souvenir View Book*, states emphatically that in 1916 the "carnival was free. Not a five cent piece was charged for any carnival attraction." It also asserted that the seven slides in the city were operated "free of charge" throughout the carnival (foreword).

42. There is no reference to such a service in either the local press coverage or the records of the SPOSCA.

43. There is contradictory information regarding the cost of carnival buttons in 1916. The *De Luxe Souvenir View Book* indicates that the events were free to all, and "Carnival Visitors Here to See Parade" (*Dispatch*, February, 1, 1916) suggests obliquely that this might have been true for visitors. Yet a St. Paul resident complained in a letter to the organizers that there *were* costs involved in the acquisition

of buttons in 1916 (Waters, letter to St. Paul Outdoor Sports Carnival Association). In 1917 buttons cost a dollar each.

44. The city's schoolchildren took over Harriet Island on February 4, 1916, and participated in a number of carnival activities ("Carnival to Close in a Blaze of Glory," *Daily News*, February 4, 1916).

45. Waters, letter to St. Paul Outdoor Sports Carnival Association.

46. "Kids Don't Need Buttons to Slide," *Pioneer Press*, January 23, 1917.

47. Anonymous carnival organizer, letter to Martin F. Ernest, January 11, 1917, box 3, SPOSCA. There are six such letters in the records, each stating the situation in precisely the same way. The association also hired guards in 1917 to watch the Cedar Street slide in the week leading up to the carnival as well as during the carnival days (invoice for money paid to the Theil Detective Services Co., February 6, 2017, "Accounts, Jan. 25, 1917 to February 8, 1917," box 8, SPOSCA).

48. There is evidence to suggest that only a limited number of carnival buttons were produced each year. Note that counterfeit buttons were being sold in 1917, perhaps to ease the shortage ("Kids Don't Need Buttons to Slide"; "Would You Slide or Skate?").

49. For examples of paid events, see information on the boxing match on the last day of the 1916 carnival ("King of Winter Will be Given Throne Today," *Pioneer Press*, February 5, 1916); a front-page advertisement for the two-night run of the carnival pageant ("Tonight at the Auditorium . . . ," *Pioneer Press*, February 2, 1917); and box-office receipts for the nightly "Blue Paradise" performance at the Metropolitan Theater, during the 1917 carnival (L. N. Scott papers, box 4, SPOSCA). A small number of the events at the auditorium and elsewhere were listed explicitly as "free" in the souvenir program and in published calendars of events, which suggests that paid tickets were the norm. For an example, see "The Carnival Today," *Dispatch*, January 31, 2017.

50. "St. Paul's Wonderful Carnival Pageant," (Advertisement), *Dispatch*, February 1, 1917 (emphasis added).

51. "Carnivals Are Costly," *Daily News*, January 31, 1916; "Most Successful Trade Stimulator," *Pioneer Press*, January 28, 1916. The $10 figure is quoted in both of these articles and in a letter sent by the association late in 1916 to some of the marching club leaders from the previous year. On the $13 cost in 1917, see "Big Outdoor Fete Benefits Businesses," *Pioneer Press*, January 21, 1917; "Carnival Will Cost About $1,500,000" and the advertisement "Carnival Costumes $10 up," both in *Daily News*, January 28, 1917.

52. Landman and Wassell, "Come to the Carnival at Old St. Paul."

53. See, for example, *Pioneer Press*, February 2, 1916.

54. *Daily News*, January 30, 1917.

55. See, in general, the newspaper coverage of the carnival days.

56. *Saint Paul Outdoor Sports Carnival, make it a hot one, Jan. 27–Feb. 5th: Official Souvenir(!) Program* (St. Paul: Webb, 1916), 3, SPOSCA.

57. "Most Successful Trade Stimulator," *Pioneer Press*, January 28, 1916.

58. *Saint Paul Official Souvenir(!) Program*, 1916, 5.

59. "Mayor Extends Greeting to All Carnival Visitors," *Daily News*, January 31, 1916.

60. In this sense carnival boosters reflected an understanding of place that distinguishes between physical spaces and imagined places. See my introduction.

61. *De Luxe Souvenir View Book*, 1916, foreword.

62. There are many references to solicitation in both the carnival records and newspapers. For an example of a newspaper report of the solicitation campaign, see "Parade to Take Carnival Boom to Minneapolis," *Pioneer Press*, January 20, 1916; "Fame of Winter Carnival Reaches Islands of Pacific," *Pioneer Press*, January 23, 1916.

63. Louis W. Hill, letter to Mr. Tillman D. Taylor, October 3, 1916, box 1, SPOSCA.

64. "Fame of Winter Carnival Reaches Islands of Pacific."

65. *De Luxe Souvenir View Book*, 1916, foreword; "City is Saturated with Enthusiasm for Outdoor Fete," *Pioneer Press*, January 21, 1917. The 1916 official summation assumed that much of the 1917 advertising would be done by railroads and other transportation companies with connections in St. Paul.

66. H. P. Wickham, letter to marching club leaders, October 17, 1916, box 4, SPOSCA.

67. See daily coverage by the *Pioneer Press*, the *Dispatch*, and the *Daily News* throughout both carnivals. Although the *Union Advocate* was a significant voice for workers in the city, its coverage of the winter carnivals was limited. While mentioned, the carnivals did not factor significantly in the weekly either year. As such, a full comparison is not offered here.

68. For newspaper reports of this invitation, see "Northwest to Send Big Crowds to the Carnival," *Pioneer Press*, January 25, 1916. For an image of the "Imperial Decree" (erroneously attributed to 1917), see Spraker, "Rollicking Realm of Boreas," 329.

69. "Hotels Taxed by Visitors," *Pioneer Press*, January 19, 1916.

70. Beginning in 1880, Minneapolis overtook St. Paul in population and began to rapidly outpace it in terms of industry and prestige. By 1890 there was not even the pretense of cooperation between the cities. For an excellent interpretation of the rivalry's impact, see Wingerd, *Claiming the City*, 13–18.

71. "Big Army of Carnival Boosters in Gay Togs Parades in Mill City," *Pioneer Press*, January 22, 1916.

72. "Minneapolis to Join in Carnival," *Daily News*, January 29, 1916; "Thousands Throng Mill City Streets," *Pioneer Press*, January 21, 1917.

73. "Line, Six Miles Long, Two Hours, 20 Minutes Passing Review Stand," *Pioneer Press*, January 28, 1917; *Official Souvenir View Book*, 1917 foreword.

74. In 1917 the association anticipated spending $15,000 on film and photographs for newspapers, magazines, and other publications in order to advertise the carnival and St. Paul to the outside world. See "Cost of Filming Carnival Scenes Estimated at $15,000," *Pioneer Press*, January 31, 1917.

75. *Official Souvenir Program (1917)*; "Winter Sports Carnival Visitors Welcome," *Pioneer Press*, January 29, 1917.

76. "Carnival On; None Waits Official Day," *Dispatch*, January 26, 1917; "L. W. Hill Does Lockstep with Clubs to Keep Warm," *Dispatch*, January 27, 1917; "Montana Guests Capture Carnival," *Pioneer Press*, February 2, 1917.

77. "Big Parade Opens Carnival Tonight," *Daily News*, January 27, 1917.

78. "Queen Okabena is Home Again," [Worthington, MN] *Glory*, February 8, 1917.

79. The association established a specific committee to oversee accommodations for visitors. In 1916 it went so far as to place print page ads in St. Paul newspapers informing residents that they "Must Open Homes to Carnival Visitors" (*Pioneer Press*, January 24, 1916).

80. *Dispatch*, January 31, 1917, 1.

81. "Visiting Clubs Applauded," *Pioneer Press*, January 31, 1917, 4.

82. "America's Carnival at St. Paul," *Pioneer Press*, January 28, 1917.

83. "Lauded by Eastern Magazine Publisher," *Pioneer Press*, January 31, 1917.

84. Regarding women, in both years carnival advertising largely revolved around the image of an idealized "carnival girl"; and though women were able to participate in many activities, they were marginalized in both subtle and obvious ways. The passive Queen of the Snows was no rival to the dynamic male carnival roles, and newspaper coverage of women revelers was less robust that than of their male counterparts. Women were banned from events such as blanket tossing and a celebrated boxing match held at the auditorium. For women with children, the carnival was little more than a spectator sport. Yet, compared to the city's poorest residents and its African American citizens, women were much more widely imaged and imagined as participants in the carnival—and thus as members of the St. Paul community.

85. I have scoured the printed material from the 1916 carnival and can find no indication that any African American residents or nonresidents were involved.

86. The *Appeal*'s audience was broader than St. Paul, but its advertisements and a standing column about events in the city reflected local concerns. There was no mention of either the 1916 or 1917 carnivals in the St. Paul column during the two months surrounding the events.

87. Many thanks to the independent scholar Bob Olson for informing me about the existence of these photographs in the album *Photographs: St. Paul Outdoor Sports Carnival, 1917*, which is catalogued separately from the SPOSCA at MNHS. The album does not appear to have been designed for wide circulation.

88. The two newspaper images appeared in the *Pioneer Press*, January 2, 1917, and the "Pictorial Supplement *St. Paul Pioneer Press* Jan. 21, 1917," January 21, 1917. A number of costumed participants also paraded in blackface. I am not concerned with them here, although more research is warranted on this topic as well as on the representation of Native Americans. See also *Official Souvenir View Book*, 1917, 1; and *Pioneer Press*, January 28, 1917. A few of these images can be found in the digital collections of MNHS.

89. Camera Art Company, "Photographs, St. Paul Outdoor Sports Carnival, 1917," book 3, album 242, MNHS.

90. "King Boreas II and Some Members of His Court in Country Club Pageant," *Pioneer Press*, January 2, 1917, 1, MNHS; "Boreas Rex, ruler of the carnival . . . ," Winter Carnival Supplement, *Pioneer Press*, January 21, 1917, [4], MNHS.

91. Multiple investigations of the carnival records have not revealed any details (in accounts, ledgers, or letters) about these men.

92. There is one additional image of a black man in the published records of the 1917 carnival. It depicts a black male member of the service staff pouring champagne for a white man in a photo captioned "Banquet at Carling's for the Pendleton Buckaroos," *Official View Book*, 1917. His body is cut off by the right side of the picture frame.

93. "'Night Riders' Will Attack Carnival," *Pioneer Press*, January 21, 1917; "Decorated Auto Parade is Feature," *Daily News*, February 2, 1917.

94. "'Night Riders' Will Attack Carnival"; "Almost 1,000 Autos Line Up in Parade," *Dispatch*, February 2, 1917.

95. "'Night Riders' Will Attack Carnival."

96. "8,000 Will Follow Carnival King to Minneapolis Today," *Pioneer Press*, January 20, 1917, MNHS.

97. On racial discrimination and violence in St. Paul in this era, see Peter J. DeCarlo, "Loyalty within Racism: The Segregated Sixteenth Battalion of the Minnesota Homeguard," *Minnesota History* 65/66 (Summer 2017): 208–19. On these topics and the Ku Klux Klan, see William D. Green, *Degrees of Freedom: The Origins of Civil Rights in Minnesota, 1865–1912* (Minneapolis: University of Minnesota Press, 2015); Elizabeth Dorsey Hale and Nancy M. Vaillancourt, "One Flag, One School, One Language: Minnesota's Ku Klux Klan in the 1920s," *Minnesota History* 61 (Winter 2009–10): 361–71; and Elizabeth Dorsey Hale, *The Ku Klux Klan in Minnesota* (Charleston, SC: History Press, 2013). On the twentieth-century Klan in New England, see Mark Richard, *Not a Catholic Nation: The Ku Klux Klan Confronts New England in the 1920s* (Boston: University of Massachusetts Press, 2015).

98. "Almost 1,000 Autos Line Up in Parade."

99. "Carnival Throngs Spur King Ryker; Stage Auto Parade," *Pioneer Press*, February 3, 1917.

100. "Auto Sirens Toot Derision to Cold; Parade a Success," *Pioneer Press*, February 3, 1917.

101. On the history of Union Hall, see David Taylor, "Pilgrim's Progress: Black St. Paul and the Making of an Urban Ghetto, 1870–1930" (Ph.D. diss., University of Minnesota, 1977), 244. I also discuss Union Hall in chapter 3.

102. "Wait! For the Big 3 Days Carnival!," *Appeal*, February 5, 1916; "The Big Carnival," *Appeal*, February 19, 1916.

103. "Week's Record of Happenings in Minnesota's Capitol," *Appeal*, February 12, 1916, 2.

104. "Carnival," *Appeal*, February 3, 1917; announcement, *Appeal*, February 10, 1917, 3.

105. "The Big Carnival." Despite the claims of unity coverage of these events suggests that not all African Americans in St. Paul would have had access to the various festivities in the same way. Here, market forces also seemed to shape such

access. On the connection between the black residents of St. Paul and Minneapolis, see David Taylor, "The Twin Cities from 1910 to 1980," in *African Americans in Minnesota* (St. Paul: Minnesota Historical Society Press, 2002), n.p.

106. For another take on tensions between lower-middle-class residents and elites in this era, see Robert Johnston, *The Radical Middle Class: Populist Democracy and the Question of Capitalism in Progressive Era Portland, Oregon* (Princeton: Princeton University Press, 2003). On class and community more generally in the Twin Cities, with a specific focus on women, see Elizabeth Faue, *Community of Suffering and Struggle: Women, Men, and the Labor Movement in Minneapolis, 1915–1945* (Chapel Hill: University of North Carolina Press, 1991).

107. This series of claims can be found in box 1, SPOSCA. the working-class identity of the claimants was determined by looking up their addresses and occupations in the *St. Paul City Directory*. I am grateful to Wingerd (in *Claiming the City*) for pointing me to these specific records and encouraging close scrutiny.

108. Louis W. Hill, letter to H. P. Wickham, February 13, 1916, box 1, SPOSCA.

109. There are a series of letters to local businesses in box 5, SPOSCA.

110. C. W. Bronstein, letter to the St. Paul Outdoor Sports Carnival Association, February 10, 1917, box 5, SPOSCA.

111. W. H. Burns, letters to G. M. Kennedy, February 3, 1917, and February 5, 1917, box 4, SPOSCA. A full record of all the merchants canvassed and their replies appears in the small brown journals (unlabeled) in box 12, SPOSCA.

112. Waters, letter to St. Paul Outdoor Sports Carnival Association.

113. "Everybody's Going to the Dogs," *Appeal*, February 10, 1917.

CONCLUSION: THE COMPLEXITIES OF COMMUNITY

1. Samuel H. Zeigler and Helen Jaquette, *Our Community: Good Citizenship in Towns and Cities* (Philadelphia: Winston, 1918), 14.

2. According to the textbook, in a family the "father obtains the means for maintaining the family [while] the mother keeps the home bright and clean [and] the children go to school, assist the mother, [and] perform at home such tasks as running errands." "Here, then, we have a small community." Likewise, the authors' descriptions of a school and an athletic team as communities emphasize the degree to which each member has tasks that, if performed correctly, maintain the health and smooth functioning of the whole. Because a boy "must work not for himself alone, but rather for the success of the team," that team is deemed to be a community. This notion of mutuality was implicit in the book's explanation of the town, the state, and the nation as communities. Although never trying to imply that all members of any given place know one another intimately, the authors insisted that, because people are tied together by government, services, and public works, they have a vested interest in the lives of all those in the locality (ibid., 9–11).

3. J. Lynn Barnard, F. W. Carrier, Arthur William Dunn, and Clarence D. Kingsley, "The Teaching of Community Civics" (Washington, DC: U.S. Bureau

of Education Bulletin, 1915). A research team in Chicago included Zeigler et al.'s *Our Community* in a study of the seven most commonly used textbooks on the topic ("Report of the Committee on Social Studies in the High School," *School Review* 28 [April 1920]: 283–97). There is no concrete evidence that the book was used in St. Paul schools, but a copy exists in MNHS.

4. Robert MacIver, *Community: A Sociological Study* (1917; reprint, London: Cass 1970), 22–23. I discuss this book in chapter 1.

5. In *Claiming the City: Politics, Faith, and the Power of Place in St. Paul* (Ithaca: Cornell University Press, 2001), Mary Lethert Wingerd discusses unity among St. Paulites while acknowledging that it was something other than "community" (3).

6. "Carnival Over. Next One Assured," *Pioneer Press*, February 4, 1917.

7. In *Claiming the City*, Wingerd argues that civic identity was particularly important to the city's small business owners.

8. The way in which urbanites define the boundaries of their city is largely dependent on their social status and worldview. The places that they identify with do not often match the actual geographic bounds of the city. By studying cognitive maps drawn by various residents of a given city, Kevin Lynch has shown how political, economic, ethnic, racial, and gender divisions make living there a vastly different experience for its residents (*The Image of the City* [Cambridge, MA: MIT Press, 1985]). The spaces of a city as well as the memorable or important landmarks are understood differently and hold different meaning (or none at all) for different segments of the population. This was very much the case in modernizing St. Paul.

9. Roland Warren, *The Community in America*, 3rd ed. (Chicago: Rand McNally, 1978), 5–6.

10. Pico Iyer, *The Global Soul: Jet Lag, Shopping Malls and the Search for Home* (New York: Knopf, 2000).

11. A notable example of a planned community is Disney's Celebration, Florida, with its walkable streets, front porches, and meeting rooms available to the public in the centralized town hall. For more about the town's concept and planning, see Russ Rymer, "Back to the Future: Disney Reinvents the Company Town," *Harper's* 293 (October 1996): 65–71, 75–78. Disney designed Celebration as an alternative to the more typical subdivisions with their precisely similar homes and gated entrances. The challenge was to find a way to conflate individualism and community. Celebration's driving force was much the same as that of other examples of the new urbanism: to create place-based community by design. See also Marin Lew, ed., *A Sense of Place: Physical, Natural, and Cultural Environments* (Boston: Houghton Mifflin, 2000); and Kathleen LaFrank, "Seaside, Florida: 'The New Town—The Old Ways,'" in *Shaping Communities: Perspectives in Vernacular Architecture*, ed. Carter L. Hudgins and Elizabeth Collins Cromley (Knoxville: University of Tennessee Press, 1997), 6:111–21.

12. I thank an anonymous reviewer at University of Massachusetts Press for suggesting this relevance and for offering the word *disentangled*.

INDEX

ELIZABETH ANN DUCLOS-ORSELLO is a public-facing, inter-disciplinary scholar, educator, and leader whose career has focused on issues and questions of social justice for more than twenty years, both within higher education and with a range of social service and cultural nonprofits. She is currently chair of the Department of Interdisciplinary Studies and coordinator of American studies at Salem State University in Salem, Massachusetts. A consultant and commentator on the links between the humanities, contemporary issues of inequality, and public policy, she is a two-time Fulbright scholar and a Whiting fellow who has lived, taught, and engaged in social change work in multiple countries on three continents. She holds a Ph.D. in American and New England studies from Boston University and B.A. degrees in history and sociology-based human relations from Connecticut College. An avid runner and outdoor enthusiast, she currently lives in Somerville, Massachusetts, with her husband and son.

www.ingramcontent.com/pod-product-compliance
Lightning Source LLC
Chambersburg PA
CBHW030645270326
41929CB00007B/208